PROTECTING CHILDREN:
CHALLENGES AND CHANGE

Protecting Children: Challenges and Change

edited by
John Bates, Richard Pugh
and Neil Thompson

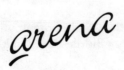

Published by
Arena
Ashgate Publishing Limited
Gower House
Croft Road
Aldershot
Hants GU11 3HR
England

Ashgate Publishing Company
Old Post Road
Brookfield
Vermont 05036
USA

British Library Cataloguing in Publication Data

Protecting children: challenges and change
  1. Child abuse 2. Abused children – Services for
  I. Bates, John II. Pugh, Richard
  III. Thompson, Neil
  362.7'6
Library of Congress Catalog Card Number: 96–80033

ISBN 1 85742 323 2

Typeset in Palatino and Optima by Bournemouth Colour Press and printed and bound in Great Britain by Biddles Ltd, Guildford

Contents

List of figures and tables

Figures

Tables

The contributors

Anne Bannister was formerly the manager of NSPCC Child Sexual Abuse Consultancy in Manchester and now freelances. She is a social worker, dramatherapist and psychodramatist. She specialized in child sexual abuse work for 15 years and trained for this in the USA. Her many publications include: *From Hearing to Healing: Working with the Aftermath of Child Sexual Abuse* (Longman, 1992).

John Bates is a senior lecturer in social work at North East Wales Institute of Higher Education. He is the author of a number of articles, mainly on the subject of information technology in the human services, and he is a member of the executive committee of ENITH (European Network for Information Technology in the Human Services).

Madge Bray is a freelance consultant and trainer. Together with Mary Walsh, she founded Sexual Abuse Childcare Consultancy Services (SACCS), and later Leaps and Bounds, a specialist residential provision integrating care and therapy for severely abused young children. She trains and lectures nationally and internationally and her therapeutic skills have won her an international reputation. She has recently completed her second book: *Sexual Abuse: The Child's Voice*.

Alix Brown is a qualified teacher and social worker. Between 1987 and 1990 she was instrumental in setting up the Shropshire Adolescent Sexual Offences Programme, which assessed and intervened with all young people who sexually abused in the county. She ran the programme, the first county-wide service in the UK. She is currently employed by the Faithfull Foundation, a voluntary child protection agency working with victims and abusers, as a principal therapist working directly with adolescents as well as training other workers and managers.

Val Capewell has a long career as a childcare practitioner. She works on a part-time basis for the National Foster Care Association as the South Wales advice and mediation worker, primarily supporting foster carers who have been subjected to allegations of physical and sexual abuse. She also works as a guardian *ad litem* and a marital counsellor.

Brian Corby is a senior lecturer in applied social studies at the University of Liverpool. A former social worker, he now specializes in child protection studies and is the author of two books on the subject: *Working with Child Abuse* (Open University Press, 1987) and *Child Abuse: Towards a Knowledge Base* (Open University Press, 1993).

Ian Crompton has worked as a co-therapist in the area of Dissociative Disorders since 1987. He is a co-founder of Chester Therapy Centre and currently lectures in social care and mental health.

Andrea Cropper lectures in social work at the University of Central Lancashire. She has worked as a generic social worker and a family placement officer in Liverpool and as a researcher at John Moores University. Her current research interests centre on developing black feminist approaches to social work research. She has co-written articles on social work assessment, research methodology and anti-oppressive practice.

Celia Doyle lectures in protection studies at Nene College and is currently researching the emotional abuse of children, conjointly with Nene College and the University of Leicester, where she is also a tutor. In addition, she is an independent practitioner, working directly with abused children and their families.

Andrew Durham has specialized in direct therapeutic social work with children and young people since 1984. Much of his work has focused on assisting young males in their recovery from child sexual abuse and he has been involved in major organized abuse investigations. He is currently the senior social worker in a specialist project and is completing a PhD thesis at the University of Warwick on the experience and impact of child sexual abuse on males.

Jill Forrest studied at Middlesex Polytechnic and qualified in social work in 1988. Initially, she worked for NSPCC before joining the social services department of the London Borough of Newham. She is currently a senior practitioner in child protection and working with children and families.

Eileen Gallagher is acting manager of NSPCC Child Sexual Abuse

Consultancy. She is a social worker and is training as a group analyst. She specializes in child sexual abuse work and has received training in the USA. She has published articles on groupwork and child sexual abuse and, with Anne Bannister, co-authored a chapter on groupwork in *The Child Protection Handbook* (Wilson and James (eds), Bailliere Tindall, 1995).

Jackie Jennings is a senior social work practitioner with a specialist child protection team based in Dudley, West Midlands. Her present practice encompasses a holistic approach to post-sexual abuse: working with all family members affected and abusers. She is highly motivated towards establishing a 'child welfare' response towards children who abuse, thus re-directing them away from the criminal route.

Malcolm Jordan is a qualified psychiatric social worker who gained his MA by research into the client's view of professional intervention. He specialized in the development of groupwork and therapeutic communities. In 1969 he became a principal lecturer responsible for a highly innovative qualifying course in residential and field social work before moving to the Social Work Advisory Service at the Department of Health and Social Security. Two years later he became Deputy Director of Social Services in Lancashire. Since 1989 he has been an independent consultant working across the UK for central and local government and independent agencies.

Barbara Kahan OBE is an independent childcare consultant who is currently Vice-president of the National Children's Bureau, where she was chair from 1985 to 1994. She was a professional adviser to the House of Commons Select Committee from 1983 to 1990, and is the co-author of *The Pindown Experience and the Protection of Children*. Her most recent book is *Growing Up in Groups* (HMSO, 1994).

Jeanie McIntee is a consultant clinical and forensic psychologist and psychotherapist. She founded Chester Therapy Centre in 1987 and the British section of the International Society for the Study of Dissociation in 1993. She specializes in assessment and recovery from trauma with children and adults.

Malcolm Millar is a lecturer in social work studies at the University of Liverpool. He researches and writes in the areas of child protection studies, probation studies, and the practical application of social work theory.

Tony Morrison is a freelance trainer and consultant in the fields of child protection and management development. He is the author of *Supervision in Social Care* (Longman, 1993), co-author of *Dangerous Families: Assessment and*

Treatment of Child Abuse (Longman, 1986) and co-editor of *Sexual Offending Against Children* (Routledge, 1994).

Michael Murphy, once a practitioner in child protection, has been the coordinator of Bolton ACPC's multidisciplinary staff care scheme since 1989. He is the co-author of *Dealing with Stress* (Macmillan, 1994) and the author of *Working Together in Child Protection* (Arena, 1995) and *The Child Protection Unit* (Avebury, 1996).

Lester Parrott is a senior lecturer in social work at North East Wales Institute of Higher Education. He has worked at a number of British universities since 1988, teaching social policy on professional, graduate and undergraduate courses. His main interests lie in the application of social policy analysis to social work practice. He is currently writing a book on social policy, social work and social care, to be published by Parallel Publishing.

Colin Pritchard is Professor of Social Work Studies at the University of Southampton. He is a psychiatric social worker by training and continues to maintain a small mental health practice. His publications are wide-ranging, including analyses of peace movements, truancy, drug misuse, a series of international studies on suicide and unemployment, sudden infant death syndrome, and child abuse.

Richard Pugh is a principal lecturer in social work at North East Wales Institute of Higher Education, and is a member of the CCETSW Welsh Committee. He has previously worked in residential and fieldwork in both the UK and the USA. While he has published widely on a variety of topics such as advocacy, coping with aggression and the impact of information technology on human services, his main fields are child protection and language issues within the human services.

Neil Thompson is Professor of Social Work and Applied Social Studies at Staffordshire University. He has child protection experience as a social worker, team leader and training officer. He is the author of a number of books, including: *Anti-Discriminatory Practice* (Macmillan, 1993), *Theory and Practice in Health and Social Welfare* (Open University Press, 1995) and *People Skills* (Macmillan, 1996).

Foreword

Barbara Kahan OBE, Doctor of Laws (Hon.),
MA (Cantab.), M(Univ.) (Hon.)

Child protection is nothing if not controversial and at the same time complex in its implications for children, families, many professionals in the services which become involved, the public, government bodies and even politicians. Child abuse has a long history, being so prevalent in some parts of the world that it has almost become a norm, while in other parts, such as Britain and North America, it has become a high-profile issue.

Over the course of approximately thirty years in Britain we have moved from widespread disbelief in non-accidental injury, and later sexual abuse, to the point where a move away from investigation towards a greater emphasis on prevention is causing anxiety to service providers, who are caught between what is seen as a failure to protect on the one hand, and an overzealous pursuit of allegations on the other. Massive investment in procedures, guidelines and interagency cooperation has been accompanied by the identification of different kinds of abuse, the acknowledgement of emotional issues for victims, staff and communities, the recognition of the long-term repercussions and problems of rehabilitation of the abused, and the reform of abusers. The title of this book clearly recognizes the challenges inherent in child protection and indicates the intention to review major developments in the field.

This book provides an edited set of readings by both established authors in the field and practitioners at the forefront of innovative practice. It seeks to integrate old and new knowledge by combining a review of the factors leading to current debates and issues with a vision of how forward movement can take place in this important area of practice. In the 18 chapters the range of topics includes not only well-known paths but also less well trod but none the less important ones. I found it valuable to have papers on organizational issues and staff care; child sex abusers and sexually aggressive youth; reforming abusers; parents; foster carers; residential care and training; issues of loss, dissociation and victims' needs, and a cluster of black, feminist and culturally different perspectives. In addition, the art of listening, and what can be learned from inquiries, together with the chapter on terror and the Stockholm syndrome, add further breadth to the span of experience and thinking. The review of research which draws upon a wide range of sources – including some of the studies contained in the Department of Health publication *Child Protection: Messages from Research* (Department of Health, 1995), which emerged while this book was in process of production – illustrates the need for more effective child protection and more reliable research.

This book should prove to be of interest to a wide audience of people involved in child protection work and in the care of children who have been abused. Such a readership is likely to include social workers; residential childcare staff; foster carers; child protection coordinators; general practitioners; health visitors; paediatricians; psychologists and nurses; police officers and probation officers; therapists and counsellors; teachers, and staff involved in the education and training of child protection workers in many settings. There are few equals to this book in the range of issues it discusses and its accessibility of presentation. It will be a valuable resource both as training material and as a 'broad read' across the subject, and will help to fill gaps in our knowledge and understanding, as well as stimulating further development in theory and practice.

Reference

Department of Health (1995) *Child Protection: Messages from Research*, London: HMSO.

Preface

The field of child protection has grown significantly since the 1960s, as an area of health and social welfare practice, as a body of theoretical knowledge and as a body of legislative and policy issues. It has developed into an extremely complex and intricate subject, characterized by a wide range of demands, challenges and dilemmas. This book seeks to play a part in helping practitioners, policy-makers and educators make sense of this immensely complex area of human services work.

Part I addresses a range of issues that are important concerns for contemporary theory, practice and policy, issues that have a bearing on the day-to-day experiences of child protection workers. The important themes to emerge from this part of the book are the need to develop anti-discriminatory forms of practice; the significance of research, and the need to evaluate outcomes.

Part II is concerned with 'Children who hurt', a deliberately ambiguous title that refers to both the hurt that children can feel as a result of abuse and the hurt that some abused children inflict on others by making the transition from abused to abuser. In many respects, we are still very much at an early stage in the development of a theoretical understanding of the intricate relationships between abuse, the pain it causes and the possible links with future abuse.

Part III has as its focus the staff dimension – that is, the range of issues that impinge on the experiences of child protection workers, the support they need and the difficulties they face. As the arguments put forward in this section confirm, there is a need for employing organizations to take far more seriously the human resources dimension of providing child protection services.

Child protection will continue to generate a great deal of concern, and we will no doubt continue to develop our understanding of this demanding field of practice. This book is presented as a step forward in developing that understanding and thereby playing a part in promoting better-informed and more effective practice.

Part I

Current issues in child protection

Introduction

The term 'battered child', which signalled the modern 'discovery' of child abuse in the 1950s and 1960s (Parton, 1985), has been replaced by broader conceptualizations of the damage that adults do to children which encompass both the sexual abuse of children and the rediscovery of the significance of neglect. However, despite the increasing sophistication of our thinking on child abuse, for many students and practitioners the immediacy of their contact with abuse, and the knowledge that they gain about it, can make it difficult for them to stand back from the sometimes harsh realities which face them. This opening section of the book has six chapters that raise issues which help to establish a broader perspective on child protection practice. They are not intended to be definitive statements, but rather are intended to raise awareness of issues which may either be taken for granted – as in Parrott's review of the consequences of child abuse – or which may simply remain unconsidered – as in Pritchard's review of the impact of intervention in reducing child mortality – or – as in the chapters by Cropper, Forrest and Pugh – are designed to re-examine familiar issues from an anti-discriminatory perspective.

The discussion and the ideas raised are not definitive statements, for the simple reason that our understandings, at both an individual and a collective level, of issues like child abuse are not static. It is obvious, from even the briefest review of post-war practice, that ideas of what constitutes abuse and what is 'good' practice have changed considerably. Not only have we been shocked by the extent of sexual abuse – which hitherto was often simplistically presented in very crude terms either as 'replacement' incest, in which daughters become the sexual partners of their fathers, or alternatively as the horrific, but thankfully rare, actions of sexual 'monsters' who prey upon vulnerable children – but we have also realized that the actions of child protection workers are not automatically beneficial in their consequences.

The phrase 'professional dangerousness' encapsulates this last idea in its narrow form: that is, where professional interventions create risks for the children they purportedly aim to protect, through such factors as errors of judgement and poor communication between professional bodies (Dale et al., 1986). However, 'professional dangerousness' can be understood in a somewhat broader fashion, as representing the risks which can arise from embarking upon forms of intervention which fail to consider the assumptions and ideas which underpin such practices.

It is in this crucial dimension that contemporary debates on child protection differ and are beginning to build a more critical understanding of what the practice of child protection entails. This part of the book introduces many of the salient issues but, as will quickly become apparent when reading the different contributions, they often raise further complexities which are not easily resolved. If this problematizes the reader's thoughts, we make no apologies, for it is our view that child protection is intrinsically an unsettling area of practice, not simply because of its dramatic nature, but because it raises very real issues about power and its exercise in professional practice.

Chapter 1 by Richard Pugh considers how social difference between workers and clients is conceptualized and may be approached and negotiated within practice. He introduces some fascinating work from other writers and tackles questions such as how to define child abuse, and what are the justifications for professional intervention. Jill Forrest, in Chapter 2, examines some of the consequences of gender expectations upon the ways in which adults and children respond to sexual abuse. Basing her chapter upon observations from her own practice, she concludes that, apart from the obvious therapeutic benefits, there is a clear case for providing post-abuse therapy for children because of its potential to reduce the risk of the abused child becoming, in turn, an abuser. She explicitly links therapy to the concept of power and suggests that such therapy should facilitate the safe expression of anger, by teaching the child non-abusive ways to exercise control over things – that is, to learn appropriate ways of being powerful.

In Chapter 3, Andrea Cropper advocates an approach to assessing and working with children and families that incorporates some of the core themes presented in the auto/biographical and theoretical writings of black feminists. She argues that, because such authors have written extensively about the personal and political dimensions of their lives in terms of race, class, gender, sexuality and social difference, an appreciation of their work will help sensitize child protection workers to the potentially inaccurate assumptions that they might make about black families, and create a better appreciation of the lived experience of their clients and of the complex factors which bear upon the circumstances of service users.

Chapter 4 by Lester Parrott begins by noting the widespread assumption that child abuse is inevitably damaging, and questions whether this is well founded by reviewing the research into the consequences of abuse. While he usefully categorizes the potential consequences into three types, Parrott's conclusion is that, while existing research is beset by the twin problems of limited generality and methodological definition, complexity remains the predominant feature in terms of the interlinked and damaging effects experienced by survivors of abuse in their childhood and subsequent adult lives.

From his review and analysis of the statistics, Colin Pritchard, in Chapter 5, shows how child deaths from adult abuse have declined since the advent of organized interventions by social work departments, the police and other agencies. He acknowledges the methodological difficulties and the limits of his analysis, but argues that there are grounds for continued optimism about the effectiveness of child protection services. These positive results are not widely known and may surprise many readers who might be reluctant to accept his conclusions – which may contradict their practical experience of increasing levels of abuse. Pritchard argues that, because social work is frequently used as a scapegoat for more general social problems, we should not ignore the growing evidence of its effectiveness.

In Chapter 6, Brian Corby and Malcolm Millar report the results of research into the nature of the relationship between child protection professionals and their clients in the light of the principles of partnership and parental participation enshrined in the Children Act 1989. In contrast to the optimism of Pritchard, their conclusions are not encouraging: in many cases a lack of clarity about what constitutes abuse, about when to intervene and about how to involve parents creates ambiguity and uncertainty about what is going on. The authors conclude that greater specificity in communications and agreements should be the foundations of better practice.

References

Dale, P., Davies, M., Morrison, T. and Waters, J. (1986) *Dangerous Families: Assessment and Treatment of Child Abuse*, London: Routledge.
Parton, N. (1985) *The Politics of Child Abuse*, London: Macmillan.

1 Considering social difference

Richard Pugh

Introduction

The practice of child protection is beset by many difficulties. This chapter considers child protection theory and practice in situations where what is conventionally described as cross-cultural and cross-national issues predominate (Boushel, 1994; Korbin, 1991); that is, where there are differences in perceptions about what constitutes satisfactory and unsatisfactory childcare. Situations where there is some perceptible difference between the formal agents of child protection and the clients raise fundamental questions about how we understand and cope with social difference. They problematize our definitions of abuse, our justifications for intervention and our conceptions of 'good' practice. This chapter proposes that conceptualizing difference solely in terms of culture and ethnicity is unnecessarily restrictive, because it ignores other aspects of difference and, most crucially, delimits the consideration of broader issues of power and social structure. This chapter considers how we think about social difference; how child abuse is defined; where child protection workers stand, and finally how such workers might begin to understand and intervene in situations of social difference. It therefore represents an attempt to use the concept of difference to link thinking about child protection more firmly into the constantly developing anti-discriminatory approach to theory and practice.

Understanding oppression

The importance of factors such as gender, race and class has been extensively acknowledged within the general literature of social work (Cheetham, 1986; Dominelli and McLeod, 1989). Within child protection literature there has been a particular focus upon the impact of child protection services upon black children and their families (Phillips, 1995). Unfortunately, some writers, in their desire to establish the harmful consequences of some forms of discrimination, have produced analyses which tend to oversimplify events. This oversimplification is most apparent in the tendency to adopt a monodimensional framework. For example, one writer might discuss racism without mention of gender or class, while another might analyse the destructive effects of patriarchal societies without recognizing that their impact may differ according to a woman's colour or class.

While each approach contributes to an appreciation of what is distinctive about racism or sexism, in their haste to reject the negative constructions of inferiority attached to particular groups the authors tend to portray all black people or all women as if they were a universal category – that is, as if they were all the same (Sibeon, 1992). Unfortunately, in rejecting the negative assumptions which derogate particular groups of people, the writers do not ultimately reject the essentialist nature of the constructs which underpin such prejudices. Paradoxically, in resisting negative attributions by attempting to replace them with positive ones, they may unwittingly reiterate the assumption of universality by claiming an homogeneity of experience and social situation for all group members. There is a fundamental problem with this approach: despite the deprecations of racist or sexist commentators, neither women nor black people are necessarily, or intrinsically, coherent, homogeneous social groups. Apart from their gender or race they may have little in common, for there may be as many differences within these categories as there are between them. Brah, in discussing the question 'Is sisterhood global?', illustrates this problem in her statement that 'we do not exist simply as women but as differentiated categories such as working class women, peasant women, migrant women' (1992, p. 131).

Arising from the problem of monodimensionality is a tendency, often unwitting, to establish 'pecking orders' of oppression (Hudson, 1989): that is, to assert the primacy of, say, race or class in the overall analysis, while other factors such as gender or disability are relegated to secondary status. This is an understandable consequence of people writing about child protection practice from their own particular social locations. After all, who else is better placed to describe the consequences of oppressive actions than those who suffer from them? However, this grounded knowledge can have problematic consequences, especially when, as Brah has noted, some writers seem to believe that:

The mere act of naming oneself as a member of an oppressed group was assumed to vest one with moral authority. Multiple oppressions came to be regarded not in terms of their patterns of articulation/interconnections but rather as separate elements that could be added in a linear fashion, so that the more oppressions a woman could list the greater her claim to the higher moral ground. (1992, pp. 136–7)

The problem with constructing hierarchies of oppression is that it oversimplifies the realities of social life and leads to a simplistic analysis of how oppressive ideas and actions actually impact upon the lives of those subjected to them. While the violence of racist thugs or rapists leaves little room for doubt about their perceptions of black people or women – in the sense that they may perceive either type of 'victim' as undifferentiated categories – much of what is oppressive in people's lives is often less dramatic and more subtly enacted. While oppression may be marked by the trauma of violence and aggression, its harmful effects are frequently more complex, both in their impact and in their implications. These negative effects, which may encompass social and material deprivation, the internalization of negative imagery and ideas, poor self-esteem and so on, are by no means inevitable. Therefore, while being black or disabled in British society may be highly predictive of group experiences, it is not inevitably so for individual members of such groups. While we can be reasonably accurate in predicting the general consequences of racism or disability, the particular experience of individuals is less certain. They may be protected by other factors or resources such as family life and social supports, political beliefs, religions and ideologies, wealth, class and occupation. For example, while white feminists have generally pointed out the negative consequences of the family, some black feminists have been more appreciative of its capacity to act as a safe place and a power base from which to engage with a predominantly white racist society. Oversimplified approaches to anti-oppressive practice carry other risks too. They may focus responsibility inappropriately. After all: 'Anti-discrimination is neither the preserve nor the responsibility of those who are discriminated against' (ILPS, 1993, p. 5). Furthermore, such approaches may allow some practitioners to avoid recognizing that, unusually, they are not the agents of change but are instead the subjects for action (Campbell, 1994).

The anti-discriminatory perspective which has been developing over the past few years has established a broader analysis which recognizes the specificity of particular forms of discrimination such as racism, while emphasizing general features which contribute to injustice and inequality, such as ideology, power, stigmatization and derogation, and at the same time pointing out the similarity of some of the consequences of discrimination in terms of marginalization, poverty and poor life-chances

(Dominelli, 1988; Thompson, 1993). The application of an anti-discriminatory perspective to the issue of child protection has immediate relevance in two ways: first, it raises the question of cultural difference in conceptions of what constitutes abuse. Secondly, it highlights the differences in power between workers and clients, and thus problematizes the relationship between them.

Social difference

In the past, accounts of injustice and inequality in respect of child protection matters tended to be presented along a single dimension of social difference, such as culture, race or class. While this was helpful in spotlighting unjust and unfair practice, it led to a rather fragmented analysis of oppression within society. The more inclusive concept of social difference has a greater utility because it:

- broadens the scope of the analysis to include many forms of difference, and thus can incorporate recognition and analysis of sexism, racism and so on;
- can enhance the analysis of the means by which difference is constructed and maintained. In this way, questions about power, social structure and location, and social definition become central to the discussion.

British society is sometimes assumed to be an homogeneous entity in which white, English-speaking, heterosexual culture is the norm, and thus all other variants are perceived as either abnormal or subcultural – in the sense that they are viewed as minority features which are pathologically different – or simply as irrelevant to the dominant mainstream. Not only are such ethnocentric representations inaccurate, but they are also self-serving devices for those people who express them. They are convenient justifications of their advocates' position, not simply because social difference can be represented as inferiority, but because it allows social problems to be seen as essentially marginal concerns which, tragic and deserving of sympathy though they may be, are not regarded as intrinsically connected with the social mainstream.

This representation of social homogeneity has, however, been extensively challenged by anti-racists, feminists and others, who have sought to point out the social differentiation which exists and who have also attempted to show how these 'problems' are inherently bound up with the social structure of contemporary British society. Therefore, adopting an approach to child protection work which recognizes the range of social variation and acknowledges that social difference will accompany many of the contacts between workers and their clients not only allows us to begin to understand what may be problematic when, for example, educated white workers work with poor, black clients, it can also encompass other variations which exist, such as differences of class and education between black workers and black clients. Thinking in this way does not deny what is specific about such situations, but it does subsume them within a more wide-ranging analysis. Adopting this higher level of generality improves the likelihood of a theory of anti-discriminatory practice which has more widespread application, but it has the accompanying disadvantage that, in doing so, we may lose sight of the important features of particular forms of oppression. Furthermore, it carries the risk that it may be misused as a sophisticated way of avoiding confronting racism or sexism within particular circumstances, by allowing unscrupulous practitioners to make an overly abstract appeal to higher-level theory.

Nevertheless, despite these risks, I believe that such an approach has considerable potential for developing child protection practice in a socially differentiated society. For example, while it recognizes that unfair recruitment practices have led to an under-representation of minorities in employment, it does not inevitably presume that a child protection worker will necessarily be a white person who somehow represents the 'normal mainstream'. Most significantly, it allows practice to be conceptualized in a manner which explicitly acknowledges the power difference between workers and clients and recognizes the reality that, however much we may attempt to 'match' clients and staff, this can never fully address the issue of difference. For, while the experiences of, for example, a black female worker and a black female client may be similar – particularly in respect of their experiences of racism – other dimensions of difference may distinguish their lived experience.

It is my contention that social difference is an inevitable aspect of any professional practice with people and that we should not seek to diminish or deny it, but should accept that such a contingency may have to be navigated and negotiated in every encounter (Thompson, 1996). This overt recognition of social difference between workers and clients opens up the possibility of more honest and direct acknowledgement of how interventions in child protection may proceed. Most crucially, it avoids any double agendas, or feelings of betrayal by clients, when workers are sometimes forced to become more authoritative in their intervention.

Social location and situated knowledge

Phenomenologists have long argued that all knowledge is partial, that it is related to the social position of the person. Anthropologists and ethnomethodologists have also developed epistemological positions which are essentially appreciative in the way they approach the question of what it is possible to know. Similarly, a central theme in the literature of emancipation, and especially in feminist accounts, is that those who wield power or seek to change things should have an appreciative understanding of the experiences of the outsider, the underdog, the excluded and marginalized. Narayan has called this insider knowledge 'epistemic privilege', by which she means that 'members of an oppressed group have a more immediate, subtle and critical knowledge about the nature of their oppression than people who are non-members' (1989, pp. 321–2). This does not mean that non-members cannot develop an appreciation of the oppressed person's position, but that this appreciation is not easily achieved, nor will it always be complete or directly felt. Acknowledgement of the epistemic privilege of insiders does not, however, imply that they necessarily 'have a clearer or better knowledge of the *causes* of their oppression' (Narayan, 1989, pp. 321–2). Otherwise, the result, as Brah notes, is that 'Assertions about authenticity of personal experience could be presented as if they were an unproblematic guide to an understanding of the processes of subordination and domination' (1992, p. 136).

The implications for child protection practice are twofold. First, it is vital that workers make some attempt to listen to the narrative offered by the people they work with. This applies to possible abusers as well as to the victims of their alleged actions. Secondly, child protection workers should not accept these accounts uncritically. If we pay no attention to the accounts of the alleged abusers, then we will certainly fail to understand what meanings, if any, abusers attach to their behaviour. This could be a crucial omission given the importance attached in UK law, and Western thought generally, to the *mens rea* – that is, the intentions that existed in the person's mind when they acted. Similarly, as Chapter 11 in this volume illustrates, if we do not appreciate the child's reality, then we may fail to understand not only what has happened to them but also, more importantly, how best to help them. Nevertheless, neither account should be accepted uncritically because, for adults, they may simply be self-serving justifications which are used to deny culpability and, for children, they may be inaccurate or mistaken stories which arise from confusion and misunderstanding. Our understanding of social location and situated knowledge also has to encompass an awareness of our own position. The recognition of the centrality of social difference thus provides a means by which we may begin to address some of the ideas and assumptions which inform our practice.

How is child abuse defined?

Child abuse may be defined in terms of the behaviour of the carer(s) towards a child, and/or in terms of the consequences for the child. There is no doubt that defining and intervening in child abuse is a normative enterprise, in that it relies upon some notions of desired, preferred or acceptable levels of child welfare, risk and outcome. The crucial question is: what, and whose, norms are being used? Workers who unwittingly and uncritically use as their point of reference norms derived from an idealized and stereotypical white middle-class family, or from other personal experience of childhood and family life, are more likely to make unfavourable assessments of those who differ from these norms. This is most apparent in situations when workers are working with poorer working-class or black families, where they may apply deficit models of child welfare which may bear no relationship to relevant criteria or actual risk. Such models are culturally biased in an ethnocentric fashion which almost inevitably leads to discriminatory and negative assessments of those families who do not conform to the supposed norm. A cross-cultural comparison of different societies quickly establishes that, while all societies have expectations and norms about what constitutes acceptable childrearing, there is considerable variation in terms of what is defined as abuse. For example, Emelie Olson (1981), an anthropologist who undertook fieldwork in Turkey, reported that local women expressed concern about her practice of allowing her 18-month-old daughter to play outdoors in a tub of water in warm weather, because of their belief that small children could easily catch a chill and die. Yet they saw nothing unusual in their advice to her to praise and kiss her daughter's genitals when bathing her, as an appropriate expression of 'positive motherly action' (Korbin, 1991, p. 69). To what extent would an explicit consideration of meaning enter into our response to Olson's example? Would we automatically regard the act of a mother kissing her daughter's genitals as 'dirty', obscene, invasive or, alternatively, in a slightly more 'enlightened' fashion, would we think that this was an inappropriate but understandable attempt to value and appreciate her daughter's body? To what extent would we consider the mother's account of her behaviour?

Korbin, in a review of cross-cultural perspectives on child abuse, states that:

> Cross-cultural variability in child rearing beliefs and behaviours makes it clear that there is not a universal standard for optimal child care nor for child abuse and neglect. This presents a dilemma. Failure to allow for a cultural perspective in defining child abuse and neglect promotes an ethnocentric position in which one's own set of cultural beliefs and practices are presumed to be preferable and superior to all others. On the other hand, a stance of

extreme cultural relativism, in which all judgements of humane treatment of children are suspended in the name of cultural rights, may be used to justify a lesser standard of care for some children. (Korbin, 1991, p. 68)

Korbin begins to address the complexities of this question by suggesting that there are three ways in which we can define child abuse. Thus, abuse may be said to occur when:

- people do not follow the culturally acceptable behaviour expected within their own culture;
- practices deemed acceptable in one culture are rejected as being abusive or harmful in another;
- social conditions 'such as poverty, inadequate housing, poor maternal and child health care, and lack of nutritional resources either contribute powerfully to child maltreatment or are considered maltreatment in and of themselves' (Korbin, 1991, p. 69).

Child protection intervention in British society is primarily conceptualized as being about the first category of definition, while the second category only becomes recognized as an issue when the perception of social difference is signalled by language, race or some other distinctive indicator of ethnicity and culture. Consequently, much of what may be significant is ignored when the markers of difference are not recognized or are overlooked – for example, when a client's first language is not English but he or she is, none the less, perceived to be competent in it as a second language. The third category of abuse is not usually seen as the preserve of personal social services and is typically perceived as being about general social welfare, since good conditions for parents and carers equate with good conditions for their children. Of course, as writers like Parton (1985) and Gil (1976) have noted, there may be telling reasons why governments and welfare agencies do not espouse the conceptions of child welfare and protection implicit in this third category.

Parton, reviewing the social context of child protection, succinctly notes that: 'Ideologically the way that the problem has been constructed blames the parents and social workers and absolves society and the state from issues of social distribution' (1985, p. 169). While any further consideration of children's life-chances and general welfare is beyond the scope of this chapter, we should not ignore this aspect, and should note that, when pursued, it may lead to some surprising observations. For example, given the greater number of child deaths caused by road traffic accidents, why do we feel more moral outrage about abuse by parents and carers than about the injuries or deaths that are directly or indirectly caused by the actions of poor drivers or by the omissions of traffic planners and the police? Boushel has noted that within a European context, the British approach to child abuse can be characterized as an overly punitive one which pays little regard to the 'amelioration of the personal and social factors underlying it' (1994, p. 176).

Taking difference into account in assessments

The perils of ethnocentric assessment were made plain in the death of Tyra Henry (see Chapter 3 in this volume) and continue to be a problematic area of practice (Phillips, 1995). In the absence of grounded knowledge, too many workers seem prepared to fill the gaps with stereotypical assumptions and inaccurate 'knowledge'. Even when they obtain accurate information, they may still be uncertain of how to use it, and what sense to make of it. Boushel has noted that, while the Department of Health has instructed workers to 'incorporate a cultural perspective' into their assessments, they have not provided much 'guidance on how "cultural variations" might be relevant to the assessment process' (1994, p. 179). Fortunately, Korbin, proceeding from her review of the research into different cultural patterns of childrearing, has made constructive suggestions as to how child protection workers might amend their assessments about people who are different from them (Korbin, 1991, pp. 70–4). She proposes three dimensions which should be examined when making such risk assessments, namely:

- the value attached to children in general within a specific culture, and the ideas held about specific categories of children which may increase vulnerability;
- the embeddedness of childrearing in wider social networks;
- the pace and extent of social change.

Vulnerability

Korbin suggests that child abuse is less prevalent 'in cultures where children are highly valued for their economic utility, for perpetuating family lines and cultural heritage, and as sources of emotional pleasure and satisfaction' (1991, pp. 70–1). However, in all societies, including these, some categories of children are more vulnerable than others. Children with health problems, those who are 'deformed' or 'handicapped', those who are unwanted, or those who are 'born under unusual, stigmatised, or difficult circumstances' are more vulnerable to neglect and abuse. Additionally, in industrialized nations particular stages of 'normal' development, such as 'toilet training' and adolescence, where oppositional behaviour or non-compliance with carers' wishes is more likely to occur, are also risky. Gender, too, is also associated with risk, typically where preferences are for male rather than female children – but not exclusively so, as sometimes there may be higher expectations of boys, which leads to harsher punishment if such requirements are not met. Behavioural expectations and particular personality characteristics may increase the level of vulnerability according to how these are perceived within specific societies.

Finally, diminished social support appears to increase the risk of abuse in many cultures. Thus, children born outside marriage, stepchildren and orphans are generally more vulnerable. It should be noted that any judgement about the likelihood of increased vulnerability can only be made with some 'insider' knowledge of how these categories are perceived within a particular culture. For example, economic utility alone can lead to the exploitation of children as workers by exposing them to high levels of health risk and by depriving them of opportunities to develop their formal educational skills.

Embeddedness

The potential for risk in any situation can be reduced by the extent to which childrearing is embedded within wider social networks. At its simplest this is evident when people other than the parents either assist or take a direct hand in looking after the child, since this tends to mitigate 'the consequences for children of having an inadequate or aggressive parent' (Korbin, 1991, p. 72). Somewhat surprisingly culturally acceptable patterns of childcare which appear to enhance children's safety are child-lending, fostering and informal adoption, although these measures need to be understood within their cultural context, since children who are redistributed for economic reasons are more likely to be at risk if they 'fail to be useful'.

Korbin suggests that urbanized industrial societies with smaller living units are less safe for children because of the relative social isolation, and particularly when there is less consensus about what constitutes acceptable childcare. Hartz (1995), in a study of conflict resolution patterns in Hawaii, notes that, while Polynesians as a rule cherished their children, in the traditional village children who faced the prospect of being physically punished by their parents could escape their fate by simply moving around to another house in the village, where a friend or relative would shelter them. If they actually succumbed to the physical punishment they would shout out loudly so that neighbours and relatives could hear what was happening to them. In such circumstances it was considered acceptable for other people to intervene. Korbin similarly notes that, amongst rural Hawaiians, 'relatives do not hesitate to yell from one house to another if a spanking has gone on long enough or is too severe for the child's misbehaviour' (1991, p. 74). The point is that urban life, with its smaller family units and less tightly knit societies, offers fewer opportunities for informal intervention, support and assistance. These aspects of urban life, when coupled with the view that childrearing is a private and not a public responsibility, increase the risk of abuse.

Rapid social change

Korbin suggests that rapid social change itself increases the risk of abuse. This increased risk is believed to arise from the breakdown of traditional structures and values. The social networks and patterns of obligation noted in the previous section are diminished or destroyed at the very time that carers are subject to greater stresses. Korbin does not uncritically accept this position and suggests that such change is often unfavourably contrasted against an idealized backcloth distinguished by the 'assumption of a lack of deviance in small societies' (1991, p. 74). Nevertheless, social change may well reduce the value attached to children. For example, when people move from agrarian to industrial societies, children change from being a productive asset, in terms of their potential as labour, to being a drain upon family resources in societies where schooling is compulsory until well into their middle teens; that is, they are potentially devalued by the change in circumstances.

We should be wary of romanticizing the 'old ways', for while it is all too easy to see how societies undergoing rapid change may begin to 'discover' their own child abuse, there is little doubt that such discoveries are linked to changing perceptions of what is considered acceptable childcare. Mejiuni, writing of Nigeria, explicitly makes this point: 'Many adults appear to have warped notions and wrong perceptions both of their duties to their children/wards and the children's responsibilities to them' (1991, p. 143). Interestingly, Mejiuni's justification for intervention derives not from an explicit acknowledgement of civil rights, but is expressed in terms of the greater good of the society: 'The extent to which children will be able to partake in nation building either as leaders or followers when they become adults will depend upon the type of nurturing they have received' (1991, p. 144).

Korbin's work usefully points child protection workers towards a much wider assessment of their social situation, but in my view her dimensions for risk assessment are probably most usefully employed not to replace the more traditional methods of assessment used by workers and agencies, but to extend or amend them. Boushel's work (1994, p. 179) provides one example of how this might be accomplished. Specifically she has developed the dimensions into a framework which has four factors:

- the value attached to children;
- the status of women and carers;
- the social interconnectedness of children and carers;
- the extent and quality of the safety nets available.

This approach develops the socially situated analysis of child abuse even further away from narrow perspectives on child protection which conceptualize abuse solely as the result of individual pathology. From this position Boushel argues that not only will workers make more accurate assessments of risk, but that they will make better plans for intervention because they can recognize other protective factors and strategies involving more collective and community-based actions. However, as Simpkin (1979) has noted, we should not be naive as to the potential political implications of developing our notions of assessment and intervention in this manner – it will very likely lead to conflicts with our 'political masters' and with critics who disapprove of any moves which appear to politicize what they presume, or prefer to pretend, are non-political problems.

Where do we stand?

Korbin does not address the issue of cultural dominance and the question of which culture is promoted and policed within a particular society, nor does she address the question of cultural difference within a given society. But it is precisely these questions which may cause difficulty in situations of social difference within contemporary practice. For example, while it may be generally accepted within UK society that committing actions which kill children is unacceptable and is thus reflected in the use of the criminal law to prosecute offenders, there is less agreement about acts of omission such as withholding life-saving treatment on religious grounds. However, child protection practice does not revolve solely around immediate life-or-death issues but also involves less clear-cut issues of neglect, physical punishment and emotional abuse, and while there may be widespread agreement about the extremes of behaviour, it is likely that many cases are far more ambiguous. What would we think if we directly encountered the practice recommended to Olson by her Turkish counterparts? Why do we forbid the genital mutilation of girls but permit it – albeit in a much less severe form – in circumcision of boys?

To some extent we may choose to dodge these difficult issues by seeking refuge in an 'apparatchik' stance: that is, by claiming, as Davies (1981) did, that it is our job to enforce the laws, not make them. Unfortunately, it is not that simple. This is a naive and disingenuous stance because it suggests that all behaviours are neatly defined into discrete categories of permitted and prohibited actions, whereas in the multiple processes of law enforcement there is considerable space for idiosyncratic interpretation, selective application and personal and institutional bias (Cicourel, 1968; Heidensohn, 1985). Furthermore, the uncertainty of interpretation and response in child protection practice is additionally complicated by the fact that such practice is conducted within an ever-changing society, one which is continuously creating and re-creating itself and its ideas of what constitutes acceptable practice by parents and workers. While statute law, case law precedents and formal policies do establish 'rules' by which we may judge adult behaviour towards children, this is, in part, constructed by our own practice. So, while some ambiguities and uncertainties may be 'tested' formally by the court, or informally by the media and wider professional opinion, much of our practice is effectively shrouded from the wider public gaze by the restrictions of confidentiality, and by the covert assumptions and invisible processes of thought which precede and accompany our actions. Davies' stance simply fails to acknowledge these sociological aspects of practice and barely recognizes the extent to which workers themselves may be important actors for changes in policy and statute.

Whether we like it or not, our knowledge is situated: that is, it is related to our specific social location along the various dimensions of difference – our position in terms of occupation, gender, language, race and so on. What, therefore, is the justification which allows us to sift, screen and ultimately accept or reject different narratives? In part, it probably derives from our own moral and social perspectives, which in turn arise from our acceptance of social norms regarding acceptable childrearing practices. Potentially, the most powerful justification might derive from our professionally privileged knowledge about the harmful effects of child abuse upon its victims (see Chapter 4 in this volume).

The crucial question for the development of an anti-discriminatory practice is: how do we acknowledge the reality of cultural variation without adopting an extreme cultural relativism in which anything goes? A conventional response is to make reference to notions of civil rights: thus documents like the UN Charter on the Rights of the Child are cited in support of our duty to intervene. This of course begs the question of whether these legitimizing devices are themselves simply social constructions which reflect particular discourses about human society. In my view, proponents of the anti-discriminatory perspective should be quite adamant in rejecting the kind of simplistic multiculturalism which leads to a stance of uncritical relativism – a position which effectively neutralizes the possibility of intervention. Instead of proposing a more-or-less explicit rights-based approach to social action, we should accept that at the heart of the anti-discriminatory perspective is a moral choice, namely a fundamental commitment to the core value of human equality. Therefore, as I have argued elsewhere (Pugh, 1996), despite accepting the socially constructed nature of all knowledge, the anti-discriminatory approach ultimately derives its legitimacy from an examination of the consequences of human actions. It is our knowledge of the damaging consequences of child abuse within Western societies that provides our most secure justification for intervention, and we should not allow the sophistries of postmodernism to deflect us from this 'common-sense' appreciation of actions and consequences (O'Neill, 1995). This is a complex area which warrants a more extensive discussion. However, for those readers who wish to venture further, Malik (1996) has provided an interesting exploration of this aspect of social action, and he too, while accepting the constructed nature of human thought, argues that amongst the multiple accounts of the social world, there are both more and less accurate renditions of it.

Approaching social difference

The preceding discussion has been rather analytical, and the implications for practice may not be readily apparent. This section attempts to pick up some of the relevant points which workers should consider in their practice.

When a worker and client clearly perceive difference between each other, the recognition may trigger other underlying assumptions and expectations of each other's behaviour, attitudes, beliefs and competence. Conversely, when they do not jointly perceive difference, they may presume a similarity of shared ideas and attitudes. Problems are likely to arise when the perception of similarity is mistaken, and a sense of confusion or betrayal is not an uncommon response amongst clients who thought that they were 'getting on well' with their workers. Davis and Proctor (1989) suggest that clients who perceive that they differ from their worker are likely to have three concerns:

- Can I trust this person? (Does this person like/dislike or respect me, or people like me? The client's perception of the likely response to these questions will determine the extent to which they, in turn, are prepared to trust the worker.)
- Is this worker competent? (Does he or she have the knowledge and skills to help me, or deal with me fairly?)
- Does this worker understand my social world? (Does he or she know about people like me? Is this person a credible person whose advice and suggestions may be valid?)

Research undertaken in the USA has shown that perceived trust, competency and validity are socially structured (Davis and Proctor, 1989). For example, male workers are often perceived by clients as being more competent than women. Black workers may be thought by black clients to have more goodwill and to be more trustworthy than white workers. However, we should be wary of assuming that this will hold for all similar situations. For example, Jaffe (1995), in a study of the influence of ethnic stereotypes upon clients' preferences for workers amongst Sephardi (Israelis of Middle Eastern origin) and Ashkenazi (Israelis of Western origin), found a clear preference amongst both groups for Ashkenazi workers. This initially seems surprising given that the Sephardi are, in many respects, marginalized within Israeli life and might therefore be expected to express a preference for workers from their own ethnic group, but it clearly raises complex questions about employment opportunities, social contact, socialization, and perceived social and professional status within an unequal society. Unfortunately, little research has been done into the perceptions and expectations held by ethnic minorities within British society.

In view of this, an open and explicit acknowledgement of difference is probably best made early in the initial encounter. For example, when a white worker meets a black client, questions or comments such as 'Do you think my being white will affect our working together?', or 'If you think at any time that I don't understand what you mean because our backgrounds are different, I hope you will tell me', signal the willingness of the worker to consider the relevance of what is different between them. The message conveyed is: I will work hard to understand your situation and I recognize that the difference between us may raise sensitive and difficult issues. Most importantly, the worker is signalling that he or she realizes that the client may well have valid reasons for doubt or suspicion. Professional courtesies are very important. Proper introductions, titles and handshakes (where appropriate) should be used to convey respect. An authentic professional demeanour which is based upon the worker's personality but conveys a professional seriousness of purpose can be undermined by superficial attempts to relate to clients using inappropriate argot, slang or dialect. Culturally appropriate attending skills and knowledge relating to expectations about eye contact, interruptions and turn-taking in conversation, and other non-verbal behaviours, should be acquired and used. There are considerable cultural differences in the extent to which different groups respond to aspects of practice such as directness, self-disclosure, empathetic understanding and disagreement. For example, workers with little experience of non-European cultures should be aware that some of the 'traditional' Western principles of practice such as confidentiality and individualization may simply be regarded as irrelevant or obstructive by some clients from African cultures (Silavwe, 1995).

Conclusion

From the preceding discussion it is clear that an anti-discriminatory practice encompasses many of the general rules for good practice, where careful listening, accurate feedback, consultation, reflection and reliability demonstrate the worker's understanding and commitment, but it goes further in embedding these rules within a broader appreciation of the demographics and biographies of both workers and their clients. Thus, workers should strive to:

● inform themselves about the complexity of social location and social diversity for both themselves and their clients;
● have some understanding of, and sensitivity to, the oppressive experiences of particular groups without being overly deterministic in their expectations in respect of any given individual;
● be aware that their own position is not neutral, either in terms of their own location within service agencies, or in terms of an explicit commitment to anti-discriminatory practice;
● understand the importance of hearing the narrative of the other person, but not accept these accounts uncritically.

We should acknowledge that our existing formal knowledge base is in many respects inadequate.

There are a number of areas where existing knowledge is limited, in particular in the British context, where there is very little published material on how different ethnic communities conceptualize abuse. This is rather different from the USA, where there is much more information and interest in how abuse might impact upon children of different backgrounds. This difference could relate to the circumstances of abuse as well as the child's reactions to it. Sanders-Phillips, in her research in Los Angeles, found that there appeared to be significant differences in the susceptibility to and level of depression between black and Latino girls who had been abused. She suggests, for example, that: 'Cultural sanctions against premarital sex may also decrease self-worth in Latino girls who were forced into premarital sex' (1995, p. 701). Ho (1990) has suggested that, because Asian women in the USA have been socialized into placing family harmony above their own personal well-being, they put up with higher levels of male violence in their homes before seeking help and protection for their children.

Similarly Boushel suggests that the position and experience of abuse victims within Irish travelling communities is related to the internal norms of the group. Thus, where there is a 'high value on marriage' and few opportunities for women to sustain themselves outside the group, 'the options facing vulnerable women and children within the travelling community are limited' (1994, p. 186) and the experience of abuse may differ accordingly. The point is not to 'discover' differences in abuse rates amongst different ethnic groups – in fact, when adjusted for socioeconomic circumstances, US studies appear to show little variation – but to sensitize ourselves as workers in a British context to the possibility that children who have been abused may respond differently according to their particular ethnic background, and to begin to develop responses and strategies for intervention which take account of these differences. However, with all of this recognition of difference it is vital to remember the point made earlier, that there may well be very important commonalities amongst clients. Similar experiences of oppression, of poverty and of situation may prove highly significant in terms of problem analysis, intervention, advocacy and self-help.

Finally, the recognition that the pursuance and development of an anti-discriminatory child protection practice is both a political and a moral enterprise requires that a worker's personal commitment to equality should be more than a superficial statement of adherence. As Archard (1993) has indicated, it requires a rethinking of our notions of what childhood itself is, for no longer can we sustain romanticized constructions of it as a state of innocence and incompetence. Good practice therefore implies that we do not simply do things *to* and *for* children, but that as far as possible we attempt to work *with* them.

References

Ahmed, S., Cheetham, J. and Small, J. (eds) (1986) *Social Work with Black Children and their Families*, London: Batsford Academic.

Archard, D. (1993) *Children: Rights and Childhood*, London: Routledge.

Boushel, M. (1994) 'The Protective Environment of Children: Towards a Framework for Anti-Oppressive, Cross-Cultural and Cross-National Understanding', *British Journal of Social Work*, 24 (2), pp. 173–90.

Brah, A. (1992) 'Difference, Diversity and Differentiation', in Donald and Rattansi (1992), pp. 64–79.

Campbell, B. (1994) 'A Personal Urge to Control', *The Independent*, 26 October, p. 15.

Cheetham, J. (1986) 'Introduction', in Ahmed et al. (1986), pp. 1–38.

Cicourel, A. (1968) *The Social Organization of Juvenile Justice*, New York: Wiley.

Compton, B. R. and Galaway, B. (1989) *Social Work Processes*, Pacific Grove, CA: Brooks Cole.

Davies, M. (1981) *The Essential Social Worker: A Guide to Positive Practice*, Aldershot: Arena.

Davis, L. E. and Proctor, E. K. (1989) *Race, Gender and Class: Guidelines for Practice with Individuals, Families and Groups*, Englewood Cliffs, NJ: Prentice Hall.

Dominelli, L. (1988) *Anti-Racist Social Work*, London: Macmillan.

Dominelli, L. and McLeod, E. (1989) *Feminist Social Work*, London: Macmillan.

Donald, J. and Rattansi, A. (eds) (1992) *Race, Culture and Difference*, London: Sage.

Gil, D. G. (1976) *The Challenge of Social Equality*, New York: Schenkman Publishing.

Hartz, D. T. (1995) 'Comparative Conflict Resolution Patterns Among Parent–Teen Dyads of Four Ethnic Groups in Hawaii', *Child Abuse and Neglect*, 19 (6), pp. 681–9.

Heidensohn, F. (1985) *Women and Crime*, London: Macmillan.

Ho, C. K. (1990) 'An Analysis of Domestic Violence in Asian American Communities: A Multicultural Approach to Counselling', *Women and Therapy*, 9, pp. 129–50.

Hudson, A. (1989) 'Changing Perspectives: Feminism, Gender and Social Work', in Langan and Lee (1989), pp. 70–96.

ILPS (1993) *Working with Difference*, London: Inner London Probation Service.

Jaffe, E. D. (1995) 'Ethnicity and Clients' Social Worker Preference: The Israeli Experience', *British Journal of Social Work*, 25 (5), pp. 615–33.

Korbin, J. E. (ed.) (1981) *Child Abuse and Neglect: Cross Cultural Perspectives*, Berkeley, CA: University of California Press.

Korbin, J. E. (1991) 'Cross Cultural Perspectives and Research Directions for the 21st Century', *Child Abuse and Neglect*, 15 (1), pp. 67–77.

Langan, M. and Lee, P. (eds) (1989) *Radical Social Work Today*, London: Unwin Hyman.

Malik, K. (1996) 'Universalism and Difference: Race and the Postmodernists', *Race and Class*, 37 (3), pp. 1–17.

Mejiuni, C. O. (1991) 'Educating Adults Against Socioculturally Induced Abuse and Neglect of Children in Nigeria', *Child Abuse and Neglect*, 15 (1/2), pp. 139–45.

Narayan, U. (1989) 'Working Together Across Differences', in Compton and Galaway (1989), pp. 317–28.

Olson, E. (1981) 'Socio-economic and Psychocultural Contexts of Child Abuse in Turkey', in Korbin (1981).

O'Neill, J. (1995) *The Poverty of Postmodernism*, London: Routledge.

Parton, N. (1985) *The Politics of Child Abuse*, London: Macmillan.

Phillips, M. (1995) 'Issues of Ethnicity and Culture', in Wilson and James (1995), pp. 108–26.

Pugh, R. G. (1996) *Effective Language in Health and Social Work*, London: Chapman and Hall.

Sanders-Phillips, K. (1995) 'Ethnic Differences in Psychological Functioning Among Black and Latino Sexually Abused Girls', *Child Abuse and Neglect*, 19 (6), pp. 691–706.

Sibeon, R. (1992) *Towards a New Sociology of Social Work*, Aldershot: Avebury.

Silavwe, G. W. (1995) 'The Need for a New Social Work Perspective in an African Setting: The Case of Social Casework in Zambia', *British Journal of Social Work*, 25 (1), pp. 71–84.

Simpkin, M. (1979) *Trapped in Welfare*, London: Macmillan.

Thompson, N. (1993) *Anti-Discriminatory Practice*, London: Macmillan.

Thompson, N. (1996) *People Skills*, London: Macmillan.

Wilson, K. and James, A. (eds) (1995) *The Child Protection Handbook*, London: Balliere Tindall.

2 Gender expectations and child protection practice

Jill Forrest

Introduction

Different gender expectations for boys and girls are widely recognized, particularly in terms of such things as patterns of dress and behaviour. Powerful social pressures operate which influence the ways in which adults think about children and which also influence children's expectations of themselves. I have found that young children quickly conform to gender expectations, so that even when parents make a special effort to address this problem, by offering their children a variety of toys, employing different role models and using non-sexist language, children are often inhibited or discouraged by other adults or children from pursuing activities outside the gender norms.

This short chapter examines some of the consequences of gender expectations upon the ways in which adults and children respond to sexual abuse. It is intended to increase awareness of the ways in which these socially structured ideas may be reproduced and reinforced, and it attempts to link abuse of, and by, children into broader issues of power and powerlessness. In this context, childhood can be understood as a powerless phase in the human life course during which we are dependent on others for our physical and emotional needs, and have little or no control over life decisions. When the powerlessness of childhood is exacerbated by the oppression of abuse, then correspondingly the degree of helplessness is greatly increased. A damaged sense of self, a lack of personal autonomy, and a sense of uncertainty and confusion about adult roles and responsibilities are common amongst victims of abuse.

What do adults think?

There is little doubt that many adults who accept conventional gender expectations of adult male and female sexuality attempt to make sense of the sexual abuse of children in these terms. Consequently, in a society in which boys learn expectations of aggression and predatory sexuality, while girls are taught a more passive role, adults may trivialize, dismiss or deny sexually abusive behaviour by young males as simply 'boys being boys'. For example, the behaviour of one 13-year-old boy who attempted to bugger a 7-year-old boy was described and assessed by the police and by the parents of both children as 'a childhood prank', 'a game that got out of hand', and as 'a misunderstanding'! This response may, of course, derive from a more widespread denial of children's sexuality in our society, although arguably each of the parties involved may have had rather different reasons for characterizing this attempted rape as child's play. The behaviour of boys who sexually abuse girls is also frequently interpreted by means of the conventional gender expectations. It is perceived as a 'normal' urge, wrongly expressed or inadequately controlled, a misguided extension of supposedly 'normal' behaviour.

Conventional gender expectations, when applied to girls who are victims of sexual abuse, result in considerable sympathy for those who fit the preconceptions of passivity and weakness, and who are therefore viewed as understandably tearful victims. However, abused girls who breach conventional expectations, and who are perceived as being in some way either sexually provocative or precocious, may be blamed in much the same way as some adult victims of rape are, being described as 'slags' or as having 'asked for it'. I once overheard a male colleague say to another male colleague: 'No wonder she has been abused, did you see the way she was dressed?' In a similar fashion, the out-of-role behaviour of girls who victimize others is either dismissed as 'play' or treated with total disgust or bewilderment.

How do children respond?

If the abuse suffered is that of sexual abuse, then the child's feelings may be independent of their gender, but the way they express these emotions will be shaped by it. Boys seem to be more likely to express their distress through externally directed, more active behaviour, which may include aggression and violence towards other people. In contrast, girls' responses appear to be more passive and internally directed: their distress may be expressed tearfully, by running away or, in severe cases, by self-mutilation.

Additionally, children's perceptions of why the abuse happened, and its consequences, may also be gender-based. For example, some boys who have been abused by men have subsequently asked: 'Does it mean I'm a "poof"?'

Victims of sexual abuse will look for situations which help them regain some feelings of control. New behaviours may be tried out by the child, and they will experiment with such behaviour until they understand its processes, variations, what it feels like, whether it is enjoyable, fun, satisfying or painful, and so on. It is likely that any behaviour which gives an abused child power or allows the expression of powerful emotions will be reinforced in that child. The child's experience of the behaviour and its consequences will determine whether the behaviour is reinforced or abandoned by the child. For a child who has been abused and who has not had help to come to terms with and make sense of the experience, there are, in both the long and the short term, two negative possibilities:

- to enact sexual behaviour by continuing in the role of victim;
- to become a victimizer themselves.

While these potential outcomes exist for girls and boys alike, it is my belief that the gender expectations prevalent within our society tend to steer boys towards an abusive victimizing role and girls into a perpetuation of the victim role. There are serious implications for the safety of the victims and of other children whenever either of these two possibilities occurs. Children who have been sexually abused may re-enact some of the behaviours they have seen or been subjected to. These re-enactments may include both victim and aggressor behaviours. As noted in the previous section, adult social reactions to boys and girls when they re-enact elements of their experiences will often be quite different. However, in the absence of any decisive adult censure, control and support, a victimizing child of either sex may be perceived by their less powerful peers as being powerful, and he or she may continue to abuse younger children, physically and sexually with virtual impunity.

Some consequences of abuse

When a child exhibits sexually victimizing behaviour they have power over the victim. If adults ignore this behaviour or minimize it by calling it sexual experimentation and thus unwittingly allow it to continue, then the victim becomes powerless. Alternatively, if adults react in a shocked, angry, anxious or horrified manner, the victimizing child may understand that the adults are unable to cope with his or her behaviour. This realization can thus reinforce a potentially powerful pattern of behaviour.

It is especially difficult for children who live in families where there is an expectation that boys will grow up to abuse others, and that women and girls will always be powerless victims. If a boy remains in such a family, then he is likely to reproduce such expectations, and if his mother escapes from such a household with him, then the behaviours which he has already learned may act as unwelcome reminders of what has gone before. The boy's unwanted behaviour may consequently be perceived as deliberately abusive and somehow inevitable.

The consequences of failing to realize or respond effectively to abused children may continue into those children's adult lives. Undetected and uncontrolled, boys may continue into adulthood as abusive men, men who remain a risk to all children with whom they come into contact. Such men may deny their own abusive behaviour, and may also apply the same denial to abusive behaviour by other males and thereby fail to protect children from the depredations of other men. In fact, involving other men may even provide some sort of comforting rationale, a means of avoiding labelling their own behaviour as illegal or abusive.

Similarly, if girls are not taught that they have a right to assert their wishes, or at the very least that they have a right to say 'no', if they never experience non-abusive relationships or realize that such relationships exist, then they too may carry the consequences of abuse into adult life. Abused girls who are not helped to come to terms with their experiences may, as mothers, be afraid to touch or hug their own children because they fear that the child may interpret this as abuse. Some mothers may remain afraid that they may actually abuse their own children. In contrast, other women who have suppressed their abusive experiences may, as adults, miss or deny the symptoms of abuse in their own family or household. Those who have continued in a passive victim role may, in their adult life, replicate risky relationships based on submission to more dominant men. Their capacity to recognize and resist both their own continuing experiences of oppression, as well as that of their children, is thus severely impaired.

Conclusion

While it is by no means inevitable that children who are subjected to abuse will themselves become involved in abuse in their adult lives, there is a higher risk of this being the case than with children who did not suffer abuse. Therefore, apart from the obvious therapeutic benefits to the children, there is a clear case, in terms of prevention, for providing post-abuse therapy for children, therapy which incorporates work on the issue of re-enactment of behaviour. Children need to have boundaries set for their own behaviour which are realistic in terms of their age and gender. Such therapy should facilitate the safe expression of anger and teach the child non-abusive ways to exercise control over things: that is, to learn appropriate ways of feeling powerful. This work must include an assessment of how gender roles are affecting the child, and should help them challenge the gender expectations which may have shaped or reinforced their particular patterns of thought and behaviour.

While girls are more likely to need help in the overt expression of anger and boys in expressing their sorrow, the eventual goal is to reach a point in therapy where they can place responsibility for their experience of abuse on their abuser whilst taking responsibility for their own re-enactment of behaviours. From this point they have choices about what they will do in the future. All victims, male and female, have the potential to make the transition from victim or victim/abuser to survivor, but this is made more likely with skilled help.

3 Rethinking practice: Learning from a black feminist perspective

Andrea Cropper

Introduction

Major developments in child protection, such as the Children Act 1989 and the numerous official inquiries into cases of abuse, have stimulated many child protection professionals, especially those working with children and families from diverse backgrounds, to rethink their approach to their work. However, some agencies and professionals seem unable and unwilling to develop holistic, integrated approaches to assessment of such individuals and families – approaches which incorporate an understanding of the nature and operation of power and oppression. In such instances, those working in this arena need to reassess their own values and methods, and attempt to understand the important relationship between them.

This chapter advocates an approach to assessing and working with children and families that incorporates some of the core themes presented in the auto/biographical and theoretical writings of black feminists. Some of these writers, such as Brah (1992), Collins (1990) and hooks (1981, 1984, 1989), have written extensively about the relationship between their values and their methods for understanding social science and social relationships. Their analyses focus upon the personal and political dimensions of lived experience relating to race, class, gender, sexuality and social difference. A common feature of their work has been the desire to view these social divisions not as additive systems but as interlocking systems of oppression, a standpoint which promotes a more thorough analysis of difference and of the social reactions to it. Thus, an appreciation of black feminist perspectives is more likely to sensitize workers to the lived experience of their clients and to encourage a more developed understanding of the complex factors which interact with and act upon their clients' lives.

Learning from our mistakes

The 1980s witnessed several major child abuse inquiries; it was a volatile time for those involved in child protection. These inquiries highlighted important concerns about how agencies and workers were investigating child abuse, and about how they sought to protect children who came from backgrounds different from those of the workers involved. These inquiries alerted us to the existence of stereotyping within the assessment process and to the problems which have arisen when professionals have assumed universal categories of race, culture, class and gender. In such instances, workers have assumed rather than assessed (Thompson, 1993). Sometimes this has resulted in a failure to protect black children in abusive situations because workers have based their assessments upon cultural assumptions made about particular 'racial' groups. Such assumptions may be punitive or liberal in their perspective, but both are likely to prove dangerous in practice.

Ahmed et al. (1986) have noted the tendency to base assessment on such assumptions and have highlighted severe discrepancies in the way black families and individuals have been dealt with. Ahmed (1989) has also noted the prevalence of punitive and coercive approaches to black families. In some cases, black children have been unnecessarily moved from their families when workers, and not just white workers, have used their own assumptions about family life as a baseline in their assessment, and have thus failed to recognize the strengths of black families. This may partly account for the notably higher proportion of black children in care than white children (ABSWAP, 1983). Such misguided and mistaken assumptions may operate in different and apparently less punitive directions, as, for example, in the case of Tyra Henry. Here the black grandmother was not seen as an individual but as a stereotype, albeit a positive one in this instance – as the 'all-coping indestructible African Caribbean matriarch' – an assumption which, as events sadly demonstrated, contributed to a failure to recognize the dangerousness of Tyra's situation, because of the overestimation of the protective influence of the grandmother (Lambeth, 1987, pp. 108–9).

Relevant themes from black feminist perspectives

This section outlines some of the relevant ideas found in the auto/ biographical and theoretical writings of black women – women who have advocated that 'Understanding does have to be founded on an analysis of real interconnecting, systematic, material oppressions as well as the personal experiences of their effects' (Clifford and Cropper, 1994, p. 53). The following subheadings are used simply as a device for identifying some of these core ideas found within the literature and are not intended to represent the entirety of the perspectives, nor to imply that each idea is somehow a separate entity. They are clearly interlinked, both theoretically and in their implications for practice.

Non-universal categories and the interconnection of oppression

Black feminists have been prominent in emphasizing the various ways in which oppressions interconnect and overlap, and they have criticized feminist and anti-racist theories which have excluded dimensions of race, class, disability and sexual orientation from their analyses (Collins, 1990; hooks, 1981, 1984, 1991; Lorde, 1984). What has also been critiqued are perspectives which advocate a hierarchy of oppressions in which racism comes first, while some of the others, if mentioned at all, trail far behind (Kershaw and Logan, 1994). Thus, what is most significant is the recognition that the category of 'woman' is not universal, and that an analysis of women's position must look at how a woman's situation is affected by interconnecting issues of race, class, disability, sexual orientation, age, and so on. For example, a woman's experience of living in poverty may be further compounded by race and disability (Glendenning and Millar, 1987). Black feminist literature has examined the effects of racism on black people's lives and raised awareness that, for example, being black in Britain is different from individual to individual and community to community. It is vital for workers to connect biography, culture, structure and history when working with clients, as it is evident that black people are not a homogeneous group – the common dimension is that, while all black people are subject to racism in its various forms, the personal experience of individuals will differ according to other factors in their lives. Cosis-Brown (1992) has cautioned against any stereotyping that assumes certain individuals as a type.

Identity and difference

Analysing difference and concerns with issues of identity have been at the forefront of black feminist literature. Approaching and working with social difference is made more complex by the reality of shifting identities and cultures, where individuals' identities and positions are not static but are fluid and can change over time (Lorde, 1984). This can best be seen in the case of black women who have multiple identities and who may align themselves with different groups such as black groups, women's groups, lesbian groups or disabled groups at different times. Workers who perceive individuals simply as members of a single social category will inevitably limit the scope of their assessments. There are obvious issues here around identity in terms of children in care. The care process can have profound implications for a child's self-image and identity. Research on black children has suggested that many of them have an early awareness of the negative images of their blackness (Maxime, 1986; Milner, 1983; Varma, 1993). In addition to whatever other problems they may face, these children have the pervasive effects of racist stereotyping and negative and derogatory imagery to contend with. Workers should therefore acknowledge the lived experience of black children and be aware of the impact this may have upon the children's development and upon their perceptions of adults and authority figures.

Mother-blaming

While feminist writers have raised professional awareness and challenged sexist assumptions and stereotypical notions about women's roles, the incorporation of such ideas into practice is often quite superficial. Braines and Gordon (1983) have pointed out that much of the literature on child protection is preoccupied with the mother's responsibility for abuse and protection. Apart from the obvious fact that this attribution of culpability is inherently problematic, it tends to devalue the role of other significant people and agencies by pathologizing women as 'poor mothers' who have apparently 'failed' to protect their children from men. Women abusers who do not fit into the stereotypical notions of 'woman' and 'mother' are generally treated differently and more harshly, as though they are doubly at fault by being abusers and by not conforming to the conventional stereotypes of women. Furthermore, mother-blaming is problematic because, at one level, issues of poverty, isolation, racism and stress are conveniently ignored while, at another, it downplays the potential contribution of other individuals, especially within 'non-Western' family structures.

Narrative and standpoint

Black feminists have advocated that the narrative form is crucial to their ways of understanding, assessing and communicating (Collins, 1990). Black women, being at the 'sharp end' of discrimination, can speak with some authority about their lives and the experience of marginalization and disadvantage. Their accounts of their lives have produced a triangulation of knowledge, experiences and perspectives that can be used by others to understand the problems they face. Thus, the special knowledge gained by oppressed individuals who occupy what has been termed as the 'outsider within' position in society (Collins, 1990; hooks, 1981, 1984) allows other more powerful people to appreciate the underside of oppression. Being the 'outsider' brings with it a certain kind of knowledge concerning those who are in dominant positions as well as the different knowledge of the dominated. Collins (1990) argues that this ontological knowledge and experience should be used as a valid viewpoint on the social world. She also puts forward the need to develop an interlinking of theory and lived experiences which can acknowledge and respect differences without fixing them outside history or contemporary social relations.

Narratives need to be viewed in both personal and political contexts. Accurate assessment and informed intervention are dependent upon hearing the voice of the other person and require an appreciation of the wider context in which that voice is speaking. It is imperative to give people a voice – to hear what they are saying and how they are saying it. Historically, it has been difficult for many clients to tell their stories, especially those people who have been perceived as different, deviant and 'difficult'. In the case of children who have been abused, the formal guidelines for interviewing still impede these young victims' narrative and make it difficult for their voice to be heard through the constraints of gathering formal evidence. In working with children, adults should be aware of their relatively powerful position and should thus seek ways of enabling children to communicate, as well as reflecting upon the language they use and the pace of conversation. One example from my own practice involved a black girl who was showing me her life-story book. Towards the end of the book, there were some typed notes which described how her mother had schizophrenia, and in a welter of social work jargon recorded the reasons for the girl's admission into care. When I asked the child what this page was, she told me that she did not want to look at that page because it was boring and she could not read some of the words, nor understand them. Clearly, this child was not being allowed to tell her story and record it in her own voice.

Reflexivity and power

Linked to the analysis of difference and social divisions are issues concerning reflexivity and power. The concept of reflexivity is not a new one, and although it was developed by feminist writers (Stanley, 1990; Williams, 1989; Bhavnani, 1993) other writers have included issues of reflexivity and power within their perspectives (Freire, 1972). Reflexivity refers to the process by which individuals need to acknowledge their own role and position in any social interaction, and the effects that this has upon the interaction itself, upon themselves, and upon the people with whom they are interacting. It is important for workers consciously to locate themselves within the intervention and interaction – that is, to become aware and take cognizance of their own position, perspective and values, and to appreciate the other person's perceptions of them. Thus, in any client/worker relationship it is necessary for us to be aware of the influence we have as workers – workers who occupy specific positions in terms of profession and other social differences – upon the individuals and situations we are assessing. This is important because these perspectives and values will determine which 'facts' we select from our interactions and how we subsequently choose to interpret them. My own research into fostering and adoption assessments highlights the complexity and fluidity of such power issues. I was a black woman interviewing mainly white, female, working-class applicants for fostering and adoption, but unusually perhaps, I was the one who had power by virtue of my formal role of practitioner/researcher.

The personal as political

Black feminists have highlighted how black women's lives and oral narratives interconnect and cannot be separated from the social, political and economic aspects of the society they live in. In most cases black women do not have a choice about whether to separate their personal lives from wider, external societal issues. Again, this was a feature of my research in which black, disabled and gay interviewees appeared to have some understanding of this concept and spoke about how being black, disabled or gay had implications in both their personal and outside lives. For example, black women's experiences are shared with, and are part of the lives of, others, particularly when they live within black communities.

Contemporary policy and practice

Much of the literature of the 1980s failed to make reference to black children and families and those from various other ethnic minority groups whose diverse life experiences will be compounded by racism and who may encounter such racism from the agencies which strive to maintain their care and welfare. This literature therefore made little attempt to develop an analysis of oppression and power in both personal and structural terms. For example, the Department of Health (1988) booklet *Protecting Children* made only very limited reference to race and, while the Children Act 1989 requires 'due consideration' to be given to a child's race, religion and culture, some have interpreted these requirements in minimalist terms. Within the formal knowledge base of social work, explicitly anti-racist and feminist approaches to theory and practice have attempted to challenge race- and gender-oppressive theories and practice at both personal and institutional levels (Dominelli, 1988; Dominelli and McLeod, 1989; Thompson, 1993). One major theme within this literature is that the categories of race, gender, class, disability, age and sexual orientation are not viewed as single-factor issues in isolation from each other. Other writers have also highlighted the strengths of various individuals and communities who had previously been portrayed as problematic and pathological (Ahmed, 1990), and this has encouraged workers to reassess some of the more common stereotypical assumptions. For example, Asian women have provided analyses on roles and relationships within their cultures which present quite a different picture from the simplistic portrayals of them as quiet, passive women, repressed by arranged marriages (Bhavnani and Coulson, 1986).

Some social work agencies have dealt with difference by trying to match workers and families, particularly in terms of race and gender divisions. While it is useful for children and families, particularly in the sensitive area of child abuse, to be matched with individuals who can share and understand experiences of racism, sexism and other oppressions, it is essential for *all* workers to have an understanding of how oppression operates. It should not be a foregone conclusion that all black people and all women are able to recognize race and gender oppression, particularly given that we are all subject to the internalizing of racist, sexist and other oppressive stereotypes. Black workers alone cannot solve all problems, some of which have been created by the oppressive practices of such agencies. Thus, black workers may be isolated, marginalized and exploited within some agencies, having difficult cases to attend to and advise upon, and receiving limited support.

Making assessments

While official policy on child protection advocates a comprehensive assessment in order to 'understand the child's and family's situation in order to provide a sound basis for future assessments' (Department of Health, 1988, p. 21) and thus acknowledges the importance of workers understanding the cultural context, workers should be wary of cultural relativism and an overreliance on cultural explanations (Channer and Parton, 1990). If not, such analyses may 'detract attention both from significant emotional factors as well as structural factors, such as class and race' (Ahmed, 1981, cited in Gambe et al., 1992, p. 32). Despite efforts to incorporate issues of race and culture when working with black families, there is an unfortunate tendency to omit other dimensions of social difference. Such reductionist approaches isolate and marginalize race from the other dimensions of class and gender. However, race and racism can only be fully understood if analysed in the context of these other dimensions to the lives of individuals and families (Gilroy, 1992). Furthermore, there is a tendency to construct a hierarchy of oppressions in which racism comes first and the others follow on afterwards, whereas, as noted in the previous section, factors such as gender also affect how women experience racism and being black.

The danger of these stereotyped assumptions has been that individual families and their norms, values and functioning have often not been assessed in a holistic sense, by attempting to put families and individuals into convenient 'boxes' it has had the effect of limiting workers' understanding of such clients and their situations. In the case of black families, black communities vary enormously in terms of social and cultural traditions, so that there is no single style of black family functioning. The same applies to white families, who are not homogeneous in terms of values, norms, culture and traditions. Although 'white family' is not a term that is used in the same way as 'black family' is used, it should be noted that most people would be hard-pressed to define white family norms in the way that black family norms have often been unquestionably defined. Indeed, we are usually never alerted to the fact that an assessment or report is actually about a white family, as whiteness is assumed as the norm. With both white and black families it would be equally wrong to impose middle-class, heterosexual stereotypical norms and values. It is difficult for social workers to make 'clear, comprehensive and expert judgements' (Department of Health, 1988, p. 20) if they persist in using such limited references and analyses of difference.

Taking power into account and locating the worker within the assessment

While it is important to look at individuals' life experiences, where it is possible to locate individuals within their particular, personal experiences and thus avoid stereotyping, care should also be taken to encompass a much broader framework which includes issues of power and oppression and some reflection upon the worker's own position. This points to 'a need to look at ways in which our [workers'] membership of different social categories has affected our perceptions and others' perceptions of us' (Clifford and Cropper, 1994, p. 54).

Difficulties can occur whenever there is a difference in power between client and worker. Indeed, black families themselves do feel that class is often an issue with any worker – black or white (Rhodes, 1993). The fact is that *all* workers have power over their clients by virtue of their professional and their class position. These factors potentially influence all worker/client relationships and so impinge upon all aspects of intervention. Reflexivity is a two-way process, and thus it is necessary to be aware of the influence workers will have on clients' lives and the effect clients and their situations will have on the workers'. This is particularly so within the area of child protection where the very nature of such work can lead to intense stress and sometimes burn-out. Workers need to recognize their professional status, whoever they are – their race, gender, age or other social division does not take this dimension away.

Issues of reflexivity and power are of prime importance when workers are engaged in comprehensive assessments involving family members' life histories, or are helping individuals in making sense of their own lives and actions. It is imperative that individuals are allowed to speak their narrative – that is, talk about their own lives in their own words. This avoids the immediate perils of unwittingly superimposing meaning upon the actions and motivations of other people. Listening carefully to the narratives of clients may help workers to gain insight into the individual's experiences in a way that can guard against their being influenced by assumptions and stereotypes.

Conclusion

It is my view that the broad themes I have identified as central to black feminist perspectives can be used to assist social workers and other professionals to achieve more comprehensive assessments – assessments that are not reductionist in nature. Thus an appreciation of the ideas of non-universal categories and interconnection of oppression; identity; mother-blaming; narrative and standpoint; reflexivity and power, and the personal as political should serve to raise personal awareness of these issues and potentially can be developed into a more thoroughgoing analysis for child protection practice and process – analysis which is able to acknowledge the diversity of individuals' experiences, grounded in the very different social conditions of their lives (hooks, 1981; Lorde, 1984). Furthermore, such knowledge generated from black feminist perspectives can be used to assist an understanding of the position of all individuals, whether they are black or white, female or male. This is possible because black women have been concerned about promoting multiple standpoints and have allowed for difference in a way that others have rejected or analysed in narrow terms. Incorporating some of these themes in theoretical and practical terms may pave the way for a more holistic and thorough approach to assessing children and families in the arena of child protection. Therefore, all workers are recommended to attempt to:

- make connections between individual lives and the wider social political structures and history;
- listen carefully to personal narratives, and to situate these within the broader context;
- explore areas of misunderstanding and personal ignorance by asking for explanation and clarification, and thus avoid making ethnocentric assumptions.

References

ABSWAP (1983) *Black Children in Care*, London: Association of Black Social Workers.
Ahmed, B. (1989) 'Protecting Black Children', *Social Work Today*, 8 June.
Ahmed, B. (1990) *Black Perspectives in Social Work*, London: Venture Press.
Ahmed, S. (1981) 'Asian Girls and Culture Conflict', cited in Gambe et al. (1992).
Ahmed, S., Cheetham, J. and Small, J. (eds) (1986) *Social Work With Black Children and Their Families*, London: Batsford.
Bhavnani, K. K. (1993) 'Tracing the Contours: Feminist Research and Feminist Objectivity', *Women's Studies International Forum*, 16 (2), pp. 95–104.
Bhavnani, K. K. and Coulson, M. (1986) 'Transforming Socialist Feminism: The Challenge of Racism', *Feminist Review*, 23 June, pp. 83–94.
Brah, A. (1992) 'Difference, Diversity and Differentiation', in Donald and Rattansi (1992), pp. 64–79.
Braines, W. and Gordon, L. (1983) 'The New Scholarship on Family Violence', *Signs*, Spring, pp. 490–531.
Channer, Y. and Parton, N. (1990) 'Racism, Cultural Relativism and Child Protection', in Violence Against Children Study Group (1990), pp. 105–21.
Clifford, D. and Cropper, A. (1994) 'Applying Autobiography: Researching the Assessment of Life Experiences', *Autobiography*, 3 (1), 3 (2), pp. 47–59.
Collins, P. H. (1990) *Black Feminist Thought*, London: Unwin Hyman.
Cosis-Brown, H. (1992) 'Lesbians, the State and Social Work Practice', in Langan and Day (1992), pp. 201–20.
Dent, G. (ed.) (1992) *Black Popular Culture*, Seattle: Bay Press.
Department of Health (1988) *Protecting Children: A Guide for Social Workers Undertaking a Comprehensive Assessment*, London: HMSO.
Dominelli, L. (1988) *Anti-Racist Social Work*, London: Macmillan.
Dominelli, L. and McLeod, E. (1989) *Feminist Social Work*, London: Macmillan.
Donald, J. and Rattansi, A. (eds) (1992) *Race, Culture and Difference*, London: Sage.
Freire, P. (1972) *The Pedagogy of the Oppressed*, Harmondsworth: Penguin.
Gambe, D., Gomes, J., Kapur, V., Rangel, M. and Stubbs, P. (eds) (1992) *Improving Practice with Children and Families*, Leeds: CCETSW.
Gilroy, P. (1992) 'It's a Family Affair', in Dent (1992).
Glendenning, C. and Millar, J. (eds) (1987) *Women and Poverty in Britain*, Brighton: Harvester Wheatsheaf.
hooks, b. (1981) *Ain't I a Woman*, London: Pluto Press.
hooks, b. (1984) *Feminist Theory: From Margin to Center*, Boston: South End Press.
hooks, b. (1989) *Talking Back*, London: Sheba.
hooks, b. (1991) *Yearning, Race, Gender and Cultural Politics*, London: South End Press.
Kershaw, S. and Logan, K. (1994) 'Heterosexism and Social Work Education', *Social*

Work Education, 13 (3), pp. 61–81.

Lambeth (1987) *Whose Child? The Report of the Panel Appointed to Inquire into the Death of Tyra Henry*, London: London Borough of Lambeth.

Langan, M. and Day, L. (eds) (1992) *Women, Oppression and Social Work*, London: Routledge.

Lorde, A. (1984) *Sister Outsider: Feminist Theories*, New York: The Crossing Press.

Maxime, J. (1986) 'Some Psychological Models of Black Self-Concept', in Ahmed et al. (1986), pp. 100–16.

Milner, D. (1983) *Children and Race: Ten Years On*, East Grinstead: Ward Lock Educational.

Rhodes, P. (1993) *Racial Matching in Fostering*, Aldershot: Avebury.

Stanley, L. (1990) *Feminist Praxis*, London: Routledge & Kegan Paul.

Thompson, N. (1993) *Anti-Discriminatory Practice*, London: Macmillan.

Varma, V. (ed.) (1993) *How and Why Children Hate*, London: Jessica Kingsley.

Violence Against Children Study Group (1990) *Taking Child Abuse Seriously – Contemporary Issues in Child Protection Theory and Practice*, London: Unwin Hyman.

Williams, F. (1989) *Social Policy: A Critical Introduction*, Cambridge: Polity Press.

4 Researching the effects of child abuse

Lester Parrott

Introduction

Much research time and effort have rightly been directed to the detection and investigation of child abuse. However, for practitioners working with those who have been abused, there is a relative dearth of information about its effects, both long- and short-term, upon which to base appropriate intervention (Oates and Bross, 1995; Reder et al., 1993). In the absence of such information, many practitioners may develop their knowledge of such effects from their personal experience of practice and from the acquisition of the 'common sense' stock of knowledge about child abuse. This 'common sense' is likely to presume as a 'fact' that child abuse is damaging in its consequences, and that it can so damage children that they, in turn, may become abusers of others. It is not the intention of this chapter to reject that assumption, but it is my aim to attempt to clarify which effects are well established by research and to point up some of the limitations of that research. For example, in Chapter 7 in this volume, Bannister and Gallagher, in describing work undertaken with children who sexually abuse other children and noting the effects of previous abuse as an important factor to be considered in the causation of abuse, are careful to acknowledge the limitations of our 'knowledge'. This caution is well founded for, as research by Dobash et al. (1993) has shown, 77 per cent of the perpetrators studied had not been abused themselves.

While there is a growing body of research in the USA, in the UK, as the report *Child Protection: Messages from Research* (Department of Health, 1995) has identified, there remains a shortage of information that can be used to guide child protection practice after the initial stages of investigation and detection. It is the purpose of this chapter to provide a review of recent research into the effects of child abuse, with a view to highlighting issues which will be of use for practitioners in working with the effects of abuse on children. These effects, which may be manifested in childhood or later in adult life, can usefully be categorized as being of three types – that is, the consequences for the victims in respect of:

- sexual and criminal behaviour;
- mental health;
- parenting behaviour.

These divisions are made in order to make the studies easier to understand. They are not intended to oversimplify or misrepresent the reality of abuse, nor are they seen as being mutually exclusive consequences – clearly, the effects may be complex and interwoven.

There is no discussion of possible developmental delays resulting from traumatic experiences in childhood, but suffice to say that much of the literature is relatively limited in terms of the timespan of recording and observation. However, Gibbons et al., who undertook a study which examined the effects of physical abuse on children nine to ten years after the abusive events were discovered, found that their data:

> pointed away from the conclusion that physical abuse in early life had a direct [or long-lasting] effect on children's development. It seemed rather that physical abuse was in some cases an important sign of a number of other generally damaging circumstances, in particular of a harshly punitive, less reliable and less warmly involved form of parenting. (1995, p. 67)

Of course, there are some events, such as severe injuries, which are so traumatic that their effects cannot but be found in later childhood or adult life, and it should be noted that this study did not attempt to investigate the more subtle, but perhaps more pervasive, effects of emotional abuse upon personal esteem and identity. What follows, then, is a review of the research material divided into the three broad categories of the consequences of abuse, as listed above. In each of these areas the results of research will be discussed and the veracity of their findings will be described as the researchers assess them. This is followed by a brief review of some of the methodological problems involved in this area of research, and a summary of the main implications for practice.

Sexual and criminal behaviour

Much research has attempted to describe possible links between the experience of childhood sexual abuse (CSA) and the victim's subsequent involvement in abusive or inappropriate behaviour. In Friedrich's (1993) review of the literature, he outlines a range of studies which use diverse methodologies based on empirical assessments of sexual behaviour in relation to children. These include reviews of personal records; parent reports; the relationship of abuse variables to sexual behaviour; psychological assessment of the child, and direct observation of the child's behaviour. Friedrich concludes that there is an increasing body of research which has demonstrated that sexual abuse is linked to increased sexual behaviour in the victim following the abuse. In particular, increases in this behaviour appear to be related to specific abuse factors such as the number of perpetrators, and to more general behaviour disruption. However, one problem is that the type of assessment method used relates to whether or not sexual behaviour is observed in the first place. Some methods are less reliable than others. Commenting on the use of children's drawings to infer experiences of abuse, Friedrich noted that mixed results were obtained and were less significant than direct observation of children. As he remarked:

> Direct observation of children led to relatively consistent findings on increased sexual behaviour. It appears that drawings, for example, are one more step removed from the child than the more proximate behaviour observed either by parents or other observers. (1993, p. 64)

The limitations of this method are obvious: the subjective interpretations of these drawings may say more about the viewer than about the artist. We should be wary of inferring abuse from what may be quite benign representations of family life or general life experiences. Similar difficulties have also been highlighted in observing the play of children with 'anatomically correct' dolls and then interpreting its significance as a sign of abuse. Everson and Boat (1994) found a wide range of interpretations between professionals as to what forms of play constituted evidence of sexual abuse. Howitt (1992) describes this research and highlights some of the differences. For example, while 'Half of the social workers saw the laying of the dolls on top of each other as abnormal – only one fifteenth of law enforcement officers did' (p. 88)!

In concluding his review, Friedrich notes that increased sexual behaviour by sexually abused children is consistently recognized and that more research needs to be devoted to assessment and intervention and the longer-term implications for the children. This conclusion mirrors that of Hallett and Birchall (1992) for a UK context: 'sound empirical evaluations of outcomes of treatment options are lacking' (p. 326).

Adams et al. (1995) studied a group of 499 'seriously mentally ill' children receiving treatment at a psychiatric hospital. The subjects were categorized as follows:

no inappropriate sexual behaviour   (n = 296)

inappropriate sexual behaviour   (hypersexual, n = 82)
                                           (exposing, n = 39)
                                           (victimizing, n = 82)

Information was taken from hospital records in the form of chart reviews. Although there are obvious methodological problems arising from the nature of the sample (thereby prompting caution about the extent to which it is possible to make any wider inferences), the study had the benefit of using a comparison group (no inappropriate sexual behaviour) to highlight which clinical features were specific risk factors for the inappropriate behaviour group, rather than those more broadly associated with mental disorder. Overall, 82 per cent of those with inappropriate sexual behaviour had some history of being sexually abused, but in the comparison group only 36 per cent had similar histories. Within the inappropriate sexual behaviour group with more severe problems (exposing and victimizing) there was a clear association with a number of factors, such as developmental delays, lower IQ scores, other behavioural difficulties, and also having been abused. It was clear that there was a stronger association between having been sexually abused and displaying inappropriate sexual behaviour than other factors. The researchers found that the greater the severity of the history of abuse, for example in terms of the number of perpetrators involved, then the greater the chance of involvement in the more serious forms of inappropriate sexual behaviour.

Widom and Ashley Ames (1994), using analysis taken from criminal records in Indiana, attempted to assess the long-term criminal consequences of childhood sexual abuse. They compared cases of validated childhood sexual abuse with a group consisting of physically abused and neglected children, and with a control group who were matched for age, race, sex and class. They concluded that, compared with other types of child abuse and neglect, childhood sexual abuse does not uniquely increase an individual's risk for later delinquent or criminal behaviour. However, when compared with the control group, both groups of children who had been abused were significantly more likely to commit a sexual offence. Where these three characteristics were found together (neglect, and physical and sexual abuse), then victims were more likely to run away than was the case for those experiencing sexual abuse only. It is significant that the majority of both the male and the female sexually abused children in this study did not have an official criminal history. We should therefore recognize, as the authors note, that 'Delinquency and criminality represent only one possible type of outcome associated with childhood sexual abuse' (1994, p. 315).

This is an important finding, as it suggests the multifaceted nature of the effects of child abuse in later life and directs us to be sceptical of attempting to highlight one consequence as being necessarily more significant than another in the experiences of survivors of abuse. One encouraging finding was that a relationship with a significant and supportive person may act as a buffer for the long-term consequences of abuse. This raises crucial issues for future research, as examining cases where children appear to overcome, or have been protected from, negative consequences of their early childhood experiences may have considerable implications for how social workers attempt to prevent and work with the damaging consequences of abuse. Furthermore, it suggests that the status of 'victim' is not an inevitable nor an irreversible consequence of childhood abuse. Child protection workers should, therefore, more readily consider the potential benefits to be gained by working in the long term with survivors, and also acknowledge the potentially valuable work of survivor groups who have been able to step away from and challenge the status of 'victim' so readily imputed to them by some professionals.

Mental health

The traumatizing effects of childhood sexual abuse (CSA) on mental health have been widely noted. It is accepted as axiomatic by many practitioners that it carries a legacy which feeds into long-term psychological harm. This appears to be borne out by the prevalence of CSA amongst those seeking help with psychological problems (Davenport et al., 1994).

The study by Davenport et al. attempted to gauge whether there was a consensus as to what abuse people considered to be most severe in terms of its consequent effects. The authors wished to assess whether these views coincided with wider, more grounded, empirical research and observation. Their sample, which consisted of professionals in the field, students, and patients with eating disorders who themselves had a high incidence of CSA, showed a high level of agreement between respondents as to what factors contributed to CSA. The people in the sample were also asked to identify the relative strength of the relationship between the duration and forms of abuse and the consequences, by distinguishing between those factors which they perceived to be less serious and those which were deemed most serious. The results, as one might expect, showed that the abusive act itself was seen as a highly significant element. Thus, abuse which involved physical contact abuse was rated more serious than non-contact, but the use of force to overcome resistance to CSA was considered to be potentially even more traumatic. Less predictably, the variable which received the most consistent results was the disclosure of CSA and its effects upon the victim. This traumatic effect was not limited simply to the initial response at the time of disclosure. In fact, there was broad agreement that a lack of continuing familial support was the worst post-abusive environment for the CSA victim.

To professionals who are considering what kind of support would be most beneficial for a victim, this finding suggests that interventions such as family therapy and groupwork may be more effective than individual support offered in isolation. This should not diminish the overall importance of disclosure itself as profoundly therapeutic, since, as Davenport et al. indicate, such disclosure can be extremely helpful in reducing feelings of shame, stigma, guilt and personal blame. Speculatively, however, it seems that the broader acknowledgement that abuse has taken place and the social support offered by significant others is most helpful in diminishing the traumatic effects of CSA on a victim.

The existence of a consensus on the relative importance of the different factors associated with abuse should not be taken as evidence of the inevitability of a victim being damaged by even the most traumatic events, nor of the relative innocuousness of seemingly trivial incidents – although, clearly, the possibility of agreement between professionals and their clients about the effects of CSA will be important for the process of helping. For example, such agreement means that the client will have a greater chance that their feelings and expectations will be understood and met by the worker. The importance of this finding is crucial in enabling professionals to distinguish those factors which either contribute to or hopefully mediate against abuse at various stages of the abuse cycle. In developing this line of research, it may be productive to distinguish between the primary and post-abuse situation and therefore identify those interventions which are of most help at the respective stages of abuse and recovery.

Rowan et al. (1994) studied 47 survivors of CSA who had sought help. The authors attempted to examine the relationship between the seriousness of CSA experienced and the subsequent development of post traumatic stress disorder (PTSD). Using a standardized measure of PTSD, they found significant correlations between the intensity of the abuse in both duration and severity and a diagnosis of PTSD and its level of severity. The problem with the study, as the authors note, concerns the influence of other childhood/adult traumas in the subjects' lives which might have affected the development of PTSD. As the authors remarked: 'Given the report of these other traumas, it might have been expected that these other traumas would have been significantly related to the PTSD measures' (p. 59). Therefore, we should be wary of mistakenly attributing cause and effect to incidents which may have had their roots in the past and which may also have been significant in forming the current level of trauma. Davenport et al. (1994) suggest that researchers undertaking studies should, in the future, obtain more extensive measures of other trauma experiences. For practitioners, this observation highlights the importance of obtaining accurate histories of family and client experience, and implies that we should be careful not to oversimplify the possible interlinking of different factors in constructing our understanding of problems, causes and possible therapies. Wind and Silvern (1994) tried to address this issue by studying how differences in the personal experiences of parental warmth and childrearing affected female survivors' psychological difficulties in relation to their childhood physical and sexual abuse. They found a clear differentiation between victims' perceptions of parental warmth – which strongly influenced the relationship between intrafamilial child abuse and levels of self-esteem and depression – and the association of abuse with post traumatic stress syndrome – which was independent of perceived parenting.

Brayden et al. (1995) attempted to study the lasting influence of CSA upon adult mental well-being and feelings of physical self-esteem. They studied the hospital records of women with a history of mental health problems and searched for differences between those reported as having been sexually abused in childhood and those with no recorded history of such abuse. The authors were somewhat surprised to find that childhood sexual abuse was not a good predictor of how sexually abused women felt about their emotional and psychological health after family and other demographic variables were taken into account. However, despite this lack of a direct independent association between this hypothetical concept and CSA, the levels of physical well-being and worth were lower for sexually abused women than for non-abused women when other explanatory variables were controlled.

Interest in the impact of the severity of CSA experienced by its victims has been stimulated by the controversies about the existence of ritualized forms of abuse. Lawrence et al. (1995) attempted to assess the impact of such abuse in relation to women who had been sexually abused in childhood. Their study was an empirically based assessment of the consequences of self-reported CSA which examined whether there were differences between women who in childhood had experienced ritualistic forms of abuse (CRA) and those who had experienced non-ritualized forms only (NRA). The study found that the CRA group exhibited and experienced significantly higher levels of trauma, which related to factors such as the duration of abuse and the number of perpetrators. Although the study made no claim as to the veracity of the CRA group's claims, the symptoms reported were consistent with profiles of individuals who have suffered other, more easily discernible forms of traumatization.

La Fontaine (1995), in her research on ritualized abuse, found that many of the children who reportedly had been subjected to CRA had suffered extreme levels of traumatization as a result of their experiences, but that there was little evidence that CRA, as distinct from NRA, was a significant factor. More pertinently, the levels of trauma appeared to be linked to the seriousness of the abuse, in terms of factors such as the number of perpetrators and the practices involved, rather than to any ritualized components. However, because these cases were rather extreme ones, the impact on the children was in turn intense and, for many workers, highly disturbing. La Fontaine suggests that the effect of this on professionals was for them to 'seek evidence of an event of assault or abuse commensurate with the magnitude of the damage' (p. 75), to the extent that they sought, or were susceptible to, notions of unusual ritualized practices. The practices were, in La Fontaine's view, mostly known forms of sexual deviation, all being behaviours depicted in existing child pornography. Furthermore, these demonized explanations tended to obscure more significant factors, such as the extreme poverty and deprivation in which many of the children lived.

The impact of such evidence of traumatization and its effect on workers is notable in the response of workers to therapeutic issues. Recognizing the scope and scale of the distress felt by the children and the effects this trauma has upon workers themselves requires that workers are clear about their own feelings of abuse, given that some may have experienced abuse themselves. In this context, self-help groups for practitioners and survivors of abuse may well be an important source of support in dealing with this kind of trauma (Lloyd, 1993).

Parenting behaviour

There are two dimensions to this type of effect. First is the effect of abuse upon the child's parent(s) and their subsequent response to the child and his or her behaviour. Second is the longer-term effect upon the abused individuals in adult life when they themselves become parents – that is, upon their capacity to parent their own children.

Recent work in the UK has focused on the impact of abuse upon the mothers and carers of abused children. Two studies by Monck and colleagues both examined the effects of 'treatment' plans on such children and their carers, and found that, while there was little change in the children's feelings of depression and suicide after intervention, there were significant improvements in the carers' self-esteem and parenting skills. Monck and New (1995), in a study of a group of mothers of children subjected to CSA, attempted to examine the efficacy of groupwork compared with family work alone, but were unable to come to clear conclusions in this respect. Although their evidence was not conclusive, the clinicians involved in assessing the participants' progress did claim improvements for those additionally involved in group therapy. The children were able to share their feelings about their abuse with others, and mothers were said to have made progress with their own feelings regarding their children's abuse. Mothers reported fewer behavioural problems in their children and that their relationship with their children had improved. Differences in the researchers' and the clinicians' findings may not necessarily invalidate the group approach. As Monck et al. (1995) suggest, it is possible that groupwork may well deepen mothers' and children's understanding of whose responsibility the abuse was, yet it may not lessen the feelings of depression which may arise in the short term as a result of this increase in understanding. Thus, if the research was carried out over a longer term, the benefits described above might become more apparent. The positive message from this research is that interventions of whatever kind (group/family or both) could reduce feelings of depression in carers and so enhance their capacity to cope with their children's behaviour, 'normal' or otherwise.

A common concern expressed by parents who were themselves victims of childhood sexual abuse is their fear that they will be unable to parent their own children adequately. This fear in itself can be debilitating and, in turn, may lead to problems in parenting their own children. Cole et al. (1992), in a study of incest survivors, attempted to assess the range of difficulties that such parents experienced. The study compared three groups of women, those:

- whose father was alcoholic (often associated with incest) but not abusive;
- with fathers who were not abusive nor alcoholic;
- with fathers who had involved daughters in incest.

In comparison to the other two groups, the women who had experienced incest felt inadequate as parents. They reported feelings of lack of confidence and lack of control, and felt emotionally overwhelmed by the demands of parenting. This was particularly difficult in relation to the promotion of autonomy and self-control in their children. As Cole et al. noted, parental consistency, organization and a sure but sensitive manner are usually positively associated with the development of self-control and autonomy in children. The difficulties incest survivors reported with their own children suggest the possibility of a vicious circle of feelings of inadequacy which both impairs their capacity to cope and exacerbates the difficulties they have with their children, and which in turn leads the carers to feel more inadequate and less confident in parenting.

Relationship problems with their children also fed through into survivors' relationships with their partners, as the incest victims' experience of their family of origin was significant in corroding the trust that builds between partners in adult life. Finding a positive relationship with their marital partner, as the researchers describe it, predicts feelings of confidence and control which may suggest, as noted above, the importance of supportive relationships in mediating the negative long-term effects of incest.

Some problems of methodology

For a variety of reasons, as most researchers would concede, researching the effects of child abuse is fraught with methodological difficulties. These might begin, for example, with the question of defining what actually constitutes abuse (Department of Health, 1995) and extend through to the reliability of self-report and recall studies, encompassing the whole gamut of problems traditionally associated with survey research. This section does not attempt to provide a thorough review of these difficulties but, instead aims to alert the reader to some of the more pressing problems in respect of the studies reviewed here.

Conceptualizations, design and representativeness

Ghate and Spencer (1995) note that the way in which child sexual abuse is conceptualized and operationally defined influences the overall design of the study, the nature of the questions asked and, crucially, the estimates of the prevalence of such abuse which are produced. A review of the literature shows that a wide variety of different methodologies are used. These range from self-report data (Bagley et al., 1994) or empirical research based on clinical samples using structured interview techniques (Rowan et al., 1994), to questionnaires used with groups outside the identified abused population, such as students (Davenport et al., 1994). Much of the data gathered by these studies is specific to the research design and the nature of the population studied, and so there are obvious limits to the extent to which it is possible to generalize from it. This problem of representativeness means that studies based upon, for example, samples of children and adults undergoing psychiatric treatment may be highly unrepresentative of the wider population of people who have been abused.

Research instruments, measurement and comparisons

Clearly, such selectivity has benefits in terms of targeting research but it undoubtedly influences the professional 'common sense' assessment of the effects of abuse, particularly the impact of these effects on the future physical and psychological health of those abused. This aspect is raised in a review of the empirical assessment of sexual behaviour in sexually abused children made by Friedrich (1993), who notes that increased sexual behaviour in such children is consistently identified as a consequence of sexual abuse. The problem here is that: 'The type of assessment method [used] seems related to whether or not sexual behaviour problems are observed' (p. 64) in the first place. The potentially self-fulfilling nature of such activity is obvious: the significance is that our knowledge of CSA and its consequences is affected by the ways in which researchers choose to study the problem – that is, the methods they adopt to measure the extent and prevalence of such abuse within their chosen population. Many studies do not allow effective comparisons to be made either between different populations or over the passage of time. It would be useful if researchers attempted some standardization of the research instruments used for the assessments of children both before and after therapy, and if they clearly specified the criteria for successful outcomes.

Conclusion

While these important methodological problems must be acknowledged, it should also be recognized that, in view of the low level of knowledge currently obtaining, these studies do provide some important information for practitioners wishing to understand the effects of abuse on victims. What I am arguing for in this review is an informed and critical reading of the literature, which recognizes the limitations of the studies in terms of their absolute validity, but which does not dismiss the information contained in them as having no practical value at all.

The first major point is that while practitioners are extensively engaged in the detection and investigation of child abuse, there has been less focus on more positive aspects of how to work with the consequences of abuse for both carers and children. Following in the wake of the Cleveland Inquiry and the persistent underfunding of social service provision (Schorr, 1992), part of the problem in the UK in recent years has been this imbalance of effort, where prevention and ameliorative efforts have been overwhelmed by the focus on guidelines for greater sophistication and accuracy at the assessment stage (Farmer and Owen, 1995). Although the intention of the Children Act 1989 was to create a framework for partnership in childcare interventions, as noted in Chapter 11 in this volume, this is not without its own problems. For example, not all families wish to be assisted or are in a position to be treated in the way that some practitioners may want to work with them. Nevertheless, it is probable that the best way to help children who have been abused is not through individual therapy but by supporting their carers.

This review has, for the heuristic reasons noted in its introductory section, separated out different categories of effects of abuse, but perhaps the most significant finding from the research is the multifaceted impact of the effects of abuse, rather than the isolation of single outcomes (Widom and Ashley Ames, 1994). The complex interaction of multiple factors in the abusive actions, in the child's experience and in the carers' responses should compel us to treat with caution any unitary views on the effects of child abuse which isolate that abuse from the social context in which it takes place.

Given the potential benefits of various forms of family work, groupwork and peer support, it remains questionable whether these forms of long-term intervention have any priority in many social services departments in the UK. Although recent government guidelines have indicated that social services departments may be too focused on prioritizing protection work, the problem of resources as well as the operational perspective will continue to impede developments. The dilemma that departments face in this area is acute. While a shift of focus would provide greater opportunities for workers to justify and embark upon long-term supportive work, the resource base for children's services continues to be under threat and at risk of collapse, especially in inner city areas, as successive reports into child abuse failures have documented (Parton, 1991). If government attempts to refocus social service departments onto issues of prevention are successful, then it is to be hoped that resources will be available to provide the longer-term support and intervention that this review has shown to be so crucial in working with child abuse. However, there remains a more fundamental question about whether it is appropriate to frame intervention solely within the narrow therapy-oriented model which continues to dominate everyday practice (Hallett and Birchall, 1992; Parton, 1985).

References

Adams, J., McClellan, J., Douglass, D., McCurry, C. and Storck, M. (1995) 'Sexually Inappropriate Behaviours in Seriously Mentally Ill Patients', *Child Abuse and Neglect*, 19 (5), pp. 555-68.

Bagley, C., Wood, M. and Young, L. (1994) 'Victim to Abuser: Mental Health and Behavioural Sequels of Child Sexual Abuse in a Community Survey of Young Adult Males', *Child Abuse and Neglect*, 18 (8), pp. 683-97.

Brayden, R., Deitrich-Maclean, G., Dietrich, M. and Sherrod, K. (1995) 'Evidence of Specific Effects of Childhood Sexual Abuse on Mental Health Well-Being and Physical Self-Esteem', *Child Abuse and Neglect*, 19 (10), pp. 1255-62.

Cole, P., Woolger, C., Power, T. and Danielle Smith, K. (1992) 'Parenting Difficulties

Among Adult Survivors of Father–Daughter Incest', *Child Abuse and Neglect*, 16, pp. 239–49.

Davenport, C., Browne, K. and Palmer, R. (1994) 'Opinions on the Traumatizing Effects of Child Sexual Abuse: Evidence for Consensus', *Child Abuse and Neglect*, 18 (9), pp. 725–38.

Department of Health (1995) *Child Protection: Messages from Research*, London: HMSO.

Dobash, R., Carrie, J. and Waterhouse, L. (1993) 'Child Sexual Abusers: Recognition and Response', in Waterhouse (1993), pp. 113–35.

Everson, D. M. and Boat, B. W. (1994) 'Putting the Anatomical Doll Controversy in Perspective: An Examination of the Major Uses and Criticisms of the Dolls in Child Sexual Abuse Evaluations', *Child Abuse and Neglect*, 18 (2), pp. 113–29.

Farmer, E. and Owen, M. (eds) (1995) *Public Child Protection Practice: Private Risks and Public Remedies*, London: HMSO.

Friedrich, W. (1993) 'Sexual Victimization and Sexual Behaviour in Children: A Review of Recent Literature', *Child Abuse and Neglect*, 17, pp. 59–66.

Ghate, D. and Spencer, L. (1995) *The Prevalence of Child Sexual Abuse in Britain*, London: HMSO.

Gibbons, J., Gallagher, B., Bell, C. and Gordon, D. (1995) *Development After Physical Abuse in Early Childhood: A Follow-up Study of Children on Protection Registers*, London: HMSO.

Hallett, C. and Birchall, E. (1992) *Coordination and Child Protection: A Review of the Literature*, London: HMSO.

Howitt, D. (1992) *Child Abuse Errors*, Hemel Hempstead: Harvester Wheatsheaf.

La Fontaine, J. (1995) 'The Extent and Nature of Organised and Ritual Sexual Abuse: Research Findings', in Department of Health (1995), pp. 73–5.

Lawrence, K., Cozolino, L. and Foy, D. (1995) 'Psychological Sequelae in Adult Females Reporting Childhood Ritualistic Abuse', *Child Abuse and Neglect*, 19 (8), pp. 975–84.

Lloyd, S. (1993) 'Facing the Facts: Self Help as a Response to Childhood Sexual Abuse', in Waterhouse (1993), pp. 191–207.

Monck, E. and New, M.(1995) 'Sexually Abused Children and Adolescents and Young Perpetrators of Sexual Abuse Who Were Treated in Voluntary Community Facilities', in Department of Health (1995), pp. 75–6.

Monck, E., Sharland, E., Bentovim, A., Goodall, G., Hyde, C. and Lewin, R. (1995) 'Child Sexual Abuse: A Descriptive and Treatment Study', in Department of Health (1995), pp. 76–8.

Oates, R. K. and Bross, C. D. (1995) 'What Have We Learned About Treating Child Physical Abuse? A Literature Review of the Last Decade', *Child Abuse and Neglect*, 19 (4), pp. 463–73.

Parton, N. (1985) *The Politics of Child Abuse*, London: Macmillan.

Parton, N. (1991) *Governing the Family: Child Care, Child Protection and the State*, London: Macmillan.

Reder, P., Duncan, S. and Gray, M. (1993) *Beyond Blame: Child Abuse Tragedies Revisited*, London: Routledge.

Rowan, A., Foy, D., Rodriguez, N. and Ryan, S. (1994) 'Posttraumatic Stress Disorder in a Clinical Sample of Adults Sexually Abused as Children', *Child Abuse and Neglect*, 18, pp. 51–61.

Schorr, A. (1992) *The Personal Social Services: An Outside View*, York: Joseph Rowntree Foundation.

Stevenson, O. (ed.) (1993) *Child Abuse: Public Policy and Professional Practice*, Hemel Hempstead: Harvester Wheatsheaf.

Waterhouse, L. (ed.) (1993) *Child Abuse and Child Abusers: Protection and Prevention*, London: Jessica Kingsley.

Widom, C. and Ashley Ames, M. (1994) 'Criminal Consequences of Childhood Sexual Victimization', *Child Abuse and Neglect*, 18 (4), pp. 303–18.

Wind, T. and Silvern, L. (1994) 'Parenting and Family Stress as Mediators of the Long-Term Effects of Child Abuse', *Child Abuse and Neglect*, 18 (5), pp. 439–53.

5 Two decades of progress: An international review of child protection services

Colin Pritchard

Introduction

In the 1960s, while Kempe et al. first reported the 'baby battering syndrome' in 1962 and the NSPCC research unit into 'baby battering' was established by 1968, public and professional awareness and acknowledgement of child abuse were limited. However, this innocence was shattered in 1973 by the death of Maria Colwell, which taught the UK that child abuse could be a killer and that it was a problem our society must address. Since then, a succession of highly publicized inquiries have established a general perception of both the prevalence and consequences of abuse, and the inefficiency of social work services. Subsequently, a key question in the minds of the public and politicians is: how effective are child protection services in reducing the annual toll of that most extreme consequence of child abuse, child death? Until recently there were relatively few outcome studies in respect of child protection to offset its poor media image. However, over the past decade or so there has been growing evidence that good social work works (Pritchard, 1986; MacDonald et al., 1992; Raynor et al., 1995; Sheldon, 1995). There have been, of course, a number of very important child protection studies (for example, Parker et al., 1991) and, more recently, broader studies which have explored outcome over time (Thoburn et al., 1994; Gibbons et al., 1995) or analysed variations in rates of children on the Child Protection registers or numbers in care (Little and Gibbons, 1992; Gibbons and Bell, 1994).

Crucially policy issues drive practice, not least because of the high media – and therefore high political – profile child protection has. Given the growing use of audit by the Department of Health (1992), with an increasing emphasis upon prevention, it is expected that similar 'targets' will be demanded of Social Services. Some researchers have used child death rates as outcome measures, though this is not an uncontested practice (Lindsey and Trocme, 1994; MacDonald, 1995). Evidence from such studies in the USA is contradictory. For example, claims of a reduction in child deaths being associated with an improvement and increases in the levels of reporting of abuse (Besharov, 1990) were challenged by Lindsey and Trocme (1994) and Pritchard (1992a).

There are, of course, difficult methodological and ethical problems in child protection research (Gallagher et al., 1995). Obviously one cannot compare non-intervention against intervention, and at best, therefore, it is 'special' versus standard care which can be evaluated. Yet the consequences of ineffective child protection – apart from fatality, which is relatively rare (Greenland 1987; Pritchard, 1994) – cannot be overstated. Adults with a history of abuse or neglect are disproportionately represented amongst a whole range of adult psychosocial pathology (Hawton and Roberts, 1985; Van Egmond and Jonker, 1988; Pritchard et al., 1990; Akhurst et al., 1995; Cox and Pritchard, 1995). Paradoxically, because the problem is so serious, only the most rigorous research is acceptable, but methodologically this is so problematic that it has to be acknowledged that many studies, including this work, have limitations. None the less, child protection outcomes should be reviewed nationally because, self-evidently, if there is no improvement or, indeed, matters have deteriorated, we are morally bound to consider alternative practice and policies. This chapter aims to provide such a review of child protection services by an examination of national and international trends in child homicide.

Practice outcome studies: an early positive outcome

In the late 1980s, Hampshire Social Service Department reviewed, via a retrospective analysis of the case records of 60 families on the Child Protection register, the impact of their child protection services. By definition, families on the register would be expected to be especially disturbed, and this was confirmed as the majority experienced multiple psychosocial problems, with half the mothers having experienced neglect or abuse when they were children (Pritchard, 1991). It was important to gain an independent and validated assessment of the degree of risk the children faced, and this was the first study in Europe to use the 'Assessment Scheme' of Baird (1988), which is increasingly being utilized in the USA because of its brevity and ease of use.

In the Hampshire cohort only 5 per cent of the families were assessed as being at 'Moderate Risk'; 85 per cent were 'High Risk', and a further 10 per cent were assessed at the 'Very High Risk' level. Considering these scores, and comparing them with work in the USA, it was anticipated that four out of five children would have been subjected to abuse or re-abuse, with at least half the sample being received into care. However, the Hampshire results were considerably more encouraging. In spite of the high levels of psychosocial disruption, some 90 per cent of the children had been successfully reintegrated into their family of origin and remained so for two years after the closure of the case. Nevertheless, because of the impact of the media upon our perceptions, such a positive outcome had not been expected.

A core theme in the direct work by the social workers was practical help within the essential context of a supportive and, at times, supervisory relationship. It was clear that, in the vast majority of families, despite most of them having a history of long-standing disruption, the social workers were able to engage the families in a constructive, but not sentimental, relationship. One-fifth of the families had had their children taken into temporary care, but in such a manner as was eventually perceived as caring and supportive. Initially, many of the parents needed a degree of dependency upon the social worker(s), until they were sufficiently empowered to meet the needs of their children. These themes were noted in an earlier study from the USA by Burch and Mohr (1980), who contrasted a standard level of provision against an enhanced service described as 'Positive Parenting'. Here, again within the context of an appropriate relationship, the workers utilized 'educational' principles, recognizing that their cohort of families needed to learn parenting skills, because most had never experienced them at first hand themselves.

Families who received the focused 'educational' rapport model did significantly better than clients receiving another standard child protection service, with less abuse/re-abuse, lower in-care rates and better social adjustment. This caring *and* controlling/supervisory relationship was also found in another outcome study by Zimrin (1984), in which success was essentially due to the level and strength of contact, as family aides had intensive contact over a three-month period. Quite literally the families were under daily supervision in every sense of that word, as they were given practical demonstrations of home care and childcare so that, in all cases, positive and sustaining relationships were developed, to the extent that, when the service ceased, there was measurable deterioration. Again, the enhanced service did better than the standard level of care. Of particular interest is the work of Gibbons et al. (1995), who showed that, in relation to both attitudes of the protection services and parenting styles, the quality of relationship was crucial to the long-term development of children who had been abused.

How good, nationally, is our child protection?

The results of the Hampshire study were discussed confidentially with a number of senior practitioners, who expressed the opinion that an evaluation of their own services would have similar results: at least 80 per cent of their children 'at risk' would be successfully reintegrated into their families. If such success was fairly widespread, it seemed logical that there should be some indication of improved child protection at the national level over time. The problem was how to demonstrate an event – abuse – which if prevented would not be visible. The problem was resolved by reversing the equation. Instead of attempting to measure success, indicators of failure were analysed, based on the notion that, whilst prevention by its very nature is invisible, failure can be seen amongst a number of possible criteria such as children in care or accommodated, hospital admissions, and so on.

The indicator of failure finally decided upon was not the level of reported neglect, which is fraught with methodological difficulties (Lindsey and Trocme, 1994; Greenland, 1987; Gallagher et al., 1995), but a measure of the extreme end of the abuse continuum, child death. At its harshest, one cannot argue with a 'body count', although it is recognized that there may be debates about how the 'count' is made (Greenland, 1987; Creighton, 1993; Pritchard, 1993; Lindsey and Trocme, 1994; MacDonald, 1995; Pritchard, 1996). This method is in effect epidemiological – that is, measuring mortality rates in relation to environmental factors over time. The approach reflects the Durkheimian thesis that changes in certain types of death mirror changes in society, classically in respect to suicide – a thesis which, a hundred years on, continues to have empirical support (Diekstra, 1989; Lester, 1993). The method has also been used to examine international studies of suicide and unemployment, and the sudden infant death syndrome (cot deaths) since the early 1970s (Pritchard, 1992b, 1994; Pritchard and Hayes, 1993).

Rather than compare death rates *between* countries, an individual country's mortality rate is compared over time, thus avoiding the problems of different recording and legal systems (Gelles and Edfeldt, 1986). An example best illustrates the method. In 1973, Anglo-Welsh 'All Accidental' baby deaths were 502 per million, yet by 1992 this had fallen to 172, an index of 034, equivalent to a 66 per cent reduction. To take another example, Germany had a rate of 1336 in 1973, which fell to 415 baby deaths by 1992, an index of 031. While Germany still has a higher baby accidental death rate than England and Wales, it has actually decreased at an even faster rate.

In Gelles and Edfeldt's study, baby (<1 year), infant (1–4 years) and older child (5–14 years) homicide rates were reviewed annually up to 1992. Because the actual numbers are relatively small, the inevitable annual variations are evened out by taking the average rate for a two-year period, 1973–74, and comparing this with the latest years available, 1991–92. The underlying thesis is simple: if child protection at a national level has made little or no difference, then the rates and index would remain the same – that is, an index of about 100. However, given that this time period encompasses two severe recessions, and that inequality also increased (OPCS, 1995), it is not unreasonable to expect that some forms of child abuse and neglect also might have increased (Holinger, 1987; Judge and Benzeval, 1993), and that this would be reflected in increased numbers of deaths. This study concentrates upon baby (<1) and infant (1–4) deaths, because these younger children are predominately victims of an assailant from within the family, mainly parent figures, whereas older children (5–14) are more often victims of extrafamilial violence (Bourget and Labelle, 1992; Somander and Rammer, 1991). This latter point needs to be borne in mind when considering the rationality of associating child homicide rates with the extremes of child abuse and neglect.

Child homicide in England and Wales 1973–1992

Table 5.1 is based upon OPCS data (OPCS, 1975–1994, 1986–1994), and shows the numbers of baby, infant and child deaths between 1973 and 1992. From the index of change it can be seen that there is a decline in baby deaths in particular, although the 'blip' following a recording change after 1979 should be noted (Creighton, 1993). Nevertheless, taking the simplest of statistics, the index for baby deaths is 031, equivalent to a 69 per cent reduction, while 'all children' homicide from the two years 1973/74 to the two years 1991/92 fell from 208 to 70, an index of 034 – that is, equivalent to 64 per cent improvement. However, it may be possible that some child abuse deaths may be hidden in the Undetermined Deaths (UDs) category (Creighton, 1993), and therefore the total of UDs are also included in the table. Certainly there was a marked rise in UDs in the early 1980s, followed by a decline with a peak in the later two years. However, even when all homicides and UDs are combined, the index still shows a fall of 070, a 30 per cent overall reduction. None the less, it should be remembered that 'undetermined' means just that, and we should not automatically assume that such deaths are necessarily the extreme consequence of hidden child abuse.

Rather than just look at the index of change, we can compare differences between two decades (Table 5.2). Over the twenty years from 1973 to 1992 there had been 1212 homicides, an average of 60.6 deaths per year. In the earlier decade of 1973–82, there were 770 homicides, compared with 442 for

Table 5.1   Numbers of child deaths in England and Wales, 1973–1992

Year	Homicide			Undetermined deaths (UDs)			Total deaths	
	Baby (<1 years)	Infant (1–4 years)	All (0–14 years)	<1	1–4	5–15	Total UDs	All deaths
1973	40	22	102	6	11#	39#	56	158
1974	35	40	106	8	10	22	40	146
1975	33	30	86	9	12	22	43	129
1976	36	26	85	10	11	14	35	120
1977	18	33	78	2	11	17	30	108
1978	29	38	92	11	3	21	35	127
1979	38	28	94	17	21	26	64	158
1980	13	17	47	17	13	12	42	89
1981	10	7	30	25	24	32	81	111
1982	13	17	50	23	15	24	62	112
1983	15	22	45	18	19	12	49	94
1984	9	23	50	11	22	13	46	96
1985	11	28	59	14	16	27	57	116
1986*	22	9	50	17*	10	14	41	91*
1987*	13	15	41	17*	17	22	56	97*
1988*	21	19	54	26*	19	14	59	113*
1989*	17	11	37	22*	17	18	57	94*
1990*	8	17	36	23*	17	30	70	106
1991*	11	16	41	17*	28	18	63	104
1992*	12	13	29	29*	21	31	81	110
Index of change								
1973/91	067							
1973/92	n/a		034				149	070

Sources: OPCS (1975–1994, 1986–1994).

Notes

#Corrected in 1973 to include the 15 year age, based upon the average for the age year – thus, the actual total of deaths is for 0–15 years.

*Includes neonatal deaths, that is <28 days (OPCS, 1975–1994, 1986–1994).

Total Homicides   [n = 1212] 1973–82 770 (64%) v. 1983–92 442 (36%)
Total Undetermined Deaths   [n = 1067] 1973–82 488 (46%) v. 1983–92 579 (54%)
Combined Deaths   [n = 2279] 1973–82 1258 (55%) v. 1983–92 1021 (45%)

Null Hypothesis – no significant differences over the years in relation to Total Homicides 1973–92:
Year-On-Year Total Homicides 1973–92 χ^2 = 199.62 19 d/f P = <0.0001
Year-On-Year Combined Deaths 1973–92 χ^2 = 70.67 19 d/f P = <0.0001
Therefore the Null Nypothesis is rejected at the 0.1% level of confidence.

Table 5.2   Homicides and undetermined deaths, 1973–1982 v. 1983–1992

Year	Homicides n = 1212	Undetermined n = 1067	Combined n = 2279
1973–1982	64%	46%	55%
1983–1992	36%	54%	45%
Index of change 1973/82–1983/92	056	117	082

Notes

Combined Deaths Decades 1973–82 v. 1983–92
χ^2 =69.88 1 d/f P=<0.0001

1983–92. Or, in other words, 64 per cent of all homicides occurred in the first decade.

A comparison of the Undetermined Deaths (UDs) between 1973 and 1992 shows that there were 1067 UDs, with 46 per cent (488) occurring in the first decade, and 54 per cent (579) in the second, confirming the increase in this category noted by both Creighton (1993) and MacDonald (1995). The simplest statistic, the index of change, shows that in respect of homicides the index fell to 056, an equivalent fall of 44 per cent, to be set against a rise in UDs of 17 per cent, and a fall of 18 per cent in combined deaths. On comparing the two decades, a Chi Square test yielded a highly statistical significant result (P = <0.0001), showing an unequivocal fall in the number of child deaths between 1973 and 1982 and 1983 and 1993. And, while there were undoubtedly more UDs over the period, there were also significant reductions in the child homicides.

However, to be doubly sure, the year-on-year variations contained in Table 5.1 were tested. The null hypothesis – that is, that there were no significant differences over the years in relation to Total Homicides 1973–92 – showed a highly significant Chi Square value of 199.62, which allows us to reject the null hypothesis at the 0.1 per cent level of confidence. In addition, the Combined Deaths 1973–92 yielded a significant Chi Square result of 70.67, which also supports the rejection of the null hypothesis at the 0.1 per cent level. Thus, no matter which way the figures are reviewed, there was a real fall in combined deaths, and especially amongst baby, infant and child homicides, in England and Wales between 1973 and 1992.

International comparison of child death rates in industrial nations

This section compares the English/Welsh experience with that of other industrial nations. To enable direct comparison of countries with different levels of population, child death rates per million population rather than their actual totals are used. Because this is potentially an unreliable measure in the case of countries with small populations, comparisons are made only of countries with populations of over 14 million.

From the figures in Table 5.3 it can be seen that there was a substantial fall in the proportion of Anglo-Welsh baby deaths between 1973/74 and 1991/92, an index of change of 030, equivalent to a decline of 70 per cent, whilst the total homicide index was down to 033, a fall of 67 per cent. Other countries also had substantial falls: Japan (57 per cent), Australia and Germany (44 per cent), Italy (39 per cent), the Netherlands (24 per cent) and Canada 23 per cent – though only Japan (57 per cent), Germany (51 per cent) and Australia (39 per cent) had significant falls in total homicide. England and Wales thus headed the league table of reductions for both baby and all/total child homicide. Indeed, even if all the smaller nations had been included, the Anglo-Welsh would still have led the field in this respect. However, whilst the Anglo-Welsh reduction is impressive – especially baby deaths, which fell from 114 to 34 per million, Australia, Italy, the Netherlands and Spain have a lower rate. To put this in perspective, in 1992, when both child homicide and road deaths reached record lows, for every child homicide there were nine child road deaths, and in relation to deaths from strangers the road fatalities were 30 times higher, confirming Greenland's (1987) point that, while any child death is undoubtedly a personal tragedy, child deaths are fortunately relatively very rare.

So, despite challenges to this approach (Creighton, 1993; Lindsey and Trocme, 1994; MacDonald, 1995), which admittedly has its limitations (Pritchard, 1996), we can nevertheless be confident that child murders, surely the most extreme form of child abuse, really have fallen from the highs of the 1970s.

Possible explanations for decline in child homicide

How, then, might we explain the decline in child homicide? The following section discusses some of the factors which may have influenced or determined these significant changes.

Table 5.3 Baby, infant and child (5–14 years) homicide in England and Wales and other industrial countries, 1973/74 to 1991/92 (rates per million population)

YEARS	BABY	INFANT	CHILD	TOTAL
England and Wales				
1973/74	114	25	8	147
1991/92	34	11	4	49
Index of change	*030*	*044*	*050*	*033*
Japan				
1973/74	166	50	17	233
1991/92	72	19	9	100
Index of change	*043*	*038*	*053*	*043*
Germany				
1973/74	122	18	43	183
1990/91	68	14	8	90
Index of change	*056*	*078*	*019*	*049*
Australia				
1973/74	50	24	13	87
1991/92	28	17	8	53
Index of change	*056*	*071*	*062*	*061*
Canada				
1973/74	60	29	9	97
1990/91	46	24	13	83
Index of change	*077*	*083*	*144*	*086*
Italy				
1973/74	18	5	5	28
1989/90	11	6	7	27
Index of change	*061*	*120*	*140*	*096*
Netherlands				
1973/74	33	4	5	43
1990/91	25	17	5	47
Index of change	*076*	*425*	*100*	*109*

Table 5.3   (continued)

France				
1973/74	35	11	4	50
1990/91	40	12	7	59
Index of change	*114*	*109*	*175*	*118*
USA				
1973/74	104	48	22	174
1989/90	163	52	30	245
Index of change	*157*	*108*	*136*	*141*
Spain				
1973/74	8	2	1	11
1989/90	18	3	10	31
Index of change	*225*	*150*	*1000*	*282*

Source: Extrapolated from WHO Annual Statistics (1975/1994).

Hidden deaths

The idea persists that there has been no real improvement in child death rates, either because child deaths have somehow been more effectively hidden by the perpetrators or because they have been lost in the recording practices of the relevant agencies. However, in England and Wales, over 50 per cent of baby deaths are routinely subject to an autopsy, a figure which rises to virtually 100 per cent where there is any suspicion or doubt surrounding the death of a child. This is very much the picture in the other Western countries, with autopsies carried out in almost all 'doubtful' cases (WHO, 1975–1994). Nevertheless, despite improved forensic techniques, a degree of uncertainty always remains, as it does with any other criminal offence. This supposition that welfare agencies are missing deaths is not credible given the historically unprecedented degree of professional and public attention now being given to child protection. Many measures introduced since 1988, such as 'Working Together', have emphasized the importance of interdisciplinary cooperation and communication, and have thus led to a greater degree of interprofessional scrutiny (Buchanan, 1994; Hallett, 1995). Of course, there are still weaknesses in these procedures and variable levels of cooperation between professionals and parents (Thoburn et al., 1995) but, despite the discipline almost making an art of self-denigration, the changes in child protection policy and procedures do appear to have had some positive results. It may be asked, however, why, at a time of the fiercest scrutiny of child deaths, there should be an increase in undetermined deaths in England and Wales. Could it be that UK courts, because of events in Cleveland and Scotland, have become more reluctant to intercede by sanctioning the removal of children from potentially dangerous situations? We do not know. But, while it is possible that a few child abuse deaths will be successfully hidden by their perpetrators, it has never been more difficult to achieve this and it is surely mistaken to assume that the majority of UDs are homicide.

Socioeconomic context: The interaction of poverty and mental disorder

One aspect must not be overlooked and that is the cumulative impact of poverty, which from what we know about family breakdown should have led to an increase in child abuse and neglect (Jones et al., 1987; McLloyd, 1990; MacFate et al., 1995). While the vast majority of abuse and neglect cases obviously do not end in death, overall child mortality is, none the less, correlated with poverty, both in the USA (Holinger, 1987) and in England and Wales (Judge and Benzeval, 1993). In their seminal work, Judge and Benzeval examined all types of children's deaths from the ages of 1 to 15 between 1981 and 1985, and their analysis showed, unequivocally, increased deaths amongst children of parents in receipt of benefits. This category of family had three times the child death rate of families from social classes 1 and 2, and were even 44 per cent higher than those in class 5.

Another problem which interacts with poverty is that of mental disorder and its interface with child abuse and neglect. This may be considered controversial but, in Kempe's original work which alerted the Western world to 'baby battering' (Kempe et al., 1962; Kempe and Kempe, 1978), in an effort to emphasize the ubiquitous nature of such abuse, the author played down the psychiatric dimension – although later research shows that a significant number of abusers do have mental health problems (Kaye et al., 1990; Somander and Rammer, 1991; Bourget and Labelle, 1992; Samuels et al., 1992; Wilczynski and Morris, 1993; Meadow, 1994). In a careful review of international research, Stroud (1996) showed that more than 40 per cent of all child killers came from this cohort. While citizens in general are in far greater danger from motorists than they are from people with mental health problems – who are far more at risk from themselves – we should not ignore the fact that, in the presence of a mental disorder, especially a personality and/or a paranoid disorder, the risks to those immediately around the disordered person are raised.

Whilst there is a clear need to improve and better fund community care services for people with a mental disorder (Pritchard, 1992c), there is evidence that the best modern community psychiatry is effective (Butler and Pritchard, 1990; Lester, 1993) – a fact which is implicitly recognized by government in their targets to reduce suicide by substantial margins (Department of Health, 1992). Child protection services usually respond promptly when dealing with the interface of child protection and psychiatric disturbance, and I suspect this is an important feature which is reflected in the overall reduction of child deaths. This fact is partly grasped by some critics: 'whilst intervening we might, incidentally as it were, prevent some deaths' (MacDonald, 1995, p. 496) – this is exactly what I believe occurs.

The probable contribution of improved child protection

MacDonald (1995), while accepting that the trend of improvement in the rate of child deaths may be valid, questions whether the evidence supports the assertion that it is child protection services that have contributed to the decline. There is a range of empirical evidence which shows some forms of social work practice to be effective (MacDonald et al., 1992; Sheldon, 1995; Raynor et al., 1995), and particularly in respect of child protection (Burch and Mohr, 1980; Pritchard, 1991; Zimrim, 1984; Gibbons et al., 1995). Despite recent criticisms that the initial contact with the statutory services is almost adversarial and inquisitorial for many families (Thoburn et al., 1995), practice experience suggests that, once child protection services are involved, the situation will either be maintained or improved – children generally are protected from extreme harm. When services pursue the twin aims, embodied in the Children Act 1989, of protection and the prevention of family breakdown, their interventions also contribute to the amelioration of those stresses which at their most extreme lead to severe physical injury and even death. It must be remembered that this evaluation is postulated upon the notion of a continuum of damage, with the accompanying recognition that effective early intervention not only limits some of the least severe consequences, but also ameliorates the worst ones. The Department of Health (1992) have already established the concept of health targets aimed at reducing 'preventable deaths' generally, and have thus made public and political the use of mortality statistics as indicators of success or failure. It may not be long before such targets are established and accepted for child protection services also.

In conclusion, the critics who seek to reject and rebut this approach to the evaluation of child protection policies and services have yet to establish a plausible alternative explanation of why child homicides have fallen in England and Wales. Admittedly the data may be imperfect, the methodology not ideal, and there is urgent need for more practice-related research, but there are grounds for continued optimism that current child protection services have brought about a reduction of child deaths. We should, therefore, give some credit to those front-line professionals who, along with their clients, face the risks. Social work has a bad press (Franklin and Parton, 1992), and the discipline is frequently used as a scapegoat for more general social problems. Sometimes we are our own worst enemy: we ignore the growing evidence which can be found in consumer studies, such as those made of probationers (Bailey, 1995; Cox and Pritchard, 1995; Ford et al., 1996), single homeless people (Pritchard and Clooney, 1994) and so on, that clients generally are appreciative of the help they receive from social workers. Hence it is time to give due acknowledgement to the commitment and dedication of a service which seeks to bring about change and improvement in the lives of children and families, which cumulatively has brought improvements and which, at the extreme end of the continuum, saves lives. If these efforts remain unrecognized, we run the risk that our work will become increasingly bureaucratized in ways which will limit and erode our efforts to reach out to vulnerable people, and will thus further undermine our effectiveness.

A note about methodological issues

There are a number of difficulties surrounding measurements in respect to national and international child death rates. All are essentially related to recording systems and possible changes over time (Gelles and Edfeldt, 1986). The first ever international review of child homicides was criticized in respect to changes in OPCS methods of recording (Creighton, 1993; Lindsey and Trocme, 1994; MacDonald, 1995). These are answered in substantial detail, although readers are encouraged to review such criticisms, as well as the reply (Pritchard, 1996). The following notes briefly outline the main issues, although crucially it should be noted that this chapter has incorporated the earlier criticism, and thus permits a greater degree of confidence in the results.

Actual numbers of child deaths over time are used in the temporal analysis for England and Wales (see Tables 5.1, 5.2), though of course they do not account for the changes brought about by variations in population: hence, as England and Wales are two of the few countries, from the mid-1980s, to have had an increase in births, the raw numbers do not show this modifying factor. Conversely, I have used child death rates per million population from WHO (see Table 5.3) for the international comparisons. These rates are derived for each sex, summed and then divided by two to give the overall rates per million. It should be noted that, in every country reviewed in this sample, baby boys are more often victims than baby girls.

Readers might be surprised to find a variation between OPCS and WHO figures. This is partly due to the fact that 'undetermined' deaths are truly that, and that at any given time a number are 'in process'. Incidentally, neither OPCS nor the Home Office figures match. The key, therefore, is to compare the same data set over time. I choose the 'medical-social'-oriented OPCS because of its closer match to WHO, thus facilitating international comparisons. In respect of the Spanish figures (Table 5.3) mismatch may occur because of the possibility that unfavourable social indices might have been suppressed under the older illiberal regime; we do not know for certain that such was the case, but it is important to recognize this contingency. Similar factors might have operated in respect of both Greece and Portugal.

The most important methodological issue are the changes in OPCS Series DH 2 on Causes of Mortality (OPCS, 1975–1994), which removed, from 1986 onwards, those neonatal deaths which occurred in the first 28 days of life. However, in Series DH 6 on Childhood Mortality Causes (OPCS, 1986–1994), these neonatal homicides and UDs are given. Tables 5.1 and 5.2 have therefore incorporated the neonate deaths accordingly.

References

Akhurst, M., Brown, I. and Wessley, S. (1995) *Dying For Help: Offenders at Risk of Suicide*, Wakefield: Association of Chief Probation Officers.

Bailey, R. (1995) 'Helping Offenders as an Element in Justice', in Ward and Lacey (1995), pp. 127–38.

Baird, C. (ed.) (1988) *Development of Risk Indices for Alaskan Family Services*, Washington DC: National Council on Crime and Delinquency.

Besharov, D. J. (1990) *Recognizing Child Abuse*, New York: The Free Press.

Bourget, D. and Labelle, A. (1992) 'Homicide, Infanticide and Filicide', *Clinical forensic Psychiatry*, 15 (3), pp. 61–73.

Browne, K., Davies, C. and Stratton, P. (eds) (1988) *Early Prediction and Prevention of Child Abuse*, Chichester: Wiley.

Buchanan, A. (ed.) (1994) *Partnership in Practice: Child Protection*, Aldershot: Avebury.

Burch, G. and Mohr, V. (1980) 'Evaluating a Child Abuse Intervention Programme', *Social Casework*, 61 (2), pp. 92–9.

Butler, A. and Pritchard, C. (1990) *Social Work and Mental Illness*, London: Macmillan.

Cox, M. and Pritchard, C. (1995) 'Troubles Come Not Singly but in Battalions: the Pursuit of Social Justice and Probation Practice', in Ward and Lacey (1995), pp. 88–112.

Creighton, S. (1993) 'Children's Homicide: An Exchange', *British Journal of Social Work*, 23 (6), pp. 632–4.

Department of Health (1992) *The Health of the Nation: A Strategy for Health in England*, London: HMSO.

Diekstra, R. F. W. (1989) 'Suicide and Attempted Suicide: An International Perspective', *Acta Psychiatrica Scandinavia*, 80, pp. 1–24.

Etherington, S. (ed.) (1986) *Social Work and Citizenship*, London: BASW.

Ford, P., Pritchard, C. and Cox, M. (1996) 'Consumer Views from Probationers: A Renewal of Advise, Guide and Befriend?', *Howard Journal*, in press.

Franklin, B. and Parton, N. (1992) *Social Work, the Media and Public Relations*, London: Routledge.

Gallagher, B., Gibbons, J. and Creighton, S. (1995) 'Ethical Dilemmas in Social Research: No Easy Solutions', *British Journal of Social Work*, 25 (3), pp. 295–311.

Gelles, R. J. and Edfeldt, A. W. (1986) 'Violence Towards Children in the USA and Sweden', *Child Abuse and Neglect*, 10 (4), pp. 501–10.

Gibbons, J. and Bell, C. (1994) 'Variation in Operation of English Child Protection Registers', *British Journal of Social Work*, 24 (6), pp. 701–14.

Gibbons, J., Gallagher, B., Bell, C. and Gordon, D. (1995) *Development After Physical Abuse in Early Childhood*, London: HMSO.

Greenland, C. (1987) *Preventing C.A.N. Deaths*, London: Tavistock.

Hallett, C. (1995) *Inter-agency Coordination in Child Protection*, London: HMSO.

Hawton, C. and Roberts, J. C. (1985) 'Risk of Abuse and Attempted Suicide', *British Journal of Psychiatry*, 146, pp. 415–20.

Holinger, P. (1987) *Violent Death in the United States*, New York: Guilford Press.

Jones, D. N., Pickett, J. and Barboor, P. (1987) *Understanding Child Abuse*, London: Macmillan.

Judge, K. and Benzeval, M. (1993) 'Health Inequalities: New Concerns about the Children of Single Mothers', *British Medical Journal*, 306, pp. 677–80.

Kaye, N., Borenstein, N. and Donnelly, S. (1990) 'Families, Murder and Insanities: A Psychiatric Review of Paternal Neonaticide', *Journal of Forensic Sciences*, 35, pp. 133–9.

Kempe, C. H., Silverman, F., Steele, B., Droegmueller, W. and Silver, H. (1962) 'The Battered Child Syndrome', *Journal of American Medical Association*, 181, pp. 17–24.

Kempe, H., and Kempe, C. H. (1978) *Child Abuse*, Chicago: University of Chicago Press.

Lester, D. (1993) 'The Effectiveness of Suicide Prevention Centres', *Suicide and Life Threatening Behaviour*, 23 (3), pp. 263–7.

Lindsey, D. and Trocme, N. (1994) 'Have Child Protection Efforts Reduced Child Homicides? An Examination of Data from Britain and North America', *British Journal of Social Work*, 24 (6), pp. 715–32.

Little, M. and Gibbons, J. (1992) 'Predicting the Rate of Children on the Child Protection Register', *Research Policy and Planning*, 10, pp. 15–20.

Lynch, M. J. (1988) 'The Consequences of Child Abuse', in Browne et al. (1988), pp. 35–49.

MacDonald, G., Sheldon, B. and Gillespie, J. (1992) 'Contemporary Studies of the Effectiveness of Social Work', *British Journal of Social Work*, 22 (6), pp. 615–43.

MacDonald, K. (1995) 'Comparative Homicide and the Proper Aims of Social Work: A Sceptical Note', *British Journal of Social Work*, 25 (4), pp. 489–98.

MacFate, K., Lawson, R. and Wilson, W. J. (eds) (1995) *Poverty, Inequality and the Future of Social Policy: Western States in the New World Order*, New York: Russell Sage.

Madge, N. (1983) 'Unemployment and its Effects on Children', *Journal of Child Psychology and Psychiatry*, 24 (2), pp. 311–20.

McLloyd, V. (1990) 'The Impact of Economic Hardship Upon Black Families and Children: Psychological Distress, Parenting and Socio-economic Development', *Child Development*, 61 (2), pp. 311–46.

Meadow, S. R. (1994) 'Munchausen Syndrome by Proxy', *Journal of Clinical Forensic*

Medicine, 1, pp. 121–7.

OPCS (1975–1994) *Mortality Causes*, Series DH 2, London: Governmental Statistical Services [data taken from each year's publication].

OPCS (1986–1994) *Childhood Mortality: Causes*, Series DH 6, London: Governmental Statistical Services [data taken from each year's publication].

OPCS (1995) *Social Trends*, London: Governmental Statistical Services.

Parker, R., Ward, H., Jackson, S., Aldgate, J. and Wedge, P. (1991) *Assessing Outcomes in Child Care*, London: HMSO.

Pritchard, C. (1986) 'Social Work Effectiveness and the New Right', in Etherington (1986), pp. 4–42.

Pritchard, C. (1991) 'Levels of Risk and Psycho-social Problems in Families on the "At Risk of Abuse" Register: Some Indices of Outcome Two Years After Case Closure', *Research Policy and Planning*, 9 (2), pp. 12–26.

Pritchard, C. (1992a) 'Children's Homicide as an Indicator of Effective Child Protection: A Comparative Study of Western European Statistics', *British Journal of Social Work*, 22 (6), pp. 663–84.

Pritchard, C. (1992b) 'Is There a Link Between Suicide in Young Men and Unemployment? A UK Comparison with Other European Community Countries', *British Journal of Psychiatry*, 160, pp. 750–6.

Pritchard, C. (1992c) 'What Can We Afford for the NHS? An Analysis of Government Expenditure 1964–1992', *Social Policy and Administration*, 26, pp. 40–54.

Pritchard, C. (1993) 'Reanalysing Children's Homicide and Undetermined Deaths as an Indication of Improved Child Protection: A Reply to Creighton', *British Journal of Social Work*, 23 (6), pp. 645–52.

Pritchard, C. (1994) 'Connections or Coincidence? An International Comparison of Sudden-Infant-Death-Syndrome (SIDS), Baby Homicide and Childhood Malignancies in England and Wales: A New Approach to Child Protection Social Work', *Social Science Review*, 5 (3), pp. 186–218.

Pritchard, C. (1995a) 'Psychiatric Targets in Health of the Nation: Regional Suicide 1974–1990 and Employment Prospects 1990–1994 in Britain: Precursors of Failure?', *Journal of the Royal Society of Health*, 115 (2), pp. 120–7.

Pritchard, C. (1995b) *Suicide the Ultimate Rejection? A Psycho-Social Study*, Buckingham: Open University Press.

Pritchard, C. (1996) 'Search for National Indicators of Effective Child Protection in a Re-analysis of Child Homicide in Eleven Major Western Countries 1973–92: A Response to Lindsey, Trocme and MacDonald', *British Journal of Social Work*, 26 (5), pp. 545–63.

Pritchard, C. and Clooney, D. (1994) *Fractured Lives and Fragmented Policies: Single Homelessness in Dorset, A Report to the Department of Environment*, Bournemouth: Bournemouth Churches Housing Association.

Pritchard, C. and Hayes, P. (1993) 'La Morte Subite des Nourisons', *Medicine Infantile*, 100, pp. 573–86.

Pritchard, C., Cox, M. and Cotton, A. (1990) 'Analysis of Young Adult Clients in Probation and Social Service Caseloads: A Focus on Illegal Drugs and HIV Infection', *Research Policy Planning*, 8 (2), pp. 1–8.

Raynor, P., Smith, D. and Vanstone, M. (1995) *Effective Probation Practice*, London: Macmillan.

Samuels, M. P., McClaughlin, W. Jacobson, R. R., Poets, C. F. and Southall, D. P. (1992) 'Fourteen Cases of Imposed Upper Airway Obstruction', *Archives of Diseases in Childhood*, 67 (1–6), pp. 162–70.

Sheldon, B. (1995) *Cognitive Behavioural Therapy: Research, Practice and Philosophy*,

London: Routledge.

Siefert, K., Schwartz, I. M. and Ortega, R. (1994) 'Infant Mortality in Michigan's Child Welfare System', *Social Work*, 39 (5), pp. 574–9.

Somander, L. H. K. and Rammer, L. M. (1991) 'Intra-and-extra Familial Child Homicide in Sweden', *Child Abuse and Neglect*, 15 (1/2), pp. 45–55.

Stroud, J. (1996) 'Mental Disorder and the Homicide of Children: A Review', *Social Work and Social Sciences Review*, 6, in press.

Thoburn, J., Lewis, A. and Shemmings, D. (1995) *Paternalism or Parternship? Family Involvement in the Child Protection Process*, London: HMSO.

Van Egmond, M. J. and Jonker, D. (1988) 'Sexual and Physical Abuse: Suicide Risk Factors for Women?', *Tijdschrift und Psychiatrie*, 30, pp. 21–38.

Ward, D. and Lacey, M. (eds) (1995) *Probation: Working for Justice*, London: Birch and Whiting.

WHO (1975–1994) *World Health Statistics Annual*, Geneva: World Health Organization.

Wilczynski, A. and Morris, A. (1993) 'Parents Who Kill Their Children', *Criminal Law Review*, 1, pp. 31–6.

Zimrim, H. (1984) 'Do Something: The Effect of Human Contact on the Parents of Abusive Behaviour', *British Journal of Social Work*, 14 (5), pp. 475–85.

6 A parents' view of partnership
Brian Corby and Malcolm Millar

Introduction

The late 1980s and early 1990s have seen a shift in thinking within child protection practice. After fifteen or more years' emphasis on protecting children *from* their parents, social workers and other professionals are now being required to work together *with* parents to ensure the safety and well-being of their children. 'Participation' has become a key word in child protection work. Involvement of parents at child protection conferences and in the implementation of child protection plans is seen as a prerequisite of effective and ethical practice in this field. The reasons for these developments are complex. The ineffectiveness of measures to protect physically abused and neglected children (Department of Health, 1991a) and public concern about excessive professional intrusiveness in cases of sexual abuse (Cleveland County Council, 1988; Orkney Report, 1992) were important factors in this process. At a broader level, the Conservative Government's emphasis on parental responsibility and choice was influential (Eekelaar, 1991). Such ideas were acceptable to welfare professionals who increasingly valued partnership and empowerment as central elements of practice.

This chapter will examine how, if at all, this shift in thinking has filtered through to practice. Research into these developments is now beginning to emerge. Quantitative data shows that there has been a reduction in the number of care proceedings and in the use of emergency protection orders, which may suggest a shift towards greater use of voluntary agreements between parents and social workers (Department of Health, 1994). A major research study (Thoburn et al., 1995) into the implementation of policies of parental participation at child protection conferences has shown such

75

participation as working effectively to lay some foundations for cooperative work with families. Some other studies (Rochdale Area Child Protection Committee, 1993; Corby et al., 1995) are more sceptical, questioning the meaning and impact of policy in this area. Farmer and Owen (1995) have carried out research into child protection practice in the post-conference period. They found that there was persistent disagreement between parents and professionals in 36 out of 44 cases studied, and that many parents and children found the experience of investigation, attendance at conferences, and later intervention to be difficult and conflictual. Nevertheless, the authors see parental participation as one of the key means of improving child protection work.

The study presented here to some degree replicates that of Farmer and Owen in that it focuses on the experiences of a group of parents within the child protection system in a period of up to a year after the initial investigation. It is important to note that the research took place between 1993 and 1994 in an agency that had gone some way further in developing participation procedures than those studied by Thoburn et al. (1995) and Farmer and Owen (1995). On the face of it, therefore, there should have been more scope for effective participatory practice.

Method

The research data presented here is taken from a larger study of parental participation in child protection work, the initial aim of which was to examine the experiences of parents at child protection conferences. Thirty-five conferences involving 32 families were attended, and 29 of these families (3 refused) were interviewed approximately six weeks later. Twenty-four of these families were interviewed again on average ten months after the conferences. This chapter concentrates on data provided by these 24 families at these two interviews. The focus was on parents/carers' perceptions of being involved in the child protection process. They were asked about their understanding of the purposes of social work intervention, and their feelings about, and their evaluation of, their contacts with social workers and other professionals. The data presented here, therefore, is derived solely from the perspective of the consumer. It is recognized that the consumer perspective provides just one aspect of a multifaceted process, and that service users' views cannot be the sole determinant of policy (Gardner, 1989). However, in an area of activity in which emphasis is being placed on participation and on taking parents' views into account, it seems essential to draw on what parents are saying about their experiences.

In what follows, some general data on the families interviewed is presented, with an account of their experiences in the order of the events as they happened: (i) the initial investigation, (ii) the child protection conference, (iii) the follow-up to the conference and (iv) the situation ten months later. Finally, the implications of these findings for child protection policy and practice are discussed.

Data on the families

Sixteen of the 24 families in the study had been involved with social service departments before the investigations which led to the conferences we attended, and 10 had been the subject of previous child protection investigations. The conferences were held because of allegations of physical abuse (11), sexual abuse (9) and neglect (4). In 20 cases, allegations were based on incidents of abuse that had, in the opinion of the professionals, already taken place. In 4 cases, there were concerns that there was a risk that abuse might occur. Children were registered in 15 of the cases and not registered in 9. The alleged abuser was interviewed in 10 cases. Those interviewed in the remaining cases were largely non-abusing parents (usually mothers) and, in 3 instances, the grandparents who had taken over the care of the allegedly abused child. In 9 of the cases, the alleged abusers (all males) had left home.

The experience of investigation

Being subject to a child protection investigation is almost certain to be an unpleasant experience for parents, whether they be the alleged abusers or not. It is likely to challenge their ability to fulfil a fundamental social role. There is the threat that children may be removed from their care, and there is the fear of criminal proceedings and public disgrace. Nevertheless, following the experience at Cleveland, there has been a greater emphasis on listening to the wishes and feelings of parents (and children). The focus of current practice is on working to secure the cooperation of parents and to ensure their children's future welfare.

In this study, only one of the people interviewed was regarded as a serious child abuser. Over half of interviewees were non-abusing mothers. Nearly all the parents we spoke to who were alleged to have abused their children were believed to have committed minor acts of violence. Given this, it might have been expected that the wishes and feelings of our respondents would have been genuinely taken into account in accordance with the spirit of the Children Act 1989 and the Cleveland Report. However, if this did happen, it was not reflected in the experiences reported by most of the respondents in this study.

Fifteen respondents experienced the child protection investigation negatively, 7 positively and 2 were ambivalent. A variety of reasons were given for the negative responses. In 5 cases, social workers were considered unsupportive: 'I didn't feel like anyone was giving me support.' Five parents/carers felt inadequately informed: 'They blame me, but won't tell me what's wrong with the child.' Three parents/carers felt that social workers were overreacting to events: 'They stirred it up like a hornets' nest' – 'It was as though she was deliberately digging, nit-picking about things.' In the remaining 2 cases, the complaints were of a more general nature. Experiences were described as 'frightening' and 'daunting'.

A key factor at this stage was the number of changes that took place in the household: 14 of our 24 respondents reported these. In 9 cases (4 physical abuse, 5 sexual abuse), male adults (all alleged abusers) had moved away from households. In 4 cases, children were placed with grandparents, and in 1, the grandmother moved in with the family.

In half the cases where these changes took place, they were unwelcome to the non-abusing parent. This was particularly so where physical abuse was alleged: in these cases, parents felt aggrieved, but accepted that they could not offer any resistance to the professionals' assessment. In sexual abuse cases, there was more agreement between parents/carers and professionals that exclusion of the alleged abuser was the best course of action. In these circumstances, the non-abusing parent was more rejecting of the alleged abuser.

The general impression gained from most of these parents/carers was that professionals were not sensitive to their clients' individual needs, being dominated by concern for procedures. Consequently, parents felt that they had little influence on events and that their normal parental control and responsibilities had been abruptly suspended.

Those that experienced the investigation more positively referred to the supportive qualities of social workers, and to the clarity and the patience shown by these workers and other professionals in explaining their involvement: 'I don't know what we would have done without the social worker' – 'I have nothing but praise for them this time.'

Nearly all of these respondents were considered to be non-abusers and their children's names had not been placed on the child protection register.

The child protection conference

The 1991 *Working Together* guidelines (Department of Health, 1991b) recommend that parents and children should attend conferences, and stress that their exclusion from such discussions needs to be 'especially justified' (para. 6.15). This thinking is in line with the philosophy of partnership embodied in the Children Act 1989, and some see it as useful in empowering parents and involving them more fully in the child protection process (Family Rights Group/NSPCC, 1992).

In the area studied, all parents/carers and children over 13 years of age attended the whole of child protection conferences. Social workers were required to encourage participation, to explain the way in which conference business was conducted and also to help prepare parents and children as best they could. Immediately before conferences, parents and children met with the conference chairpersons, and further briefing took place.

Parents/carers were asked how adequately they had been prepared for conferences by social workers. Although half felt that social workers worked well to prepare them, it is notable that only 5 of the total sample described their experiences of attendance in positive terms. Some respondents queried whether it was possible to be well prepared for an experience of this sort: 'I don't think that you can be [well prepared]. Nothing against the social worker, but you are so emotional and in a state of shock.'

Nineteen of the 24 respondents considered the conference experience to be threatening or confusing. Nearly half found it worse than they had expected. Many of them found it hard to express themselves in the conference setting, and those who did put forward their views felt that these contributions carried little weight. Several felt that the professionals at the conference had already made up their minds about the outcome. These parents/carers clearly did not feel that they had participated in the sense of being empowered. Significantly, of the 5 who felt positively about their experiences, only 1 was a suspected abuser.

Notwithstanding these findings, most parents/carers felt glad that they had attended conferences, because they could hear what was being said about them. These views could be used to argue the success of the parental participation policy, but, if so, the standard for participation is being set at a low level, in that it does not require any *active* involvement on the part of parents (see Daines et al., 1990).

These findings do not portray the conference as engaging parents/carers in the child protection process. Indeed, there is some suggestion of an alienating effect, in that parents are confronted with the reality of their lack of power.

After the conference

The post-conference period provides an opportunity to involve parents/carers more fully in the child protection process, even if the investigation has been a difficult experience for them and the child protection conference too threatening to allow meaningful participation.

Parents/carers were asked in first interviews what had happened in the six-week-period following the child protection conference. The focus was on the extent to which their views and feelings were taken into account and the degree to which they felt in control of events – in short, how far they considered themselves to be working in partnership with professionals.

Immediately after the conference, the social worker was the main point of contact for parents/carers. In addition to social work contact, 2 families were allocated a family aide. Other professionals (particularly health visitors and school teachers) were seen at core group meetings (see below). Five families said that they had received no visits during this period (all registered cases) and 6 that they had received one visit only. Some of these were happy at this limited contact and would have seen professional intervention as interference. Others felt frustrated by the fact that little seemed to be happening: 'The funny thing was that after the conference we never heard a flipping thing.' The remaining 13 families reported between 2 and 6 visits during this six-week-period. Some welcomed this degree of involvement, but a few felt that they were being swamped with visits.

Two key issues emerged from the comments about this stage of the child protection process. First, it was clear that many families were looking for help, and second, that almost all wanted to have more control over events.

With regard to the first issue, 4 families unequivocally reported that their contact with social workers during this period was helpful. The following comments demonstrate the sort of response they valued: 'I could ring her whenever I wanted to – she would visit sometimes to see how I was, which was very nice' – 'She was a friend more than a social worker.' Nine families specifically referred to the lack of help they received: 'I did ring her up and ask her to come and she said "No". We want someone to sit down and talk to on our own.'

All these respondents wanted their social worker to give them time and listen to their problems. In many of the remaining cases, it seems that parents/carers had already made a judgement that the social worker was not helpful and so did not consider it appropriate to seek support from that source.

The second main issue relevant to the post-conference period concerned the extent of parental control over events. Many parents/carers felt that they had little such control, and little understanding of what was happening. Five said they were unclear about what social workers were trying to achieve. Eight said that they were unclear about the visiting intentions of the professionals. For those who felt in need of help and support from their social workers, this was particularly frustrating. Many parents had low expectations and accepted what was happening in a fatalistic way, such as this mother who was visited by a family aide twice a week: 'It wasn't forced on me, but I'm not happy about it – no-one likes being told how to bring up their own kids, do they?'

Issues such as these might have been tackled at core group meetings of the kind recommended in the 1988 *Working Together* guidelines (Department of Health and Social Security, 1988). These meetings, convened by key workers (that is, social workers), and attended by other relevant front-line professionals, parents/carers and children (where appropriate), are intended to translate conference recommendations into a practical form in cases where registration of children has taken place. The participation of parents in these meetings is seen as an important means of involving them in any action to be taken. According to the parents/carers in our sample, such meetings were held during the six-week post-conference period in 10 of the 15 cases involving registration. None of the parents who had attended these meetings felt that the meetings had helped to clarify aims.

The overall impression of this stage of intervention from the parents/carers' perspective was one of confusion, uncertainty and lack of control over matters such as agreed goals, expectations and time-limits. In some cases, there was little or no activity after the conference, particularly if children's safety had already been achieved by removing alleged abusers from ongoing contact with them. In other cases, where there were continuing concerns, there was more activity, but the focus was on taking steps to ensure the safety of the child by, for example, provision of family aides, contact with family centres, and monitoring by individual social workers. Most parents felt only marginally involved in the process, and the majority felt that they were not being helped.

Ten months after the conference

The pattern set in the early post-conference period generally persisted up to the time of the second interviews. Parents/carers reported either no (or limited) contact (11 cases) or that visiting had been maintained throughout the whole period (12 cases). There was one 'no response'. The key issue seemed to be whether or not the child had remained in the same household as the alleged abuser. Twenty parents/carers felt that the contact they had with professionals was problematical. Most felt that they had little control over events and little understanding of the intentions of the professionals. This was particularly true with regard to the timing and content of visits, which were very much in the hands of the social worker: 'We only see her once in a blue moon when she fancies it' – 'She come [*sic*] in for fifteen minutes, said, "Hello, you're all right", and then left' – 'They said they'd do regular visits – then in May last year they stopped calling.'

Only 8 respondents said that they had some agreement with their social workers about the frequency of visiting. In 13 cases parents/carers felt there were no clear plans, and 15 felt confused about what was expected of them.

Another feature of parents/carers' contact with social workers during this period was that it tended to be crisis-focused. In 11 of the 24 cases, there were further causes for concern, including 2 incidents of abuse. Other concerns included additional children being born; 'potential abusers' moving into households; disputes over contact between parents/carers, and carers' illnesses. Events such as these precipitated visits by workers where previously there was little or no contact.

Throughout this period, 17 of the parents/carers reported feeling blamed and 16 said that they felt judged by the professionals: 'I'm just an item, I'm not really being asked what I want. I don't feel like I'm the girls' mother' – 'They've made me feel inadequate as a parent. I haven't been counselled. I haven't had any help. I've done a good job from my point of view looking after the kids because I've had them all my life.' This feeling of inadequacy was echoed by many of the parents/carers, including non-abusers as well as alleged abusers.

In general terms, these parents/carers did not feel involved in the child protection process. Indeed, the opposite was true in most cases. If anything, the picture was bleaker at ten months after the conference than before. Issues of blame and responsibility often remained unresolved. There was still a good deal of bitterness in some cases over the fact that individuals had been forced to leave the family home (very few had returned by the time of the second interview). Few parents expressed the feeling that they had been helped by the protection process, and this was true of several non-abusing parents as well as of those suspected of being abusers. There continued to be a lack of clarity about the purposes of visiting, and little certainty about how long intervention would continue.

Discussion

For many parents (particularly those who are suspected of abusing their children), the experience of child protection intervention is a negative and problematic one. The overwhelming impression given by parents/carers of their experiences of the child protection system was one of alienation. Two factors seemed to prevail: confusion and disappointment. The confusion resulted from uncertainty about what was required to demonstrate good parenting. The disappointment resulted from a general lack of provision of the help and support that parents had somehow expected to be part of professional intervention.

Given the values underpinning the social work profession, these feelings may be surprising. Why did the social workers in our study seem to fail to engage most of the parents with whom they worked? It could be that they were particularly incompetent practitioners, lacking the skills needed to work with people in conflictual situations. However, there was no evidence to suggest that this was the case. A more plausible answer is that the tasks of investigation and policing which are an important part of the child protection role cannot easily be reconciled with the qualities of empathy, sensitivity and support which are normally accepted as part of good social work practice (see Horne, 1990). This is not a new issue for the social work profession and has been the subject of much debate elsewhere (see Davies, 1994). Recently, applying the concepts of participation and partnership with parents (and children) has been put forward as a practical response to managing this 'old conflict'. However, the findings of the study presented in this chapter raise considerable doubts about the effectiveness of such an approach.

While there are more participative structures in the child protection process than before, for example parental (and child) attendance at child protection conferences and at core group meetings (and the local authority in the area under investigation had a thorough approach to the implementation of a participation policy), very few of the parents/carers in this study felt that these mechanisms gave them a genuine sense of working in partnership. Ironically, the main impression gained was of social workers busying themselves to meet the increased bureaucratic demands of participation. For instance, at the investigation stage, many social workers were seen as concentrating on issues such as writing reports and briefing parents about conference procedures, but in the process significantly failing to respond to parents' needs for support and understanding in what was often a traumatic experience. At each of the later stages of intervention (conference, the immediate post-conference period and ten months later) parents generally perceived a lack of responsiveness to their particular concerns and needs. It is notable that Farmer and Owen's (1995) study had findings that were similarly negative in respect of parents' responses to participation. However, they, like Thoburn et al. (1995), have faith in the potential benefits of participation, provided it is based upon the efforts of appropriately skilled practitioners and supportive agency policies.

As noted already, our study was conducted in an agency that was more advanced in implementing its participation policy than were those agencies studied by Thoburn et al. and Farmer and Owen, and we have no reason to believe that the professionals involved in the practice we researched were any less committed to participation (or any less skilled at implementing it). This leads us to feel that our findings have particular significance precisely because they are drawn from an analysis of those qualities and procedures which would normally be regarded as good participatory practice. We are, therefore, less optimistic about the benefits of participation under current arrangements and question whether a system developed to protect children from their parents can accommodate participatory/partnership approaches without some substantial rethink of the aims and purposes of social work intervention in this field of activity.

At present, the child protection system is tending increasingly to focus on the assessment of risk (Department of Health, 1988), and the main theoretical base for this assessment is one of individual pathology (Corby, 1991). The reason for this emphasis lies in the recent history of child abuse and child protection work which, through public inquiries, has highlighted the dangerousness of parents (Dale et al., 1986). Unfortunately this focus can reinforce professional power and inhibit cooperative work with parents. In these circumstances, it is rare for parents to get clear messages from social workers about the acceptability of their parenting. Restructuring of families can seem a safer option for social workers than working with families as a whole. Parents' needs for help and support can remain unmet, partly because they have low expectations, and partly because the provision of such help becomes a low priority in child protection work. It is very hard to see partnership working effectively under these conditions.

Conclusion

What are the ways forward? One suggestion may be that social workers need to adopt a more sensitive and responsive approach to the parents/carers they are working with. This might be brought about by training which is focused on the individual skills necessary to achieve this goal. However, while more training in this aspect of practice should not be discouraged, such an addition is unlikely to be sufficient because it does not address the deep sense of uncertainty that is associated with the way in which child protection practice is currently conceptualized and structured. Judging from our study, there is a fundamental lack of clarity about when harm to children should be deemed sufficiently abusive to warrant professional intervention – particularly in cases where neglect and moderate physical injury are concerned. Because of this, there is vagueness about what is required of parents/carers in order for them to demonstrate that they can look after their children safely.

It is essential that professionals operate with definitions of child abuse which can be clearly communicated to parents. Besharov (1981) and Wald (1982) have defended the value of more precise definitions of abuse. This is not easy to achieve (see Giovannoni and Becerra, 1979), but if it is not addressed communication and shared understanding between parents and professionals in child protection work will continue to be deeply problematic. Professionals should be in a position to give parents unambiguous messages about what is expected of them as parents. Protection plans therefore need to be clear, specific, properly shared with parents and, ideally, agreed upon by those parents. Greater clarity in these respects would have benefited many of the parents/carers and children in this study, and it would have given social workers a better basis for intervention.

Although the tensions and dilemmas which are to some degree inherent in child protection practice cannot be entirely eliminated, communication with parents/carers can be enhanced as a result of working to diminish any ambiguity and its associated indecision. If professionals were clearer about what they meant by 'abuse' and the continuing risk of it, the conditions for a limited form of parental participation would be improved. The details of such changes must be the subject of further analysis and debate, but it is important that this is done as speedily as possible. The sense of alienation shown by many of the parents/carers in this study is not conducive to any form of partnership, and the lack of clarity, which is partly responsible for this alienation, does not provide a good basis for effective work with children and families.

References

Besharov, D. (1981) 'Towards Better Research on Child Abuse and Neglect: Making Definitional Issues an Explicit Methodological Concern', *Child Abuse and Neglect*, 5, (4), pp. 383–90.

Cleveland County Council (1988) *Report of the Inquiry into Child Abuse in Cleveland 1987*, DHSS Cmnd. 412, London: HMSO.

Corby, B. (1991) 'Sociology, Social Work and Child Protection', in Davies (1991).

Corby, B., Millar, M. and Young, L. (1995) 'Parental Participation at Child Protection Conferences', *Journal of Health and Social Care*, 3 (3), pp. 197–200.

Daines, R., Lyon, K. and Parsloe, P. (1990) *Aiming for Partnership*, Ilford: Barnardo's.

Dale, P., Davies, M., Morrison, T. and Waters, J. (1986) *Dangerous Families: Assessment and Treatment of Child Abuse*, London: Tavistock.

Davies, M. (ed.) (1991) *The Sociology of Social Work*, London: Routledge.

Davies, M. (1994) *The Essential Social Worker*, 3rd edn, Aldershot: Arena.

Department of Health (1988) *Protecting Children: A Guide for Social Workers Undertaking a Comprehensive Assessment*, London: HMSO.

Department of Health (1991a) *Child Abuse: A Study of Inquiry Reports 1980–1989*, London: HMSO.

Department of Health (1991b) *Working Together Under the Children Act 1989: A Guide to Arrangements for Inter-Agency Cooperation for the Protection of Children from Abuse*, London: HMSO.

Department of Health (1994) *The Children Act Report 1993*, London: HMSO.

Department of Health and Social Security (1988) *Working Together: A Guide to Inter-Agency Cooperation for the Protection of Children from Abuse*, London: HMSO.

Eekelaar, J. (1991) 'Parental Responsibility: State of Nature or Nature of the State?',

Journal of Social Welfare and Family Law 1, pp. 37–50.

Family Rights Group/NSPCC (1992) *Child Protection Procedures: What they Mean for your Family*, London: Waterside Press.

Farmer, E. and Owen, M. (eds) (1995) *Child Protection Practice: Private Risks and Public Remedies*, London: HMSO.

Gardner, R. (1989) 'Consumer Views', in Kahan (1989).

Giovannoni, J. and Becerra, R. (1979) *Defining Child Abuse*, New York: Free Press.

Horne, M. (1990) 'Is it Social Work?', in Violence Against Children Study Group (1990).

Kahan, B. (ed.) (1989) *Child Care Research, Policy and Practice*, London: Hodder & Stoughton.

Orkney Report (1992) *The Report of the Inquiry into the Removal of Children from Orkney in February 1991*, London: HMSO.

Rochdale Area Child Protection Committee (1993) *Parental Participation in Child Protection Conferences*, Rochdale: Rochdale ACPC.

Thoburn, J., Lewis, A. and Shemmings, D. (1995) *Paternalism or Partnership: Family Involvement in the Child Protection Process*, London: HMSO.

Violence Against Children Study Group (eds) (1990) *Taking Child Abuse Seriously*, London: Unwin Hyman.

Wald, M. (1982) 'State Intervention on Behalf of Endangered Children: A Proposed Legal Response', *Child Abuse and Neglect*, 6 (1), pp. 3–45.

Part II

Children who hurt

Introduction

The human services have travelled a long and sometimes bumpy road in gaining understanding of the impact of abuse on individual children and of how, as welfare professionals, we should respond to that abuse. The shared and contested assumptions about the respective roles of the state and of families, coupled with our ambivalence towards the status of childhood, have led to practices that were often as damaging as the abuse itself.

Social work in particular has needed to develop the capacity to look at itself critically and rethink many of the reactions and responses that social workers, their agencies and society as a whole prescribed. For example, the fact that children might abuse each other is a facet of children's behaviour that has only relatively recently been conceded. In Chapter 7, Anne Bannister and Eileen Gallagher recognize the reluctance of many professionals to take this matter seriously. They argue persuasively the necessity for workers to treat the phenomenon earnestly and they present details of their research which raise some profound questions. This research confirms that some of the children who do abuse others were abused themselves, which is a point supported by Celia Doyle in her work.

In Chapter 8, Doyle presents illustrations and explanations of the behaviour of children trapped in abusive relationships, offering an analysis based on knowledge gained from the experiences of adults trapped in hostage situations – a phenomenon that has come to be known as 'the Stockholm syndrome'. This brings a new dimension to our understanding of why children who have been hurt might protect and collude with their abusers and respond to their circumstances in unusual ways. The parallels between the experiences and responses of hostages and those of children who have been abused raise interesting questions about the psychology of abuse.

Some aspects of this analysis are developed by Neil Thompson in Chapter 9. He points out that, for many children, experiencing abuse can be seen to

89

involve a range of losses and, at such times, a child's sense of meaning, purpose and direction may be profoundly shaken. He draws on our knowledge of loss and bereavement, arguing that child protection workers need to recognize that children, their families and, indeed, staff themselves are likely to experience significant grief that should be addressed. The failure to take seriously the loss dimension of child abuse and child protection, Thompson argues, can lead to important aspects of the situation being overlooked.

One thing that human services staff have learned over the years is that child abuse is rarely, if ever, clear-cut, and that the impact of abuse on individual children is difficult to forecast. What does appear to be crucial, however, is the quality of the response after the abuse has come to light, and how that response can lead to redressing some of the painful experiences that went before. In Chapter 10, Jeanie McIntee and Ian Crompton offer a psychological paradigm to aid understanding of the effects of trauma. Although they admit that trauma is an inevitable part of the human condition, for some the pain of trauma can be so severe that a 'dissociation' of the event can occur, leading in extreme cases to a psychological disorder (Dissociative Identity Disorder or 'DID'). This dissociation of the event can create for the person an apparent lack of differentiation between people, places and time. McIntee and Crompton take their analysis a step further and describe a therapeutic intervention with an abused person who has DID, and conclude their chapter with writings from survivors.

Helping to restore an abused child to emotional health demands, amongst other things, giving power back to the child. For this to happen effectively it is crucial that the voice of the child is heard. Madge Bray and Richard Pugh write powerfully in Chapter 11 of how child protection workers must listen to the child's reality and develop sensitive and authentic approaches to communicating with children.

Many of the contributors to this section of the book are from specialized services, but it is impractical to imagine that all hurt and damaged children could be cared for by experts. Abused children need, therefore, innovative and creative responses from local services. In Chapter 12, Alix Brown and Jackie Jennings report on an imaginative project with young male abusers. The workers used a short-term focused groupwork approach that involved role play, support and education. The chapter provides a number of strategies and ideas for other workers to develop, and the outcome offers a picture of cautious optimism. Finally, in Chapter 13, Andrew Durham describes his experiences of managing a therapeutic group for young boys who were victims of an organized paedophile conspiracy. This groupwork was especially testing as the delay in bringing the perpetrators to court meant that his support work ran the risk of contaminating evidence. His practical account is a tribute to the creative and imaginative resources of the workers involved.

7 Children who sexually abuse other children

Anne Bannister and Eileen Gallagher

Introduction and background to the research

The Child Sexual Abuse Consultancy in Manchester, England, is managed by NSPCC (National Society for the Prevention of Cruelty to Children) and for eight years has been running a programme of assessment, management and therapy with sexually abused children. In recent years there has been an increase in the number of children between 8 and 12 years of age who were referred because they may have been sexually abusing others. Their histories, and their needs, were so varied that we decided more information was required.

Studies of children and young people who sexually abuse others

Definitions of abuse

The National Children's Homes set up a Committee of Enquiry in 1990 to look at the problem of children who sexually abuse other children (National Children's Homes, 1991). They found difficulties with the issue of definition but believed that, if the concepts of true consent, power imbalance and exploitation were explored, then an understanding of what constituted an abusive event would become easier.

One of their first recommendations was that all professionals should take seriously allegations of sexually abusive behaviour by children against other children and proper investigations should be made.

This enquiry was followed by a 'Survey of Treatment Facilities for Young Sexual Abusers' (National Children's Homes, 1992). Again definitions were varied, many facilities using a legal definition which did not then apply to children below the age of criminal responsibility (10 years in England and Wales). This definition colluded with the denial and minimization of abusive behaviour in children under 10 years of age.

We decided that our definition for inclusion of children in the research was that a child should be 12 years or under, and should have acted in a sexually abusive way with another child. We defined 'sexually abusive' as meaning that force or coercion had been used upon another child to ensure participation. We took into consideration the issues of power imbalance, exploitation and true consent.

Who are the children who abuse?

Glasgow et al. (1994) studied children alleged to have sexually abused other children, but found that by far the largest number of children reported for abuse was in the 13 to 17 age band. They found that almost all the reported young people were male. They concluded that 'high risk' children might be identified very early on so that intervention might prevent their sexually abusive behaviour.

Cantwell (1988) found that, although it was clear that young children were abusing others, there was a great reluctance to accept the behaviour as potentially serious. Most of her 'perpetrators' were male, but in her 'cycles of abuse' she found some abused girls who, in turn, molested younger children.

Ryan (1989), looking at the effects of childhood sexual abuse, quoted many studies of adult and adolescent abusers which have shown that abusers claimed that they began molesting other children by re-creating their own experiences of abuse.

Two studies in Washington State (Kahn and Chambers, 1991; Smith, 1988) each found that a third to half of the abusing children had been sexually abused themselves and half had been physically abused. Both studies found a high proportion of prior aggressive behaviour, although no prior serious criminal behaviours. Again most children were male, the racial composition reflecting the census figures for the state. Smith found that many had witnessed violent or abusive behaviour within the family.

What intervention is available?

Debelle et al. (1993) studied the literature on intervention programmes for juvenile sex offenders (mainly in the USA) and concluded that most therapeutic strategies for these young people had been derived from experience gained with adult sex offenders. The authors suggested that programmes suitable for adults might not be suitable for adolescents.

The NCH Survey of Treatment Facilities (National Children's Homes, 1992) found that treatment in the UK was extremely variable. Staff felt that they were doing worthwhile work because it prevented further abuse, but that much abusive behaviour by young children was going undetected or unrecognized.

Toni Johnson (1988) describes SPARK (Support Programme for Abuse Reactive Kids) at Children's Institute International in Los Angeles. This programme is for children from 4 to 13 who have a pattern of sexually overt behaviour in their histories, and who have used force or coercion to commit sexual offences against other children. Children and parents are assessed, using extensive tests, and mandates are given by the courts to keep families in therapy, much of which is in groups and is largely behaviourally orientated.

The Leaps and Bounds project in Britain provides residential care for some young sexually abusing children, and individual therapy is also provided (Ogden, 1992). The project recruits and prepares adoptive parents and offers post-adoptive support.

In *Sexualized Children* (Gil and Johnson, 1993), the authors agree that people working with this group of children need a firm grounding in both victim and offender dynamics, and they endorse intervention either individually or in groups. They confirm that the therapy must reduce the problematic behaviour of such children and explore the underlying psychological concerns. They stress the involvement of carers and schools in the process.

At NSPCC Child Sexual Abuse Consultancy we assess all children using interviews and creative therapy techniques (Bannister, 1992a; Bannister et al., 1990). We also use these techniques in individual and group therapy and, in addition, we run a confronting behavioural programme for each child alongside this. Carers are involved as much as possible.

The research focus

Our research focused on:

- children's histories to see if patterns could be detected which might alert us to children who were 'high risk' for future abusive behaviour;
- the offences themselves to see if a behavioural sequence could be identified which might alert carers;
- the therapeutic interventions to see which were deemed helpful or otherwise by children and carers.

We included children of 12 or under who had been referred to NSPCC teams in north-west England for assessment or therapy.

Method

Sampling

We included a child in our research only if the child's NSPCC social worker was satisfied that a non-consensual abusive sexual act had taken place between the referred child and another child.

We explained to each NSPCC social worker the concept of the 'unit' which we wished to interview. This consisted of the child, the NSPCC worker and the child's carer. If the child's sexually abusive behaviour had started whilst he or she was with another carer they too were included, where possible.

The NSPCC Regional Database showed a high referral rate of adolescents who had sexually abused others, but a much smaller number of younger children. This reflects other studies, especially Glasgow et al. (1994). We found great resistance from workers and carers when we asked to include cases which had been closed for more than a few weeks. One mother was representative of other parents when she wrote: 'I am grateful for the help, but I think that bringing things up again for C would not help her as she is very concerned about talking to people about what happened.' Eventually six 'units' were included in the research.

Data collection

Our two interviewers used an interview guideline but encouraged interviewees to give as much information as possible.

Interview 1 was with the NSPCC social worker to elicit the history and details of the proposed intervention at referral. Interview 2 was with the carer at the time of the first referral and Interview 3 was with the child. These three interviews were repeated at the end of the treatment. Current carers were interviewed in instances where the carer had changed between referral and the end of treatment.

Analysis

All the data was fed into a database and analysed according to a systematic framework. Because we carried out this qualitative research using a holistic approach, the text was particularly rich and, where possible, we included direct comments from interviewees. The very small sample size and subjective nature of the analysis must be taken into account when assessing the results.

Results

Age, gender and ethnic group of children

Half of the children in our study were aged 11 and half were aged 12. The fact that this was at the upper limit of our age range did not surprise us, since we found that the greatest resistance to accepting sexually abusive behaviour in children concerned younger children. We should, however, bear in mind Cantwell's point (1988) that early abusive acts which are ignored can mean that many more children are abused.

Five of the children in the study were males and 1 was female. With our small sample we cannot compare percentages with other much larger studies, but our picture is similar to other studies cited.

We had 1 child who was African Caribbean in our sample; the others were white. This ratio of 1 black child to 5 white children reflects the ratio of black/white children referred to NSPCC Child Protection Teams in north-west England.

One child in the study was in Special Education and 1 other was in a special needs class of a mainstream school.

The children's histories

Five of the children had reported that they had been sexually abused. In 2 children it seemed likely that this abuse had begun when the child was aged 2 years or less. The duration of abuse ranged between a few weeks and three years. The people who abused the children were close and extended family members, family friends or other carers. All abusers were male. The sexual abuse the children had suffered included violent penetrative acts, mutual masturbation and being shown pornographic material.

Half the children were physically abused, occasionally in bizarre ways. At least 1 child had been seriously neglected. These figures (for sexual and physical abuse) are not dissimilar to figures in studies already quoted, but the figure for sexual abuse is higher because most children are referred to NSPCC teams due to their own abuse, rather than their abuse of others.

All the children had suffered other trauma which they felt was significant. Half had been abandoned by their birth fathers early on in their lives. Two fathers or father figures had abused several children in the family, and this had been witnessed by the subject child. Another child had witnessed his father beating his mother. Two children described poignantly how they had felt emotionally abused by their father or father figure. These events are in addition to the fact that some fathers or father figures had been the instigators of physical or sexual abuse of the subject children.

Although we were not told of any physical or sexual abuse by mothers, 1 mother had contributed to the serious neglect of her child. Only 1 child had disclosed his or her own abuse to the mother, most having disclosed to teachers, NSPCC workers or foster parents. This could indicate poor emotional ties between mother and child. Several children expressed anger at mothers who had not protected them or their siblings. Two mothers appeared to have an overprotective relationship with the child.

Sibling relationships were problematic. One subject child had sexually abused a sibling and there was very severe sibling jealousy in 2 other cases. One child had been sexually abused by older siblings. Some children expressed a sense of loss about siblings who had died or whom they had never known or from whom they had been removed. There was little contact with remaining siblings, and only in the case of the child who had been abused by older siblings was it possible to state that siblings were also sexually aggressive.

Many children today live with lone mothers or in reconstructed families (Clarke, 1994). Half of our children were living with both natural parents at the time of the first abusive incident. One was with a lone mother, 1 with a mother and stepfather and 1 with adoptive parents. At the time of our research interviews the situation had changed for 2 children – 1 child had moved from two natural parents to a single foster parent, while the other child had moved from a mother and stepfather to residential care.

All the children had exhibited aggressive, angry behaviour in their past. In 4 cases this was severe (lighting fires, running away, bullying, racially abusive language, sexually abusive language to women). These findings are similar to those of Smith (1988).

Five children were described as bullies of siblings or schoolfriends. One mother said: 'He is very dominating, he is always threatening people . . . like his dad . . .'

Four children had threatened teachers and their parents with physical violence. Two of the children had undoubtedly been bullied themselves. One of these had also bullied others. One child said: 'I get called fat and black and the teachers won't do anything . . . I cry on my own.'

In fact, every child had been involved in bullying either as victim or aggressor or both. However, a recent study (Butler and Williamson, 1995) found that bullying was a common experience for many children, and so it may not be especially significant. The anger or repressed anger that this suggests, however, should not be ignored, since most subject children described feeling particularly angry at the times when they sexually abused other children.

We asked about other sexualized behaviours: 1 child had used sexually abusive language to a female carer, and another had grabbed the breasts of a female carer. Another had suggested anal sex to two different professional male carers. These children had also masturbated in public and used sexually aggressive talk to adults and children

The abusive incidents

Four basic behaviours were described, with some additions. Two children had aggressively attempted to overcome another child and to simulate intercourse. Another 2 children had aggressively attempted to fondle another child's genitals; 1 had persuaded another to participate in mutual masturbation. Three children had aggressively attempted to penetrate another.

Some children had perpetrated different sexual behaviours on several occasions. The highest number of recorded incidents for 1 child was 22. Several children had 4 or 5 recorded incidents; 1 child had only 1 recorded incident. The incidents had occurred when the children were between 8 and 11. All incidents had been witnessed by teachers, other children or other adults, except for 1 between siblings. In this case the victim reported it to a social worker and the abusing child admitted it. Victims were siblings, schoolfriends or cousins, although 1 child chose victims from a wider circle of acquaintances.

Most victims were female, although 2 children had each abused children of both sexes. Most incidents were reported immediately. This is, of course, different from abuse perpetrated on children by adults. This is seldom reported immediately and is hardly ever witnessed.

Although there was much variation in the frequency and severity of the incidents, it is clear that all the children had expressed strong angry feelings in other ways, some more violently than others. We have noticed this in our clinical work and it is implied in the SPARK programme (Johnson, 1988). This is expressed well in the Dysfunctional Response Cycle described by Ryan (1989) as a response to being sexually abused.

Ryan describes early life experiences of helplessness, loss and betrayal being re-experienced in current events such as situations of humiliation and powerlessness, which trigger 'bad feelings'. These feelings move on through withdrawal to anger and then to attempts to control or blame others. Plans are then made to express the anger through sexual assault, exploitation (bullying), drug abuse, eating disorders, violence and so on. Ryan quotes Summit's 'accommodation syndrome' (Summit, 1983) to explain how sexual abuse not only involves emotional betrayal and psychological distress but may also meet a vulnerable child's need for attention, thus creating psychological confusion. Female victims often internalize their control-seeking behaviours, whereas male victims externalize them with aggressive behaviours.

Our clinical experience leads us to believe that psychological confusion and feelings of guilt and isolation are present not only in sexual abuse but also in emotional abuse. Emotional abuse is notoriously difficult to define (Bannister, 1992b), but may occur when a carer appears to provide a nurturing, non-abusive environment, but then secretly exploits a child to provide nurture for him- or herself. It may also occur when a carer ignores or diminishes the impact of loss upon a child.

In this study we asked a question of all participants (workers, carers and children) about the events immediately preceding the reported incident of abuse. The answers appear to fit into the Dysfunctional Response Cycle. One child said: 'My mum and dad were having a fight. I was frightened. I went out and saw M (the victim) and took her to the park.' Another said: 'I felt mad and were getting me own back for what happened [to me].'

The therapy received by the children

Four children had received some previous intervention, although this had sometimes occurred before their own abusive incidents had taken place. Three had been seen by psychiatrists – mostly for short assessment periods – for behavioural difficulties which sometimes included the sexual aggression. One had been seen by a psychotherapist (in relation to their own victimization) some time before the abusive incident had happened. One child had been seen by an educational psychologist.

Two of the children were seen for short periods of up to three months by NSPCC as part of an assessment carried out for the local authority. They were included because the assessments were seen to have a therapeutic component by workers, carers and children. In each case further intervention had been recommended by NSPCC. The other 4 children had been assessed and were being, or had recently been, helped by NSPCC. The duration of this work was from six weeks (terminated when a child refused to attend further sessions) to eight months. All therapy was individual, but sometimes more than one worker was involved. One child received parallel work on his own victimization and on his victimizing behaviour by two separate therapists. Another had a worker observing the therapy, and another had two workers to offer gender choice to a child.

All work was described as 'creative therapy' or was assessed as this. Drawings, drama, stories and puppets were used. In 4 cases (including one of the short assessment cases) educative or behavioural work had also been included in order to address offending behaviour.

This diversity of therapy is reflected in previous studies (Debelle et al., 1993). Debelle et al. point out that there is little to show that one approach or component or combination is better than another. It would seem that a very flexible approach, individually tailored to each child, has the best chance of success at present. What does seem to be important is the wide knowledge and experience necessary in the workers providing the therapy to enable this to happen.

The most comprehensive treatment programmes do include individual, group and family work. Behavioural and cognitive changes in children must be reinforced by systems changes in families, and the children must have a chance to practise these changes in groups with other children. Most workers with behaviourally disturbed children recognize symptoms such as dissociation and post-traumatic stress disorder, and it is clear that workers must be trained to help children to deal with these. Donovan and McIntyre (1990) stress that workers must be aware of normative developmental behaviours in children in order to understand what is outside the norm. Gil and Johnson (1993) discuss transferential and counter-transferential issues which have a great bearing on work with abused and abusing children. There is no doubt that workers who do not receive training in all these areas are at a disadvantage.

Comments on the therapy received

Five of the children made positive comments about the therapy they had received at the NSPCC's consultancy centre. These ranged from: 'She really listened to me' to: 'When I had problems they were there. They understood what I said about L who abused me. We made an agreement and I was allowed to say what went into it. We made a folder of all my work and drawings and writing.'

One child said it was hard to talk about some things and that NSPCC had not been able to stop the child's own physical abuse. This same child recognized that more help was needed with 'my problem' but thought the time spent at NSPCC was 'too long'.

Most of the other children felt that the time spent with NSPCC was 'OK' or 'about right'. The 2 children who had only received assessment both recognized that further work was necessary. Some of the carers had a different view of the time spent at NSPCC. Two felt it was too short, although 1 accepted that the work had ended prematurely because the child refused to attend any longer.

Most of the children were happy to describe 'the best bits' of the therapy, such as drawing, acting out stories and using puppets. One said: 'I liked having the sessions videoed so that at the end we could see what I had done and how much better I was . . .'

The 2 children waiting for longer-term treatment from local authorities were described by their carers as being calmer and less aggressive after their assessments by NSPCC. Similar comments were made by the other 4 carers but 1 stated that, although the initial effect was calming, some of the child's behaviour had now deteriorated. One carer thought the timing of the therapy had been wrong because at the time the child was moving to a new school, which made it less effective. One carer felt that the work was: 'Not deep enough, not pushy enough, they let him decide what he was doing in the sessions, they didn't ask him much about his own abuse.'

Other carers pointed to the value of the support given to the child, the opportunity to express feelings, and the educative experience. One carer felt the child's behaviour had improved 'drastically' – he was calmer, less giggly and much less aggressive.

All the other sexualized behaviours were presented by the children far less or not at all.

Recurrence of behaviour after therapy

We did not include a follow-up period in this study. However, half of the interviews took place over a period of up to six months. One child was investigated for further allegations of sexually abusive behaviour during the research period, and was investigated for further allegations of violence after the intervention – and the research – had finished. This child said to our researcher, before the further offences were alleged: 'I think it might happen again.' Another child commented: 'I think I might need more help with this problem.' The latter was a child who had refused to continue therapy and had only had six sessions. Both 'assessment' children and their carers and workers recognized the need for further work.

The 2 remaining children present the most optimistic picture. One had not been reported for further sexually aggressive behaviour in the period of about a year which had elapsed since the end of treatment. The other, whose research interviews had taken place over four months, had no reported re-offences. Since that child's therapy did not start until nearly a year after the last offence, both carer and social worker were optimistic about the future. Both these children expressed positive hopes for the future and one said: 'I don't feel so mixed up now. I've grown up a lot.'

We believe it may be significant that these 2 children are the only ones who were offered, and accepted, a full dual programme lasting several months, where they were treated both behaviourally – for the offences – and empathetically – for their trauma. In addition, the current carers of these 2 children had been fully included in the work and were very supportive.

Discussion

We wish to focus on four areas which have raised questions in our minds and which we feel need further work.

1   Our research has confirmed the work of other quoted researchers and has confirmed our clinical experience, which is that children, their carers and childcare professionals are uneasy about taking sexually abusive acts by

children against other children seriously. We endorse the comments made by others which state that this is unhelpful to children, and that all known incidents should be investigated within child protection procedures.

2   We found, like other researchers, that the abusing children have varied histories and, as with adult perpetrators, there is no typical profile. However, in common with other studies, we found it is rare for girls to be referred as sexual abusers. We found that children who abuse others are likely to be children who have themselves been abused, and the 'abuse cycle' should not be ignored. Children who witnessed abusive behaviour in families and children involved in bullying figure largely in our sample, and also children who have especially difficult or non-existing relationships with their fathers. More research in these areas might be fruitful.

3   Children who are very angry, and have no acceptable way of expressing this, seem more at risk of expressing the anger in sexually abusive ways. This high level of anger seems to be closely connected with frustration and powerlessness. Children who are expressing anger in physically abusive ways may be in danger of committing sexually aggressive acts also.

4   As therapists, we endorse the work of most treatment programmes, which include cognitive behavioural work on the abusive behaviour in addition to more creative, psychotherapeutic work on the child's own traumatic life experience. We accept that this must go alongside supportive, educative work with carers and families. We believe it is most important for young children, whose own traumatic experiences are very recent, to be offered empathetic exploration of their concerns, in addition to the behavioural work which adolescent and adult programmes use to address offending behaviour. These younger children need to have an opportunity to express their angry feelings, in an acceptable way, in order for this to be witnessed, and then these feelings need to be processed. This is probably a better way of building rapport with a child who cannot have a full understanding of the consequences of sexually abusive behaviour. There is no doubt, however, that a programme of intervention is incomplete without a component which focuses on the abusive behaviour and provides alternative coping mechanisms.

References

Bannister, A. (1992a) *From Hearing to Healing: Working With The Aftermath Of Child Sexual Abuse*, London: Longman.

Bannister, A. (1992b) 'Set Up For Abuse', *Community Care*, 17/24 December.

Bannister, A., Barrett, K. and Shearer, E. (eds) (1990) *NSPCC, Listening To Children*, London: Longman.

Butler, I. and Williamson, H. (1995) *Children Speak*, London: NSPCC/Longman.

Cantwell, H. B. (1988) 'Child Sexual Abuse: Very Young Perpetrators', *Child Abuse and Neglect*, 12, pp. 579–82.

Clarke, L. (1994) 'At The Expense Of The Children?: Demographic Change And The Family Situation Of Children In Britain', International Sociological Association Committee On Family Research XXXIth Seminar, London, 28–30 April.

Debelle, G. D., Ward, M. R., Burnham, J. B., Jamieson, R. and Ginty, M. (1993) 'Evaluation Of Intervention Programmes For Juvenile Sex Offenders: Questions And Dilemmas', *Child Abuse Review*, 2, pp. 75–87.

Donovan, D. M. and McIntyre, D. (1990) *Healing The Hurt Child*, New York: W.W. Norton and Co.

Gil, E. and Johnson, T. C. (1993) *Sexualized Children: Assessment and Treatment*, Rockville, MD: Launch Press.

Glasgow, D., Horne, L., Calam, R. and Cox, A. (1994) 'Evidence, Incidence, Gender And Age In Sexual Abuse Of Children Perpetrated By Children', *Child Abuse Review*, 3, pp. 196–210.

Johnson, T. C. (1988) 'Child Perpetrators: Children Who Molest Other Children, Preliminary Findings', *Child Abuse And Neglect*, 12, pp. 219–29.

Kahn, T. and Chambers, H. (1991) 'Assessing Reoffense Risk With Juvenile Sexual Offenders', *Child Welfare*, LXX (3), pp. 333–45.

National Children's Homes (1991) *Report Of The Committee of Enquiry Into Children And Young People Who Sexually Abuse Other Children*, London: NCH.

National Children's Homes (1992) *Survey Of Treatment Facilities For Young Sexual Abusers*, London: NCH.

Ogden, J. (1992) 'Nipping Abuse In The Bud', *Social Work Today*, 7 May, pp. 16–17.

Ryan, G. (1989), *Journal of Interpersonal Violence*, 4 (3), pp. 325–41.

Smith, W. R. (1988) 'Delinquency And Abuse Among Juvenile Sexual Offenders', *Journal Of Interpersonal Violence*, 3 (4), pp. 400–41.

Summit, R. (1983) 'The Child Sexual Abuse Accommodation Syndrome', *Child Abuse And Neglect*, 7 (2), pp. 177–93.

8 Terror and the Stockholm syndrome: The relevance for abused children
Celia Doyle

Introduction

'I'll make you suffer just like I suffered': this is the constant message of a mother to her 4-year-old son (Doyle, 1995a). The mother herself had suffered physical and emotional abuse when she was young. Now she rains down verbal invective and denigration on her own child, blaming him for all her problems. It is difficult for many people to comprehend how parents, when they themselves know what it is like to be abused, go on to mistreat their own children. The majority of adult survivors of child abuse want their own and other people's children to have a better start to life than they experienced. Nevertheless, there are a number of such adults who, having been mistreated as children, then become abusers themselves. In a study of 110 emotionally abusing families, 73 per cent were found to have had at least one parent who had suffered substantial childhood abuse (Doyle, 1995b).

In order to understand how some former victims become abusers themselves it is helpful to understand the psychological process to which people can be subjected when they believe themselves to be trapped in a situation of terror and physical and/or mental pain. The phrase 'Stockholm syndrome' has been used to describe the way in which individuals can form an attachment to their persecutor. The victims endeavour to protect their abuser. They show gratitude and loyalty towards them, turning hostility away from their oppressor and onto potential rescuers. Some eventually adopt the abuser's values and beliefs and emulate their abusive behaviour.

The same process can be seen in children who are abused. In most cases, children are so powerless in Western society (Pilcher, 1995) that, potentially, they can be readily trapped in an abusive situation. This may be in the home – where to tell outsiders would be to betray the family – or in an institution

– where children may believe that no-one else will care for them if they complain. Alternatively, they may be trapped by people outside their home who make them swear secrecy and render them too fearful or indebted to tell. This chapter examines this process of emotional entrapment, termed the Stockholm syndrome, and its possible effects on abused children.

The Stockholm syndrome

The term 'Stockholm syndrome' derives from events during and after a bank robbery in the Swedish capital in 1973, when bank employees held hostage showed loyalty and affection to the robbers and used their own bodies to protect them from police fire when the robbers surrendered. In a similar manner, some long-standing concentration camp prisoners admired the Nazis, found justifications for their policies and tried to emulate the SS guards by copying their uniform and treating weaker or newer inmates oppressively (Ochberg, 1978; Bettleheim, 1979). This ability of abused people to form an attachment to their abusers is now so well recognized that negotiators in hostage situations will not rely on the hostages to assist in freeing themselves. 'Police negotiators cannot confide in the hostages if an assault is planned' (Ochberg, 1978, p. 162)

The syndrome can be observed in people from a wide spectrum of cultures and classes, equally in men and women, young or old. The Stockholm syndrome can similarly be seen in abused children whatever their colour, creed, class, disabilities or abilities.

There are certain circumstances when people perceive a danger and can see no immediate means of escape or source of help. In such cases – faced with a terrorist touting a machine gun and hand grenade, the perimeter fence of a concentration camp or, for a child, a powerful, skilfully manipulative adult – the only response may be to freeze.

The inability to escape can be real or perceived. Faced with a robber waving a gun, bank customers are likely to respond with frozen fright if they believe the gun is loaded. In reality, it may be unloaded or an imitation, but it is the customers' belief which is important. Similarly, adults may see that children have an easy escape route from an abuser – 'Why didn't he just tell his mother?' – but, from the child's perspective, there may have been no obvious deliverance. The child believes he is trapped and in the abuser's power.

In relation to anti-discriminatory practice, the pressures on black and ethnic minority group children have to be recognized. The position is perhaps summed up by Charmaine, whose parents originated from the Caribbean: 'I couldn't tell about my dad because I loved him and I didn't want him to get into trouble and I thought white people would make racist comments' (Rouf, 1991, p. 3). She recognized the racism inherent in a predominantly white society, and this increased her sense of entrapment.

Some children with disabilities may also have additional factors which can contribute to their sense of entrapment. Often there are practical problems about escaping, as one survivor explained: 'Because of my physical disability I can't get off my back without help, so all he had to do was force me to the ground and I was fair game for him and his friends' (Corcoran, 1987, p. 106). At other times, the messages given by society to children with disabilities serve to entrap them. Margaret Kennedy (1989), for example, explains how the effects of deafness can make some children feel isolated and rejected, leading to withdrawal and a loss of self-esteem and confidence. Being abused can lead to the same feelings and perceptions and thus the child is doubly oppressed, and even less able to seek help.

Compliance and denial

The inability to escape leads to frozen fright, which is not just a suspension of emotional response and activity. Rather, all the person's energy and attention are focused on the source of threat. In that state, the victim will become quiet and compliant. Frozen fright and obedience make sense because energy, which could be used later if flight or fight become possible, is conserved. Moreover, it is probably much safer than trying to resist when the odds are overwhelming and the abuser is determined to exert power. This is illustrated by an extract of a conversation between a researcher and a hostage taker:

> R [*Researcher*] 'But what you are saying, it seems to me, is the same thing, that what's important is that people obey you'.
> H-T [*Hostage-Taker*] 'Absolutely. You – you have to have control. If I've got six hostages and one of 'em is causing dissension in the group, to sacrifice that one draws the others into line'. (Knutson, 1980, p. 124)

Compliance is also reinforced by a process called 'psychological contrast'. Solzhenitsyn illustrates this process when describing the torture of prisoners in the Gulag Archipelago:

> The interrogator would be extremely friendly . . . suddenly he would brandish a paperweight and shout 'You rat! I'll put nine grams of lead in your skull!' Or as a variation on this two interrogators would take turns. One would shout and bully, the other would be friendly, almost gentle. Each time the accused entered the office he would tremble – which would it be? (1974, p. 448)

Similarly a hostage-taker explained how he ensured compliance on the part of his hostages: 'We played the game just like the police do . . . whoever was like guarding the hostages, one would be like the bad guy and the other one would be the soft-spoken good guy' (Knutson, 1980, p. 125).

Psychological contrast or the tactic of 'good guy/bad guy' has long been recognized as a method of obtaining a victim's submission. It occurs in many situations of child abuse. In some instances, the abuser, often a parent, is kind and caring, then suddenly threatening and exploiting. In other situations, the abuser is allied to another person who is affectionate and gentle. This is particularly in evidence where there are two parents. The non-abusing parent, feeling unable to seek outside help, does his or her best to alleviate the situation and comfort the child. It can also be identified in institutions where two members of staff are jointly involved in the abuse. Finkelhor et al. (1988) describe how the head of a nursery sexually abused the children in an overtly cruel fashion, while her assistant also sexually exploited the children but in a gentle, nurturing manner. However manifested, psychological contrast further ensures the obedience of the victims.

In this state of compliance, victims may be forced by the captors to violate or assault others. Children may be ordered to abuse other children. This occurs most commonly in large or extended families, institutions and in organized abuse. The victims are likely to have very little option but to comply. However, this entraps them further because now they are accomplices. The abuser's guilt is their guilt; the abuser's abhorrent behaviour is their abhorrent behaviour. In order to tolerate their own behaviour, the victims must minimize the seriousness of the abuse. They can only accept themselves if they believe that, in some senses, the abuse was justified. In British public and some state schools, the flogging of pupils was perpetuated for generations by making the older boys flog younger ones. As Robert Dougall wrote:

> This was the first of several canings but the worst were always from the Prefects . . . Once I cut a rugger practice and the Captain of the 1st XV, who was an enormous boy of about nineteen, damn nearly cut me in half. I was black and blue for weeks. (1975, p. 34)

For anyone, child or adult, to cause extensive injuries and severe pain to a child for a minor peccadillo is clearly abusive and yet, as Dougall added: 'It never occurred to any of us to bear a grievance. It was just the accepted thing' (p. 34).

Another early response to any horror or threat is denial. The frozen fright gives way to a sense of unreality and numbness which results in a denial of the reality or the severity of the situation. As one hijack victim recalls:

They shouted at us that the plane was hijacked . . . they told us to lock our hands above our heads. We sat like that for hours. Funnily enough nobody seemed afraid. Perhaps everybody felt as I did that it was too much like a gangster movie to be taken seriously. (Dobson and Payne, 1977, p. 232)

This is a useful temporary state which helps people from being overwhelmed by the terror of the situation.

Denial can, however, become less than helpful if it becomes an entrenched state. For some, like Sylvia Fraser (1989), the victim of sexual abuse by her father and a lodger, the denial is so complete that they develop two or more personalities in order to cope. Sylvia had one identity – a perfectly happy girl who had no memory of abuse – and a second one representing her father's lover. Other victims who have an awareness and a memory of their maltreatment may deny that what they experienced was abuse – as the extract from Robert Dougall's autobiography illustrates. They may deny the severity and pain of what happened to them. In addition, they may dismiss the serious effects of the abuse. Simon, a 74-year-old paedophile, despite several convictions including a term in prison for sexual offences against boys, felt his sexual love for boys had developed fully through habitual childhood sexual activities with other boys in a boys' boarding school. He felt it was 'normal' and in no way damaging (Li et al., 1990).

If abused children remain in a state of denial for any length of time they may dismiss the severity, pain and distress of their abuse and, like Simon, may see no harm in other children being treated in the same way. They can therefore become abusers themselves, without any recognition of the damaging nature – both to themselves and to their victims – of their behaviour.

Coping with fear and anger

Frozen fright, shock, numbness and denial are all passive emotions. This state of passivity does not always continue. These responses can be replaced by more active, and possibly more painful, emotions, notably fear and anger.

The uncomfortable feeling of powerlessness is all the greater if the victim fears the abuser. In order for the level of fear to be tolerated, it is usually repressed. In hostage situations 'Frequently these feelings of fear are transferred from fear of the hostage taker to fear of the police' (Strentz, 1980, p. 141). And, as Symonds comments:

Hostages in their psychologically traumatised state never view negotiations for their release as benevolent. The victim would immediately give all for his release but he interprets and experiences any negotiations as endangering him

... nonloving and threatening behaviour by the very people who are negotiating for his release. (1980, p. 134)

There is a similar transfer of anger. Gerard Vanders was a hostage whose life had been threatened during the siege of a train by Moluccan terrorists. He commented: 'There was a growing sense that the authorities were mishandling the situation. They sent us food, but no utensils' (Ochberg, 1978, p. 152). It was only some considerable time after his rescue that 'his negative feelings about the way the government handled the case have abated' (p. 153).

In the case of abused children, this process can lead to an anger against 'society' or the helping professions, rather than the person who abused them. It can lead to a rejection of all adults and authority figures. For children with disabilities, it may be an anger and distrust of all people who do not share their disability. One sex abuser, Nick, had had an abusive childhood and acknowledged his 'earlier hate for the adult person, just sheer hate . . . I like kids because, I didn't have any other, real great experiences with adults when I was a kid' (Li et al., 1990, p. 258).

But, conversely, anger can also be projected against other vulnerable people, especially other children, who remind survivors of abuse of their own frailty and powerlessness. This again can lead to a belief that 'weak' people deserve to be mistreated and exploited.

Hope and gratitude

Elizabeth Kubler-Ross (1970), working with terminally ill patients, noted that those faced with imminent death maintained hope. The same is true of hostages and many abused children. In order to preserve hope, those who are held captive and mistreated have to convince themselves that the person in whose power they are is basically good, and ultimately concerned about their welfare.

This means that hostages and abused people will look for evidence of goodness and suppress any reminder of their captors' malevolence. Sheikh Yamani, along with other OPEC ministers, was taken hostage in 1975 by the terrorist Carlos the Jackal. He recalled:

I scrutinised his [Carlos'] face. I found that his expression was full of mockery and sarcasm. But then I tried to convince myself that he really was being honest in his words and that because of my own fears I was reading fanciful interpretations into what I read upon his face. (Dobson and Payne, 1977, p. 103).

Similarly, from the other side of the Arab–Israeli divide, Sarah Davidson, a Jew who was a passenger on the hijacked Air France Flight 139, noted her reactions to the terrorist leader, Bose:

> [He] adopted a pleasant manner. He was a concealed enemy, pretending, tempting his victims to believe in his good intentions . . . [He was] so affable that after my conversation with him, I found myself accusing myself. (Dobson and Payne, 1977, pp. 226–7)

There is also a sense of gratitude for 'small mercies'. Of Stalinist concentration camp prisoners, Solzhenitsyn wrote:

> In the morning the jailer came in [with a pail of gruel] . . . and greeted them quite humanely – no it was even more precious than that 'Good morning!' . . . grateful for the warmth of that voice and the warmth of that dishwater, they drifted off to sleep until noon. (1974, pp. 541–2).

In some cases, abusers threaten the victims' lives. Maya Angelou (1984) recalls how, when she was only 8 years old, her mother's boyfriend raped her, then threatened to kill her and her brother if she told anyone. In hostage situations, there is 'a highly credible threat to life . . . from the moment that it's not carried out, we have the beginning of the gratitude that builds up on the return of one's life from the individual who made a credible threat and nevertheless is not acting upon it' (Bahn, 1980, p. 152). For abused children, the threat may not be directly to their life but to other things that the child holds dear. And each time the threat is not carried out, the child feels gratitude.

The victim has by now learned to view the abuser as good, well-intentioned and worthy of gratitude. This can lead to the victim believing that not only is the abuser good but their behaviour and beliefs are equally good. As noted, this process is so powerful that even some concentration camp prisoners believed that the SS guards' Nazi policy was correct and began to identify with and adopt the Nazi viewpoint. It is perhaps less than surprising that some maltreated children adopt the values of their abusers and start to abuse other children.

Deserving, deprecation and depression

The statements by Sheikh Yamani and Sarah Davidson also demonstrate another feature of the Stockholm syndrome. In both cases the speakers felt a degree of self-contempt. Many victims come to a logical conclusion that, if their tormentor is good and yet they are suffering, it must be because they are bad or have in some way deserved the ill-treatment. In the context of child abuse, this can lead children to mistreat their peers. They may believe that all children deserve to be treated badly and excuse their bullying behaviour on these grounds. Or, if victims see a child behaving as they have done, they may consider it right to punish or exploit him or her. The behaviour of the prefects in Dougall's (1975) example illustrates these points.

Victims of abuse often become depressed as they turn their anger and self-deprecation inwards. This too has its dangers. Sexual activity and some physical activities are very pleasurable, or participating in them can cause a surge of adrenalin. Several paedophiles record that they have sex with children to alleviate emotional pain and loneliness: 'I think God's given – let me do this thing [sex with children] . . . to satisfy me, to not let me suffer too much' (Li et al., 1990, p. 244). Another paedophile explained: 'I was feeling emotionally insecure, I was feeling emotionally starved really . . . and perhaps this pushed me to break the barriers of the conventions' (Li et al., 1990, p. 249). For a child who feels depression and self-deprecation, sexual activities or physical and emotional bullying of another child can provide a sense of power, of control and of satisfaction. This, however, may be a vicious circle (Doyle, 1994), because guilt about their activities can lead to further self-deprecation and internalized anger, which in turn can lead to a greater need to regain a feeling of strength, power and control, and hence to repeated abuse of other children.

Accepting and adapting

The final stage for many people trapped in a frightening situation can be one of acceptance. This was identified by Kubler-Ross (1970). She found terminally ill patients often reached the point where, although they were not happy about their situation, they nevertheless experienced a calm acceptance of it. They were no longer angry and afraid, nor particularly depressed. They did not blame themselves, nor other people.

Acceptance is a helpful adjustment for terminally ill patients. For people in concentration camps, there is value in the ability to live from day to day without wasting precious energy on anger, fear or self-deprecation, and without railing at the injustice and degradation of their situation.

However, there are dangers for abused children who reach this stage. They are less likely to complain about their treatment and are less motivated to seek to escape from their situation. They are also much less likely to be recognized by adults as having difficulties. A child exploding with anger, one who is constantly fearful and flinching away from adults, or one who is patently withdrawn and depressed will usually be noticed by adults. But a child in a state of acceptance will often seem to be functioning well, and will not attract attention.

Even if their mistreatment is discovered, they may not be offered effective help and protection. The Children Act 1989 requires a case to be made that the child is suffering, or is likely to be suffering, significant harm. Harm is usually measured by the child's responses. If a young person seems to be coping well, appears emotionally calm, makes no complaint about his or her treatment and has made developmental progress within a broad 'norm', then experts will pronounce that there is no evidence that the child is suffering, or will suffer, emotional harm. The fact that the child has been so severely or chronically abused that he or she has reached the final stage of adjustment escapes the notice of the protective agencies.

There is a final hazard for children who reach this stage. They have an unquestioning acceptance not only of their treatment but also of the values, justification and behaviour of their abusers. This means that they are less likely to view the abuse of other children as wrong. They may indeed believe that it is right and so may consider it their duty to engage in sexual activities with other children themselves, or, like the prefects described by Dougall (1975), believe it right to hurt and humiliate other young people.

Additionally, they no longer feel that they are in control of their own behaviour or destiny. They have reached a state of extreme powerlessness. For some, they are then able to justify their own loss of control and abuse of others on the basis of their helplessness as a victim. Ryan (1989) recognized this in relation to young people who sexually abuse other children, but it is also in evidence in other forms of abuse, including physical and emotional bullying (Doyle, 1995a).

Individual variations in victims' experience of the Stockholm syndrome

In studies of hostages and captives, the Stockholm syndrome is present in differing degrees and manifestations in different individuals, while some appear to be free of any sign of the syndrome. Researchers have yet to explain these differences. The length of time spent in a situation of entrapment appears not to have great significance. In a study of the victims of the hijack of TWA flight 355, the passengers' development of attachment to the hijackers was not dependent on whether the passengers had been freed after three hours or held for the full 25 hours, only being released after the hijackers surrendered (Strentz, 1980).

The depth of the sense of entrapment does not seem to be a major determining factor. This means that children from minority ethnic groups, or those whose disabilities cause them to feel a greater sense of entrapment, are not more disposed to develop aspects of the syndrome, and there is no evidence that they are more likely to abuse other children.

One important factor appears to be the nature of the relationship with the abuser. Hostages and captives who 'had negative contacts with the subjects did not evidence concern for them, regardless of time of release' (Strentz, 1980, p. 143). It appears that, where there are no positive aspects to the relationship, the syndrome will not develop. This may explain why children are often able to protest about mistreatment by a newly arrived abusive step-parent, a rejecting parent who only has a harsh disciplinary role or a casual acquaintance who mistreats them from the outset, and from whom they have received no affection or care.

Some hostages who have not developed the syndrome have had a very strong sense of identity and have created their own world, insulating themselves against the negative pressures. One survivor, a British Ambassador, absorbed himself in the role of the Queen's representative. Children who are able to escape into their own fantasy world or carve out a positive role or hold on to a positive identity may be less vulnerable. But 'as yet there is no identified personality type more inclined to the Stockholm syndrome' (Strenz, 1980, p. 145).

Children will therefore vary substantially in whether or not they will develop the syndrome. Those who do will also move through the different stages at different times and at an individual pace. Some may remain stuck in a state of permanent denial that they have suffered mistreatment, or one of perpetual anger. Others will range freely backwards and forwards between the various stages, for example at one moment showing depression, at another anger, all overlaid perhaps with a degree of denial. This variation depends on a complex interplay of circumstances: behaviour of the abuser, the victim's relationship with the abuser and, to a lesser degree, the victim's individual temperament, life experiences and inclinations. A similar multifarious set of factors is needed to explain why one child develops the Stockholm syndrome to the extent that he or she becomes an abuser, and why another child in very similar circumstances does not.

Conclusion

Many abused children perceive themselves to be trapped by a person more powerful than themselves in a situation of fear often amounting to terror. In these situations they are likely to experience a psychological process that many threatened and entrapped people experience. This process has been termed the Stockholm syndrome. It is apparent where the victims show an affection and protectiveness towards their abusers.

Sometimes the process leads to the victims identifying with the oppressors, adopting their values and emulating their behaviour. For abused children, it can mean that some mistreat other children when ordered to, in a state of compliance. It can also mean that they deny the ill effects of the abuse on themselves and other children. They view the perpetrator as behaving with justification and can come to believe that children should be treated in an oppressive manner. They can also end up accepting totally the rightness of the perpetrator's behaviour, and justify their own mistreatment of other children by citing their abuser's values and opinions, while excusing their own loss of control on the basis of their helplessness as a victim.

We should remember, though, that not all young people, even those who can be seen to develop the Stockholm syndrome, will abuse other children – just as the majority of concentration camp survivors did not identify the SS, nor do the majority of hostages threaten fellow hostages. It is only the minority who espouse the cause of their oppressors and, in turn, become oppressors themselves.

References

Angelou, M. (1984), *I Know Why the Caged Bird Sings*, London: Virago.

Bahn, C. (1980) 'Hostage Taking – the Takers, the Taken and the Context: Discussion', *Annals of the New York Academy of Sciences*, 347, pp. 151–6.

Bettleheim, B. (1979) *Surviving and Other Essays*, London: Thames & Hudson.

Corcoran, C. (1987) *Take Care! Preventing Child Sexual Abuse*, Dublin: Poolbeg.

Dobson, C. and Payne, R. (1977) *The Carlos Complex*, London: Coronet.

Dougall, R. (1975) *In and Out of the Box*, London: Fontana.

Doyle, C. (1994) *Child Sexual Abuse: a Guide for Health Professionals*, London: Chapman & Hall.

Doyle, C. (1995a) 'Emotional Abuse of Children', unpublished research findings.

Doyle, C. (1995b) 'Emotional Abuse, Research Findings and a Model for Intervention', paper presented at the 'Emotional Abuse and Failure to Thrive' study day, 31 March 1995, Brighton.

Finkelhor, D., Williams, L. M. and Burns, N. (1988) *Nursery Crimes: Sexual Abuse in Day Care*, Newbury Park, CA: Sage.

Fraser, S. (1989) *My Father's House*, London: Virago.

Kennedy, M. (1989) 'The Abuse of Deaf Children', *Child Abuse Review*, 3 (1).

Knutson, J. N. (1980) 'The Dynamics of the Hostage Taker: Some Major Variants', *Annals of the New York Academy of Sciences*, 347, pp. 117–28.

Kubler-Ross, E. (1970) *On Death and Dying*, London: Tavistock.

Li, C. K., West, D. J. and Woodhouse, T. P. (1990) *Children's Sexual Encounters with Adults*, London: Duckworth.

Ochberg, F. (1978) 'The Victim of Terrorism: Psychiatric Considerations', *Terrorism*, 1 (2).

Pilcher, J. (1995) *Age and Generation in Modern Britain*, Oxford: Oxford University Press.

Rouf, K. (1991) *Black Girls Speak Out*, London: The Children's Society.

Ryan, G. (1989) 'Victim to Victimiser: Rethinking Victim Treatment', *Journal of Interpersonal Violence*, 4 (3), pp. 325–41.

Solzhenitsyn, A. (1974) *The Gulag Archipelago, 1918–56*, London: Collins/Fontana.

Strentz, T. (1980) 'The Stockholm Syndrome: Law Enforcement Policy and Ego Defenses of the Hostage', *Annals of the New York Academy of Sciences*, 347, pp. 137–49.

Symonds, M. (1980) 'Victim Responses to Terror', *Annals of the New York Academy of Sciences*, 347, pp. 129–36.

9 Responding to loss
Neil Thompson

Child abuse is a complex, multifaceted phenomenon. However, one dimension of the subject that has received little or no attention is the status of the experience of abuse as a form of loss. This can be seen to incorporate a variety of losses, not least that of trust. This chapter examines the significance of abuse as an experience of crisis and loss, and considers a number of questions that arise from this analysis:

- To what extent can behaviours and emotional responses associated with abuse be linked to responses to loss?
- If children are not helped to grieve their losses effectively, can this result in destructive behaviours (perhaps including the abuse of other children)?
- What does the literature on loss tell us that could be usefully adapted to working with abused children?
- What are the implications of this analysis for child protection practice?

I shall explore a number of key issues in relation to the experience of loss as they apply to abusive situations. From this we can begin to develop a better understanding of the significance of loss as a factor in developing high-quality standards of practice in child protection.

Loss is, of course, closely associated with death, and much of the literature on loss relates specifically to death. Walter discusses the view that death can be seen as a form of social threat, an undermining of what we take for granted:

> Aries, like Gorer, argues that death is inevitably problematic; along with sex, it is one of the major ways in which 'nature' threatens 'culture'. Death must therefore be 'tamed', which societies traditionally do through religion and

115

through ritual. But over the past few centuries, individualism, romanticism and secularism have undermined the rituals, and the modern individual is left naked before death's obscenity. (1993, p. 35)

Death represents one of the ways in which nature impinges on society, one of the ways in which human endeavour and values can be undermined by what is, in so many other ways, a positive and beneficent force.

There is a direct parallel that can be drawn between this image and the experience of abuse at the hands of someone who is otherwise loving and caring – a parent, for example. A child, who sees the parent as a source of love, security and esteem, can, at the onset of abuse, be threatened by what appears in other respects to be a positive aspect of his or her life-world. It is not surprising, then, that such experiences should so often be characterized by confusion, insecurity and diminished self-esteem. As Corby comments:

> Clinical accounts suggest that the more closely related the abused child is to the abuser the greater is the degree of harm likely to result. Thus, intra-familial abuse is likely to have a more harmful effect than extra-familial abuse, and abuse perpetrated by a natural father more than that perpetrated by an uncle. (1993, p. 124)

There is, however, a more general parallel between the notion of death as a threat to society and culture and child abuse as a threat to social mores. In a society where children are valued, rhetorically at least, the widespread abuse of children can be seen as a destabilizing social force. The 'discovery' of child abuse in the 1960s, and of sexual abuse in the 1980s, can be seen to present, therefore, not only a threat to the children concerned, but also, at an ideological level, to the basic fabric of society (Parton, 1985).

Child abuse can be seen as a phenomenon that is closely related to loss in a number of ways and at a number of levels. For example, Stewart (1994) draws links between loss and the experience of abuse in adults. Such losses associated with abuse are many and various. They include:

- boundaries;
- trust;
- hope;
- feelings and what they mean;
- intimacy;
- childhood;
- spontaneity;
- privacy;
- self-respect;
- confidence and serenity;
- family;

- happiness;
- identity.

Although Stewart's ideas relate to his work with adults who were previously subjected to abuse, the same argument can be seen to apply to children who have experienced abuse. That is, the linkages between abuse and loss need to be understood in terms of the immediate effects of trauma as well as their long-term implications in adulthood.

The following passage from Rouf vividly captures the intense sense of loss that child abuse can instil:

> I am no longer I.
> If I look depressed he will hit me.
> He will slap my face like he did this morning.
> Doesn't he know why I'm depressed?
> He wants me to be his puppet. I am his clown.
> I am not allowed to have any emotion. (1990, p. 10)

The association between the experience of abuse and that of loss is therefore a very strong one, and yet one that has received little or no attention in the literature to date. This raises a number of issues that are very significant for child protection workers, issues that are worthy of much closer attention.

The work of Parkes (1986, 1988) presents loss as a psychosocial transition that can have the effect of shaking the entire world-view of the person experiencing the bereavement. For children, this can be seen to be particularly significant in so far as their world-view is still in the process of construction, and is therefore more vulnerable to the ravages that a significant loss can bring. We should therefore be ready to accept that a loss for a child may have profound consequences. Consequently, we should be wary of simplistic aphorisms along the lines of 'Children are resilient' or 'Children don't suffer in the same way as adults.' As Eth comments:

> Society generally views childhood as a naturally happy time, free of responsibilities and worries. But the implication that children are somehow protected from the emotional effects of traumatic events is tragically false . . . Children are, in fact, as susceptible to trauma as adults, even though their suffering is commonly overlooked. (1989, p. xi)

The tendency to underplay the significance of loss and grief in children (Thompson, 1995) can add to the pressures abused children experience, by devaluing or 'disenfranchising' their grief (Doka, 1985).

This can be better understood by reference to Prior's concept of the social distribution of sentiments. Prior (1993) argues that the experience of grief is not simply an individualized psychological process – it also needs to be understood in terms of social factors. Different societies permit or encourage different responses to grief. But what does this mean for children who have experienced loss as a result of abuse? What socially approved avenues are available for the expression of grief? Clearly, this is a difficult area to address in view of the issues of confidentiality surrounding child abuse and child protection. This is a point to which I shall return below.

A similar set of issues arises in relation to Marris's argument that the severity of grief depends, to a large extent, on the degree of social disruption caused by the loss. Marris (1986) draws links between the experience of loss at an individual level and at a community level (through public disasters, for example). He argues that a common theme is the loss of meaning that a bereaved person experiences. Meaning derives, to a certain extent at least, from our social networks. When these networks are also disrupted by the loss, then the loss of meaning can be intensified. In a child abuse situation, the response to the abuse by officialdom can be extremely disruptive of the child's social circumstances, particularly where the child is removed from home or where the perpetrator is a family member and he or she moves from the family home as a result of the abuse coming to light. Ironically, then, attempts to protect the child from abuse may well heighten the experience of loss brought about by the exposure to an abusive situation.

Having considered a number of issues that link loss with child abuse, we can now move on to explore some of the responses to loss that can also be seen to apply in many child protection situations. Responses to loss include:

- anger and aggression;
- guilt;
- depression;
- idealization;
- sleep disturbances;
- appetite disturbances;
- absent-mindedness;
- social withdrawal;
- restless overactivity.

Experienced childcare workers should have little difficulty in recognizing in this list a number of responses not only to loss, but also to abuse, thereby underlining the significance of the relationship between loss and abuse.

The overall list presents a range of important questions to be addressed in working through loss issues with abused children. However, for present purposes, I shall limit myself to considering three: guilt, depression and idealization.

Guilt can be seen as an internalization of aggressive feelings, anger turned inwards upon the self. A common response to abuse situations is for the victim to experience a sense of guilt, to wrestle with feelings that they somehow invited or effected the abuse. This is particularly significant, I would argue, in relation to sexual abuse situations. This is because the dominant patriarchal ideology incorporates and perpetuates such myths as 'she was asking for it' or 'she led him on'.

Guilt is a non-pathological response to a loss situation. As Littlewood comments:

> Guilt, over acts or omissions, is another experience which often follows the death of a loved person. Guilt in connection with not being kind enough to the dying person or not being present at the death are particularly common. (1992, p. 46)

Guilt can be seen as a means of handling a flood of intense feelings, an attempted solution rather than necessarily a problem, in the sense that it can, in the short term, play a constructive part in coming to terms with the loss. However, if it persists over a period of time, its presence may indicate complications in the grieving process.

The fact that, in child protection work, we also encounter a great deal of guilt in children who have been abused reinforces the central tenet underpinning this chapter – the importance of recognizing the experience of abuse as a form of loss.

Depression is a further basic element in grief responses which also arises quite frequently in the aftermath of abuse. Depression can be seen as a psychological response to loss. It is defined by Thomas and Pierson as 'feelings of hopelessness, sadness, tearfulness and intense ANXIETY' (1995, p. 113). They go on to comment that:

> Depression affects people in different ways. A person suffering from depression can feel sadness, low self-esteem, hopelessness or something more extreme, such as feelings of total despair, complete worthlessness, intense guilt and constant irritability. Tasks require extra effort; thinking becomes more difficult; and thoughts can centre on SUICIDE or be preoccupied with fears of serious illness. Speech and physical movements can be slowed drastically, while at the same time the sufferer is tense and restless, with pronounced interruption to sleep patterns. (1995, p. 113)

Children who have been abused may at times manifest some degree of depression through their actions and emotional responses. Again, this can be seen as part of the process of adjusting to an experience of loss. However, there is one significant difference. In mourning the loss of a loved one, the bereaved person can understand why he or she is depressed – the feelings, although profoundly negative, none the less make sense to the person concerned. In abuse situations, however, where the losses experienced are less explicitly acknowledged, any feelings of depression may be experienced as more threatening or destabilizing because the reason for such feelings is less clearly understood (by the person concerned and others involved in his or her care).

Idealization is a process that sometimes occurs when the loss of a loved one is experienced. This involves a bias towards remembering only the positives about a person's character and our relationship with him or her, while shutting out any possible negative thoughts or memories of the person who has died. A certain element of idealization is not uncommon in grief responses generally, but can, in some cases, be taken to extremes – it can become a dominant feature of the grieving process.

Once again, there is a clear and strong parallel with child abuse. For example, a child who has been abused by his or her father may see the father in an unreasonably positive light. He becomes idealized, as the traumatic feelings associated with the abuse are 'compartmentalized', set to one side because they are too painful to deal with. In this respect, idealization can be seen as a form of denial.

Extreme examples of the idealization of the perpetrator can create barriers for the child protection professional in trying to make progress in working with the child. However, even where the idealization is less extreme, there are dangers that the worker must become sensitive to. For example, it can be very problematic and destructive if the worker refers to the perpetrator in negative or derogatory terms. Despite what the perpetrator has done to the victim, the child may none the less have a very deep love, or at least strong attachment, for that person. The dilemma that the child experiences – trying to reconcile feelings of love with the experience of abuse – is a very difficult one, and an insensitive negativity towards the perpetrator may lead to a response of idealization. Such matters therefore have to be dealt with very carefully and sensitively.

The recognition of abuse as a matter of loss and grief represents an additional element of theory that pressurized child protection workers need to address in their practice. However, this recognition also gives us access to an existing body of knowledge and practice experience that can be amended and adapted to inform child protection work. I shall use the model of Worden (1991) as a worked example to illustrate the understanding that can be gained by drawing on theories of loss.

Worden's approach is based on the notion of 'tasks' that need to be achieved in order to move through the grieving process. There are four such tasks: accepting the reality of the loss; working through to the pain of grief; adjusting to an environment in which the deceased is missing, and emotionally relocating the deceased and moving on with life. I shall address each of these in turn.

Accepting the reality of the loss   This refers to the need to work through and beyond the first stage of the crisis, the 'impact' stage which is characterized by a sense of disbelief:

> This initial stage is characterised by stress and confusion and a sense of disbelief. The situation seems unreal. Comments such as 'I can't believe it's happened' or 'It hasn't sunk in yet' are not uncommon. Profound feelings of emptiness, loss and disorientation are experienced. (Thompson, 1991, p. 10)

One problem that can occur here is the use of denial to avoid accepting the harsh reality of the abuse. In younger children, in particular, this may manifest itself in the use of fantasy as a means of mediating or counterbalancing reality. Alternatively, it may be the *meaning* of the loss that is denied:

> In this way the loss can be seen as less significant than it actually is. It is common to hear statements like, 'He wasn't a good father,' 'We weren't close,' or 'I don't miss him.' Some people jettison clothes and other personal items that remind them of the deceased. Removing all reminders of the deceased . . . minimizes the loss. It is as though the survivors protect themselves through the absence of any artifacts that would bring them face to face with the reality of the loss. (Worden, 1991, p. 11)

Worden's comments here relate to the loss, through death, of a person. However, the same comments can be seen to apply to situations that involve the loss of a person through other means (imprisonment, for example) or to other forms of loss associated with abuse.

A first step towards integrating the experience of abuse can be seen as an acceptance of the reality of what has happened. This may be problematic for some children who have yet to reach a cognitive level at which they can comprehend an abusive situation. Ironically, in some abusive situations – those that come to the attention of the child protection services – the official response to the abuse may be even more confusing and difficult to understand than the actual abuse (Thompson, 1992).

Working through to the pain of grief   Loss is characterized by intense emotional pain, and it is a well-established principle of bereavement counselling that it is necessary to work through this pain in order to begin to come to terms with the loss. That is, if the pain is suppressed or avoided in some way, the necessary 'grief work' will be held back.

Depression can be seen as one way of avoiding the pain by numbing all emotional responses, leaving the person in a psychological state that resists all forms of emotional stimulation. The depression often associated with abuse can be seen to play a very similar role.

The skill of the worker can be a very significant factor in helping children to deal with painful feelings and avoid the need to repress them. A basic part of this skills base is the worker's ability to listen. This may sound relatively simple, but in dealing with a person who is grieving, there is a strong temptation to focus on *doing*, rather than listening. Active listening is more important than activity for its own sake:

> When humans are faced with a crisis, the urge-to-do can tempt us into rushing to 'make it better' with a platitude or other unhelpful response. But it is, of course, not action but reception which comforts. It is a counsellor's task to help a client give words to his sorrow.
>
> It is not easy to find the words to express grief and the listener can easily react to her own anxiety, letting it get in the way and thus prevent the words being found. There is a special quality of reflective silence within a relationship, however, which can enable the griever to find his [or her] own words. (Lendrum and Syme, 1992, p. 83)

Adjusting to an environment in which the deceased is missing   Loss brings about not only emotional changes, but also significant changes in the 'environment' or life circumstances of the person concerned. This means that an abused child has to come to terms with the changes brought about first of all by the abuse itself and subsequently, as noted above, by the abuse coming to light and being dealt with through official procedures.

Although there is no actual 'deceased' person, the adjustments to the loss can be equally demanding for the child to make, particularly as loss through abuse can lead to very significant, sometimes dramatic, changes – police involvement, for example. In addition, although an actual death has not occurred, a key figure in the child's life may have left, particularly where the abuser is a member of the family. Adjusting to that person's absence can be a major task in its own right. Where the person's absence produces a confused set of feelings (relief mixed with regret, for example), the complexities of adjustment can be extreme.

An important problem that needs to be prevented where possible is the tendency for the person experiencing the loss to avoid making the adjustment to their changed environment. This can occur, for example, where, instead of adapting to new circumstances, the individual resigns him- or herself to a narrower, more constricted set of circumstances. That is, they make little or no attempt to adjust to certain absences – preferring, instead, to exclude those aspects of their life from their new environment. They create, physically and/or emotionally, no-go areas.

Emotionally relocating the deceased and moving on with life   It is understandable that we should hold on to memories of a person close to us who has died. However, these feelings may need to be set in a new context, to allow us to move on with our lives. As Worden comments:

> The counselor's task, then, becomes not to help the bereaved give up their relationship with the deceased, but to help them find an appropriate place for the dead in their emotional lives – a place that will allow them to go on living effectively in the world. (1991, p. 17)

In situations of abuse, there can also be this task of 'emotional relocation', and may require skilled help to achieve. Johnson (1989) argues that this process of 'resorting' can be particularly significant for adolescents. The process involves reconstructing the present on the basis of changed perceptions of the past, and this is especially relevant for adolescents who are in the process of leaving childhood behind and engaging with adult responsibilities and expectations.

These, then, are the four 'tasks' of grieving, as set out by Worden (1991). Once again, we can see that there are clearly discernible parallels between loss as a result of death and the losses brought about by child abuse. This is not to say that the two sets of experiences are identical, but there are sufficient similarities for us to take seriously the lessons that can be learned from identifying abuse as a form and source of loss.

There are a wide range of implications that can be drawn from the recognition of this parallel. The most fundamental is the need for child protection workers to be sensitive to children's experiences of loss, to become attuned to the possibility or likelihood that the abused child they are working with is also a grieving child. The literature on loss and loss counselling can then be brought to bear to help increase our understanding and skills in this aspect of practice.

Another important implication is the need to recognize that such grief, where it does occur, is *disenfranchised* grief (Doka, 1985). That is, it is a form of grief that is not socially recognized or culturally codified, and therefore presents greater difficulties in finding expression. In particular, the confidentiality surrounding child abuse situations may erect substantial barriers to effective grieving, by narrowing down the range of people who can share the grief.

The experience of bereavement is often cushioned to a certain extent by the existence of culturally-specific rituals. These have the effect of helping to affirm that, although one member of the culture has been lost, the sharing implicit in the very notion of culture can be part of the process of beginning to come to terms with the loss. The absence of constructive, supportive rituals for responding to the grief associated with abuse can have the effect of further reinforcing its status as a form of disenfranchised grief.

In addition, the child is unlikely to be the only person experiencing loss and grief. My focus in this chapter has been on the abused child, but an argument could be made that everyone involved experiences, potentially at least, some degree of loss. This would include family members, other relatives and friends and, of course, staff involved in the child protection system. As Morrison (1990) has very ably demonstrated, child protection is an emotionally highly charged type of work. A profound sense of grief can at times be one of the emotions experienced – a fact that raises important questions in terms of supervision and staff care.

Perhaps one of the most fundamental aspects of the linkage between abuse and loss, and one that perhaps forces all practitioners to reconsider their approach to practice, is the notion of a quest for meaning. At times of loss, our sense of meaning, purpose and direction can be profoundly shaken, leaving us feeling insecure and vulnerable (Morgan, 1993). This, too, can be the reality of abuse – with many unanswered questions, little sense of meaning or purpose. Abuse can leave a child wondering 'Why? Why has this happened to me?', with child protection workers also at times overawed by the sense of tragedy, meaninglessness and loss that child abuse can so powerfully create within us.

References

Bannister, A., Barrett, K. and Shearer, E. (eds) (1990) *NSPCC, Listening to Children*, London: Longman.

Corby, B. (1993) *Child Abuse: Towards a Knowledge Base*, Buckingham: Open University Press.

Dickenson, D. and Johnson, M. (eds) (1993) *Death, Dying and Bereavement*, London: Sage.

Doka, K. J. (1985) *Disenfranchised Grief*, Lexington, MA: Lexington Books.

Doka, K. J. with Morgan, J. D. (eds) (1993) *Death and Spirituality*, Amityville, NY: Baywood.

Eth, S. (1989) 'Preface' to Johnson (1989).

Johnson, K. (1989) *Trauma in the Lives of Children*, London: Macmillan.

Lendrum, S. and Syme, G. (1992) *Gift of Tears: A Practical Approach to Loss and Bereavement Counselling*, London: Routledge.

Littlewood, J. (1992) *Aspects of Grief: Bereavement in Adult Life*, London: Routledge.

Marris, P. (1986) *Loss and Change*, 2nd edn, London: Routledge & Kegan Paul.

Morgan, J. D. (1993) 'The Existential Quest for Meaning', in Doka and Morgan (1993).

Morrison, T. (1990) 'The Emotional Effects of Child Protection Work on the Worker', *Practice*, 4 (4).

Parkes, C. M. (1986) *Bereavement: Studies of Grief in Adult Life*, 2nd edn, Harmondsworth: Penguin.

Parkes, C. M. (1988) 'Bereavement as a Psychosocial Transition: Processes of Adaptation to Change', *Journal of Social Issues*, 44 (3).

Parton, N. (1985) *The Politics of Child Abuse*, London: Macmillan.

Prior, L. (1993) 'The Social Distribution of Sentiments', in Dickenson and Johnson (1993).

Rouf, K. (1990) 'My Self in Echoes, My Voice in Song', in Bannister et al. (1990).

Stewart, A. (1994) 'The Grief of the Abused Male', paper presented at the Helping the Bereaved Male conference, London, Ontario, Canada, May.

Thomas, M. and Pierson, J. (1995) *A Dictionary of Social Work*, London: Collins.

Thompson, N. (1991) *Crisis Intervention Revisited*, Birmingham: Pepar.

Thompson, N. (1992) *Child Abuse: The Existential Dimension*, Norwich: University of East Anglia Social Work Monographs.

Thompson, N. (1995) 'The Ontology of Disaster', *Death Studies*, 19 (5), pp. 501–10.

Walter, T. (1993) 'Modern Death: Taboo or not Taboo?', in Dickenson and Johnson (1993).

Worden, J. W. (1991) *Grief Counselling and Grief Therapy*, 2nd edn, London: Routledge.

10 The psychological effects of trauma on children

Jeanie McIntee and Ian Crompton

Normal child development

Trauma is an inevitable experience throughout our lives but there are many things that may determine how well or how ill we survive it. For children, the cost of survival may be very high indeed. They may have to distort their developing self so severely that they are unable to gain maturity and make a successful transition to adulthood. Often the result of their trauma is never properly detected by those who care for them (Terr, 1990). This chapter will outline what happens to a traumatized child and how it is that the trauma 'doesn't show' very easily.

A child is not born with a ready-developed sense of self. This has to be acquired through experience. Just as cognitive and physical development is required before a child can move from gross jerky motor movements to finely tuned and skilled ones, so there is the necessity for cognitive structures to develop in order for the child to acquire a sense of self, to build expectations of the world, and to form patterns of action and interaction that rely on establishing a memory system. The building blocks for this sense of self and mental development, including memory, are the interactions a developing infant has with him- or herself and other objects in the environment, especially transitional objects (Winnicott, 1960) and significant human and animal objects. A child learns about turn-taking, the basis for interaction with others, through peek-a-boo games. A small child uses mirrors to learn about self but also to learn how to distinguish between self and other. This is achieved adequately between 10 and 24 months of age if development is not interfered with, prevented or skewed.

In the early developmental stages, an infant's experience is stochastic – that is, disjointed, like the frames of an old movie. Infants have to learn to build patterns and sometimes even the illusion of continuity that is necessary for their sense of well-being. Until they do this, they inhabit a world of part objects, dissociated islands of experience and extremes of emotion: things are either wonderful or terrible (Kohut, 1984; Stern, 1985, 1990; Winnicott, 1960). A great deal of development of memory and other mental processes is required to integrate the extremes of good and bad and establish gradations of perception and experience, especially in one person and especially in the self. Object Relations theorists describe how, in the early stages of development, an infant is only able to hold one extreme at once, and during the stage of attempted integration will use 'projection' (projecting feelings and attributes out onto others) and 'introjection' (bringing feelings and attributes into the self) repeatedly in attempts to accommodate an integrated mixture of both into the self. It is like the development of any skill – learning to drive, for example. At first one can only cope with one thing at a time – the clutch, the accelerator, the steering – since integrating and coordinating them takes time. Even with the steering, one either goes too far to the right or too far to the left; achieving the integration and control to move smoothly throughout the range of steering possibilities, while managing to stay mainly in the middle of the range, takes development (McIntee, 1992).

Psychological research now demonstrates that a baby is learning about some aspects of its environment even before birth, but following the birth there is a much greater opportunity for the child to utilize an increased range of experiences in its development. Stern (1985) has shown that even very new infants are beginning to make distinctions and build up a world-view that moves from gross to finer distinctions and patterns. The developing child is beginning to differentiate between self and other from around 10 months of age, but the self does not become consolidated until around 2 years of age (Mahler et al., 1975). Complete establishment of self and independent functioning may be a lifelong task, and for many it may never be accomplished.

Adolescence is a period in which the early development of self is revisited and reworked at a very fundamental level in preparation for separate living. There is a return to a dichotomous (all-or-nothing) world-view that is similar to that held in infancy. Things are perceived as extreme: pop bands may be seen as the best one week and the worst soon afterwards. There is a reworking towards integration, usually after separation as an individual at some greater level has already been achieved.

Traumatic effects

McIntee's trauma model (McIntee, 1992), schematized in Figure 10.1, is set in the context of trauma being an inevitable part of human experience, beginning with the natural trauma of birth. It is also assumed that the possibility of unwanted trauma may even occur in the pre-birth period.

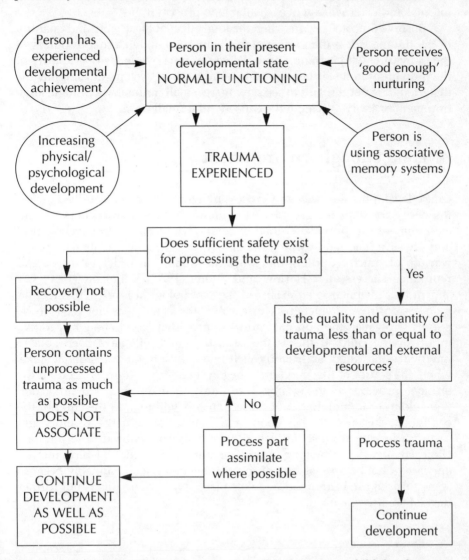

Figure 10.1   McIntee's model of trauma and its impact on child development

This model is also based on a developmental perspective that assumes that 'narcissistic injuries' (Kohut, 1984) – what we may think of as disappointments and let-downs (normal trauma) – are a necessary part of the separation process and are in fact one of the mechanisms by which individuation is achieved. McIntee (1992) describes successful accommodation of the effects of, and recovery from, trauma as the outcome of a ratio between the quality and quantity of trauma and the sum total of internal and external resources available to process it.

A positive outcome occurs when the total effect of the quality and quantity of the trauma is less than or equal to the internal and external resources of the individual who is traumatized. Where trauma overloads the capacity of the individual in his or her environmental support system, development is distorted. It is not difficult to see how many small traumata or a single large trauma may easily outweigh the capacity of a small child.

A 'good enough' environment

Child development is seen as a process by which the child intuitively takes the necessary steps for growth, if the immediately nurturing persons and environment can provide a 'good-enough' (Winnicott, 1960) psychological and physical holding. Research has shown that primate infants require the warmth of touch, cuddling and physical holding in order to thrive and reproduce successfully (Harlow and Suomi, 1970). Winnicott (1960) has shown that a similar need exists on the psychological level. While a child requires positive interaction with a carer, the carer does not have to be perfect. However, they do need to have provided 'good enough' positive input for the child. If this is the case, the child will have been able to internalize the 'good' sufficiently well to advance to the transitional stage, where the source of the 'good' may be psychologically transferred from the original provider onto an object (dummy, blanket) or onto an action (behavioural routine). Either of these transfers will remind the child of the continued existence of the 'good' and help to sustain the comfort and security derived from it, until it can be fully internalized. The authors' clinical experience of treating trauma victims suggests that the birth mother appears to hold a special significance in this holding, presumably because some form of pre-birth bonding takes place, even where this is not further developed after the birth.

Psychological holding

'Psychological holding' means providing a psychological space or relationship for the developing child. Good psychological holding should be a safe space and relationship in which the child can find nurturing and can grow. Poor psychological holding will still provide a space or relationship but instead of it being safe, it may have many inconstancies and dangers. Instead of it meeting the needs of the child, it may serve the interests of the adult.

Ideally the 'holding' should be adequately supporting but not confining. It should be like psychological scaffolding – removed unobtrusively only when it is no longer required due to the developmental achievements of the child having made it redundant. Underprotecting – taking the scaffolding away too soon – will cause the child to be low in confidence and self-achievement. Such a child will develop a false and extreme pseudo-independence or an anxiously insecure overdependence on the carer or, as an adult, on partners. When the scaffolding is held in place too long, it becomes confining, causing the child to feel suffocated and squashed. This impedes psychological development and individuation.

Adolescent separation

Pubertal development sees a reworking of the adolescent's earlier individuation with greater depth and achievement, the aim being a balanced, stable sense of self that is essential to permit intimacy and fully independent functioning suitable for rearing the next generation. Distortions at the pubertal and emerging parental stage of life will result in patterns of dysfunction that may be unrecognized by the self. Where they are recognized, they may result in under- or overcorrection. This is one of the vehicles by which dysfunction is transmitted to the next generation. An example of this is found with Annie who had suffered very badly at the hands of her physically abusive father. She recognized the problem, was determined not to repeat that pattern and very carefully chose her partner to be devoid of any of the same tendencies. The problem was that she overcorrected in her choice of partner and, although things were fine until the children came along, she then found he was leaving all of the boundary-setting to her. The failure of this to become a shared responsibility caused an imbalance in their relationship, similar to that which had existed with her parents, but with the male dominance being substituted by female dominance. The result was that Annie felt overloaded with disciplining the children and she became more and more stressed. Upon reaching the extent of her capacity to cope, she became violent towards her children in an escalating manner. Annie became very distressed because she began to realize that, in avoiding the choice of an abusing husband, she had inadvertently performed the abusive role herself, having failed to resolve the abuse dynamic.

Memory

The developmental model of memory that underpins McIntee's theory of trauma (see Figure 10.1) is associative. This means that the human brain will store experiences in some form, build them up into patterns of repeatedly similar experiences and adapt behaviourally according to these predictable patterns. For example, if you become accustomed to regular meal times, your body becomes hungry according to the pattern you have learned. Patterns have to be developed and refined through repeated experiences, where parameters and common denominators are worked out. For example, if you have been driving the same car for ten years and you change to a new one, you will quickly recognize the common items: steering wheel, accelerator, clutch, brake, gear lever. Things may differ by a small amount or by a large amount – for example, a steering wheel-based gear lever versus a floor-based lever, or manual transmission versus automatic. Knowledge of these items relies on their shape, size, colour, function and position in space in relation to each other: for example, how often do you drive a left-hand-drive car instead of a right-hand-drive – or vice versa – and go to reach for the controls in the wrong place, thus demonstrating your learned patterns of behaviour that have become automatic?

Mental map of the world

Psychological research suggests that experiential patterns are reflected by the development of internal mental constructs, an internal map or mirror to the world. An example of this would be the way a small child will build up a pattern in their brain that translates into 'biscuits are kept in the blue tin'. These internal constructs reflect the external object relationships (for example, mummy has dark hair and wears glasses) and are mediated through the subjective lens of experience of the particular infant: for example, the picture one child may draw of 'mummy' may be quite different from that drawn by another child when drawing the same person. Obviously some of the difference is accounted for by differences in the respective infants' ability to draw, but much more is likely to be a reflection of the subjective perspective of the child. Similarly, different witnesses of a road traffic accident would give differing accounts.

McIntee's model assumes that cognitive development will be needed to permit a gradual formation of these internal object relations from the gross to the refined and that two-way interactive distortions may occur. The child may bring their own experiential perspective to bear, causing distortion, or distortion could be brought about by external means. An example of a subjective distortion is the way in which children misuse language in their efforts to communicate. A friend's little girl, whilst in a cafe, said to her mother: 'I can't eat any more, I'm fed up.' It took a little while for her mother to realize she meant that she was 'full up'. An example of distortion created from outside is a client in his mid-twenties who, when first seen, had no ability to detect or label some of his bodily sensations and most of his emotions. He did not know when he was hungry or tired, and he did not know what it was like to experience happiness or sadness. He had apparently tuned out these sensations at a very early age to avoid pain. It is not uncommon to hear a child say 'I'm hungry' and to hear an adult reply 'No you're not, don't be silly!'

We are often unaware of how our perceptions and learning of patterns have occurred, and sometimes these are very difficult to change. All those who have had difficulty with changing eating or smoking patterns will understand this very well. Patterns are built up according to the subjective experience of the child within their home context. There is an interesting story about the idiosyncrasy of family patterns that became loyally repeated and became automatic, even when the need for this had ceased to exist.

A man asked his wife why she always cut the end piece off the roast joint and threw it in the bin before serving dinner. She replied that she did not know but her mother had always done it that way. The husband went to his mother-in-law and asked her why this practice was adopted and she gave him the same reply: 'Because my mother did it that way.' He then went to the grandmother and discovered that she did it because her oven overheated on one side and always burnt the joint on one side, and so the end piece on that side had to be discarded. The next two generations were loyally repeating patterns adopted without question or rationale.

Trauma and the physical and psychological processes

Trauma causes higher animals, including human beings, to produce a fight or flight response to moderate threat (see Figure 10.2). This response includes adrenalin flooding the body in order to increase the blood supply

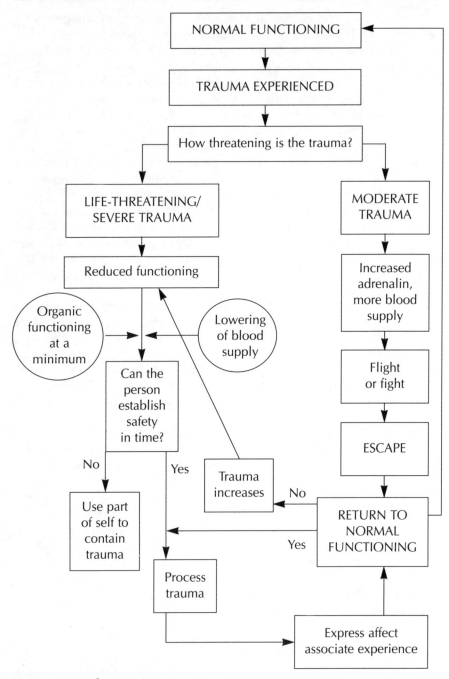

Figure 10.2   The trauma process

and enhance physical performance. Where the threat is even greater, this response reaches overload and a shutting down or freezing response is produced instead. This includes a decrease in the blood supply and an almost total reduction in organic functioning. This prevents memory and other cognitive processing from operating. It is hypothesized that the neocortex functioning is reduced to a minimum and the organism relies on more primitive, instinctive responses that are located deeper in the brain. The hypothalamus – situated at the base of the brain – is a very complex structure, responsible for the control of the autonomic nervous system, reflex integration and organization of behaviour related to survival (Carlson, 1994).

McIntee (1992) proposes that a reduction of functioning and the existence of a 'red alert', survival mode of functioning means that events are not being fully experienced and processed by the brain. The brain normally requires 20 per cent of the heart's blood supply so that, under these 'frozen' conditions, with blood supply on minimal functioning, processing cannot be performed until the danger is past and the psychophysiological conditions have returned to a more normal state.

Recovery will automatically begin once safety is re-established and the psychophysiological homeostasis has been achieved. Recovery is seen as requiring assimilation and accommodation of the events, the expression of the associated affect (emotion) and the reworking of damaged cognitive and behavioural development that may have suffered regression.

Recovery can only take place if the 'red alert' situation can be changed to one of relaxing safety, and then only if the combination of internal and environmental resources is sufficient to deal with the quality and quantity of trauma that has been experienced. If the person undergoing trauma does not possess sufficient such resources, processing will be partial or minimal.

It is proposed that loss of memory, of any degree, of traumatic events may occur for a number of reasons:

1 Processing may have been only partial and chunks of experience may not have been 'experienced' by the brain's integration-processing mechanisms. This may account for recovered memories or experiences being manifested years later in therapy or elsewhere as 'happening right now'.
2 The emotion caused by the processing may be intolerable. Denial processes, such as disbelief, may be invoked to assist with accommodation or to delay further processing. Repeated cognitive reworking and minimizing may also help in accommodating events. Recovery of these events has for the person concerned the quality of 'having always known about it but having failed to realize its significance'.

3   Processing may have occurred but in an incomplete way so that, when the emotional experience is too damaging, a repression mechanism is invoked to create either a partial or substantial amnesiac effect. Repression may overlap with the partial processing described in (1) above. It is as yet unclear if these are separate psychological mechanisms.

Dysfunctional families

An abusing family eclipses the development of the child's body or mind by requiring the child to serve the needs of the adult. This results in a loss of the appropriate boundaries, where the child's body or mind becomes used by someone else in the service of that person's own needs. This can range in severity from a parent or carer who, when a child says 'I'm hungry' or 'I hurt', denies the validity of their sensory processes, through to severe emotional, physical and sexual abuse. The loss of appropriate boundaries prevents the development of individuality and maintains the child in a somewhat undefined state, always close to 'red alert' in order to adapt to external demands.

Where the usual separation process or split into 'self and other' (usually achieved within the first two years of life) has been prevented, it may occur internally instead. This results in the most severe form of Dissociative Disorder, Dissociative Identity Disorder (DID) (formerly known as Multiple Personality Disorder). Clinical experiences of clients with Dissociative Identity Disorder show internal self structures that contain self and other development but seem to lack that individuation in the clients' external relationships. An abused child may develop a self part to whom the abuse has happened and who is experienced as 'not me'. This is either to create distance from the associated affect or because there has been a failure to process this and integrate the experience into the 'true' self. Winnicott (1960) suggests that this gives rise to manifestations of 'false self'. At the same time, there is often found to be a lack of self/other differentiation externally. Such clients are often unable to tell whether anger or other emotions are their own or belonging to someone else. In relationships they lose all sense of themselves and are subsumed by the other person, experiencing abject loss of self and existence if the relationship is not present. In cases of DID, such splits or self parts often seek expression and may take on identities and needs, therefore competing for control of the body and mind. The extent of their development appears to relate to how much they have been developed and reinforced through use. For example, if a child is repeatedly raped and has developed strong dissociation for the part of the child's self that experiences the rape, yet that part is required repeatedly to cope with these incidents, the part is likely to become experienced as a personality entity in its own right. Because of the dissociation, however, this part is unable to integrate into any more developed personality structures without therapeutic succession.

Clinical experience and self-report from DID clients (McIntee, 1994) suggest that the separating on the inside is accompanied by the building of internal object relations to reflect the external people/objects and their abusive and conflictual behaviours. The internal objects or 'parts of the self' behave conflictually towards each other. This process prevents associative and integrative functioning developing. These isolated internal objects or self parts remain isolated from each other, and their behaviour and world-view become idiosyncratic and extreme. The possibility of developing a shared reality is low and, in some cases, non-existent. The Structured Clinical Interview for DSM-IV Dissociative Disorders (Steinberg, 1994a) assesses five main aspects of experience resulting from the use of dissociation as a survival response to trauma:

1 **Amnesia** A specific and significant block of time that has passed but that cannot be accounted for by memory.
2 **Depersonalization** Detachment from one's self, for example a sense of looking at one's self as if one is an outsider.
3 **Derealization** A feeling that one's surroundings are strange or unreal. Often involves previously familiar people.
4 **Identity Confusion** Subjective feelings of uncertainty, puzzlement or conflict about one's identity.
5 **Identity Alteration** Objective behaviour indicating the assumption of different identities or ego states, much more distinct than different roles.

For discussion of the subjective experience of this see McIntee (1994).

Attempts to solve internal conflicts may occur externally via repeated, compulsive behaviours or internally by way of arguing voices or acts of self-harm. Research suggests (Kluft, 1985; Ross, 1989) that abuse would need to be early and repeated for this to occur to such an extent. McIntee defines abuse as the withholding of care, belittling and the existence of inappropriate boundaries, emotional, physical or sexual. Severe abuse can create an apparent lack of differentiation between people, places and time to the extent that past, present and future become completely malleable. This may lead to the initiation of self-abuse on the victim's part in order to give an impression of control and time process. However, this attempt at control is dysfunctional and so it fails to break the abusive cycle; instead, it merely perpetuates it, providing temporary rather than permanent relief.

The most difficult phase in the abuse cycle (see Figure 10.3) is not the abuse itself but the anticipation of it. The stress caused by not knowing what

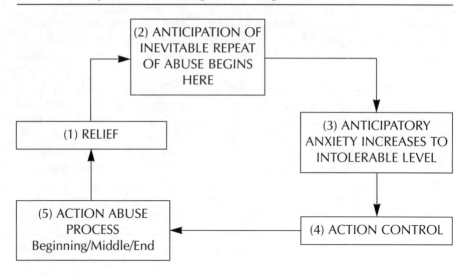

Figure 10.3   The self-abuse cycle

is going to happen, by whom, and when, provides a human being with an intolerable level and build-up of anticipatory anxiety (3). An ordinary example is the anxiety after a first date, waiting to see if a call will follow. A job interview or application may have the same effect. Often people go into 'premature closure', convincing themselves of the worst in order to avoid the need to tolerate the uncertainty, and waiting for what they feel will be a disappointing or intolerable outcome (2). For an abuse victim, it gives a sense of control to behave proactively within the abuse cycle (4). A child may deliberately 'provoke' his or her carer to the point of physical abuse since, once the abuse process has begun, the child knows he or she is nearer to the point in time at which the abuse will end. By acting in this way, the child forces the abuse cycle forward from the 'worst place' (5), which is the abuse itself, to the 'best place' (1), where the 'best place' immediately follows the abuse process. This point is so called because it marks the stage in the abuse cycle for the child which is furthest from the next incidence of abuse.

Therapeutic intervention

It is difficult for an integrated person to imagine what it is like to be non-integrated or to have Dissociative Identity Disorder. An excerpt from a client's diary may assist, and more extensive discussion of these phenomena can be found in the audiotape *People Kept Below* (McIntee, 1994):

14.09   I went shopping today and was shocked to see in the mirror a woman, obviously mature. I couldn't believe it was me. I felt really weird. Who is this mature woman?

20.09   I have just found Serenity.
          She is so beautiful.
          She can get us all together, if only we would give her a chance.
          It is her love that has kept us alive.
          She is the one I saw in the mirror in the shop.
          Serenity is chairman of the board.
          I think, constantly, she is there behind the scenes while the others are behaving and reacting.
          I fear they will try to keep her out.

Another person with Dissociative Identity Disorder, now well on her way in her recovery process, wrote the following poem as part of her therapeutic creative writing. She is describing her selves, and speaking to all of those with whom she had contact: parents, foster carers, social workers and so on. Unfortunately, because she was also abused many times after being 'taken into care', there is a double significance for her:

A PLEA FROM THE CHILDREN WITHIN

We tell you no stories, we tell you no lies, we tell you only what we see through our eyes or hear through our ears.
We are the innocent children you sent away. You are the grown-ups who chose not to listen.
We were not born with knowledge or thoughts we brought to you. We knew nothing of men's or women's private parts, of the nasty things they do.
We told you only what we had seen or been taught. We were not born so distressed or distraught with our lives in a mess.
We are human beings just like you with true feelings and thoughts. We are after all small versions of you who needed to be cared for and protected from all the evil people who did us so much wrong, not turned away or ignored just because we were small.
We are the children who never grew up because we were left with so much pain, fear and sorrow. You were the grown-ups who left us holding all the guilt and shame because you turned us away and did not listen when we came to you, leaving us believing we were all to blame.
You are the grown-ups who were supposed to be our guardians of love, care and protection instead of turning us away, calling us liars and story tellers with huge imaginations.
We are the children who ended up feeling crazy or insane, keeping

secrets because we dared not tell you as you chose not to listen when we tried so hard to tell you about our journeys through hell, causing us to become so split up and divided inside, it's a miracle we ever survived.

Because severe Dissociation has resulted from very early and severe trauma, it has interfered with, and distorted, the normal psychological developmental process. Therefore, therapy for Dissociative Identity Disorder needs to be psychodynamic in its basis but eclectic in the management of thoughts, feelings and behaviours that are dysfunctional. It should also be in the interests of maximizing integrative development. The client with DID has so much development to achieve and so much traumatic material to process that a very comprehensive package of therapy is essential. Although there are differing opinions about how long therapy will take and whether integration of subjectively separate self-parts is the desired goal, the International Society for the Study of Dissociation (1994) suggest that therapy will typically be in the region of five to ten years. Our clinical experience concurs with this view and suggests that therapy can be very demanding of both client and therapist.

There are many general principles of therapy generated by this theoretical model. The task is so comprehensive that it draws on many other theories and established techniques, bringing them together in a paradigm that informs the therapy for Dissociation, and which allows for the existence of prodigious individual differences. The less experienced and confident psychotherapist finds it hard to accommodate this level of complexity and seeks to simplify the task by concentrating on generalities that inform practice and create the illusion of security and recipes for intervention. This is profoundly limiting for the therapist, and especially for the client, who will still not experience unrestricted growth even though their therapist recognizes and knows 'what to do' with DID.

Successful work with Dissociation requires a highly skilled psychotherapist with the confidence to know that he or she does not need to know everything and that the 'doing' belongs with the client and not the psychotherapist, even when the client is suffering from such a profoundly disabling and developmentally delayed condition. Like all nurturing, it is the quality and capacity of the psychological holding of the client and the tolerance of uncertainty that permits growth in both the client and the psychotherapist. This also means that sufficiently nurturing holding is required for the psychotherapists themselves. It is necessary for every psychotherapist treating Dissociative Identity Disorder to have a supervisor with extensive experience in this clinical field. The severity of the trauma and the complexity of the therapeutic task mean that the transference and counter-transference have a quality that is often too extreme for the therapist to hold alone without distortions affecting their capacity as a therapist. It is of great benefit to have not only an experienced supervisor but also the guidance of a supervisor who does not have direct contact with the client. As expert help is not yet very widely available in the UK, this may mean resorting to the use of supervision by telephone if no source of expertise is locally available. A good theoretical framework does help client, psychotherapist and supervisor hold on to such complex and sometimes bizarre information as is generated in Dissociation cases, and to provide guidelines as to the course of therapy and its pitfalls. That a professional can develop the awareness to identify Dissociation is in itself a great help to the client and permits the professional to assist the client in locating a suitable therapist. A common mistake, once one's awareness is raised, is to experience a very strong need to rescue, or make up for, the client's past professional or service losses. This may result in beginning therapy by default, with no certainty of continuance or competence, and may do more harm than good.

For the potential therapist, new to this clinical field, there is a great advantage in demonstrating to the client that no matter how urgent or terrible the content of the client's distress, it can be held and tolerated whilst appropriate boundaries and other therapeutic considerations, like supervision, are secured.

References and recommended reading

Please note that, until recently, the best texts on Dissociation were aimed at its most extreme form, Dissociative Identity Disorder (previously called Multiple Personality Disorder) and it should be understood that Dissociation is a continuum of severity with DID at the most severe end. Therefore, many of the titles listed below may appear to be peripheral but they still contain the best information on the identification of, and therapy for, Dissociation.

Braun, B. (1986) *The Treatment of Multiple Personality Disorder*, Washington DC: American Psychiatric Press.
Carlson, N. R. (1994) *The Physiology of Behavior*, 5th edn, Massachusetts: Allyn and Bacon.
Cohen, L. M., Berzoff, J. N. and Elin, M. R. (eds) (1995) *Dissociative Identity Disorder*, London: Jason Aronson.
Harlow, H. F. and Suomi, S. J. (1970) 'Nature of Love – Simplified', *American Psychologist*, 25 (2), pp. 161–8.
Herman, J. (1992) *Trauma and Recovery*, New York: Basic Books.
International Society for the Study of Dissociation (1994) *Guidelines For Treating Dissociative Disorder (Multiple Personality Disorder) In Adults*, Skokie, ILL: ISSD.
Kluft, R. (1985) *Childhood Antecedents of Multiple Personality*, Washington DC: American Psychiatric Press.

Kluft, R. (1993) *Clinical Perspectives on MPD*, Washington DC: American Psychiatric Press.

Kohut, H. (1984) *How Does Analysis Cure?*, Chicago: University of Chicago Press.

Mahler, M. S., Pine, F. and Bergman, A. (1975) *The Psychological Birth of the Human Infant: Symbiosis and Individuation*, London: Hutchinson.

McIntee, J. (1992) *Trauma: The Psychological Process*, Chester: Chester Therapy Centre.

McIntee, J. (1994) *People Kept Below*, audiotape, Clare Hunt, 20th Century Vixen, discussion by people with Dissociative Identity Disorder in the UK.

Putnam, F. (1989) *Diagnosis and Treatment of Multiple Personality Disorder*, New York: Guilford Press.

Ross, C. (1989) *Multiple Personality Disorder: Diagnosis, Clinical Features and Treatment*, New York: Wiley.

Ross, C. (1994) *The Osiris Complex: Case Studies in Multiple Personality Disorder*, Toronto: Toronto Press.

Rowan, J. (1990) *Subpersonalities: The People Inside Us*, London: Routledge.

Steinberg, M. (1994a) *Structured Clinical Interview for DSM-IV Dissociative Disorders (SCID-D), Revised*, Washington DC: American Psychiatric Press.

Steinberg, M. (1994b) *Interviewer's Guide to the Structured Clinical Interview for DSM-IV Dissociative Disorders (SCID-D), Revised*, Washington DC: American Psychiatric Press.

Stern, D. N. (1985) *The Interpersonal World of the Infant: A View from Psychoanalysis and Developmental Psychology*, New York: Basic Books.

Stern, D. N. (1990) *Diary of a Baby*, London: Harper Collins.

Terr, L. (1990) *Too Scared to Cry: How Trauma Affects Children . . . And Ultimately Us All*, New York: Basic Books.

Van der Kolk, B. (1987) *Psychological Trauma*, Washington DC: American Psychiatric Press.

Van der Kolk, B., McFarlane, A. C. and Weisaeth, L. (eds) (1996) *Traumatic Stress*, New York: Guilford Press.

Winnicott, D. (1960) 'Ego Distortion in Terms of True and False Self', in Winnicott, D. (ed.) (1960).

Winnicott, D. (ed.) (1960) *The Maturational Process and the Facilitative Environment*, London: Hogarth Press and the Institute of Psychoanalysis.

Winnicott, D. (1971) *Playing and Reality*, Harmondsworth: Penguin.

Zulueta, F. de (1993) *The Traumatic Roots of Destructiveness: From Pain to Violence*, London: Whurr.

11 Listening to children: Appreciating the abused child's reality

Madge Bray and Richard Pugh

How ignominious to be a child. To be so small that you can be picked up. To be moved about at the whim of others. To be fed or not to be fed. To be cleaned or left dirty. Made happy or left to cry. It is surely so ultimate an indignity that it is not surprising that some of us never really recover from it.

Felice Leonardo Buscaglia

Introduction

Buscaglia's words alert us to the powerlessness of childhood, to the total dependency of infancy and to the effects which may persist into adulthood. To begin to work effectively with abused children we must hear the child's voice and listen to it. We have to begin to appreciate how the world looks from a child's perspective. If we fail to take this step into the world of children, then we do violence to their experience by superimposing our own meanings and intentions without any consideration of their understandings of what has happened, or is happening, to them. That child protection is a contentious field is without doubt but, in all of the debates and arguments, we should be careful to hear what children themselves have to tell us. Otherwise, the consequence, as Boyle has noted, is that amidst 'the clamour of professionals crossing swords, it is hardly surprising that the voice and the experience of the abused child is the most silenced voice of all' (1991, p. xi). This chapter therefore considers some of the barriers to effective communication. Its core theme is that, without an appreciation of the reality of the children with whom we work, we will adopt approaches and procedures which will be insensitive, ineffective and even counter-productive. In short, we will fail children.

143

Being prepared

Preparing oneself to work with abused children is not an easy task. There is no easily learned process for the task is never completed – it requires a continual willingness to be open to change and to appreciate the reality of another person's experience. It must be recognized that this type of work cannot be sustained successfully without organizational commitment and support. The emotionally charged content of child protection and therapy goes to the very heart of the worker's sense of self. Without adequate support and opportunity for reflection it can prove overwhelming. Nevertheless, we can identify some of the significant issues and indicate their likely consequences.

Barriers to communication

We focus here upon some of the most common barriers to communication with children who have been abused. Probably the biggest barrier arises from the reluctance of adults to acknowledge the relative powerlessness of children. In daily life children cannot fail to be aware of this imbalance but, because of their particular experiences, abused children may be extremely sensitive to this. They may have learned to watch adults very carefully indeed for the slightest signs of disapproval, aggression or threat. In its most extreme form this can be seen in the ultra-quiet and conformist behaviour described as 'frozen watchfulness'. In contrast, the insecurity of other children may lead them to adopt behaviour which tests the adults' reactions. Thus a child who has been sexually abused by several adults may greet a new person by overtly sexualized behaviour, such as tongue kissing, and sexual rubbing of themselves or the adult. In doing so, they may be repeating previously learned patterns of behaviour which they believe are either normal or necessary in such situations, or alternatively, are checking out the adult as a potential threat. Such behaviours are often misinterpreted by workers. In our experience they are as much about the exploration of power, and attempts to make sense of the child's inner confusion, as they are about sexuality.

While workers can never entirely abolish the power difference between themselves and their clients, they can minimize it to some degree (Pugh, 1996) and, most importantly, can communicate to the child their willingness to proceed on the child's terms. Workers should be sensitive to:

- how they physically position themselves in relation to children;
- their language and the words they use;
- their tone of voice;

- their appearance;
- their gender;
- how they introduce and present themselves.

It is crucial to allow children the space and the time to develop conversations as they wish. This, of course, is where the use of toys and other forms of play create opportunities for workers to be with children and engage with them in relatively non-threatening ways. This is not play therapy as such, but is better described as play-related communication (Wilson et al., 1992).

Avoiding direct questions and intrusive eye contact, together with responses which echo the child's statements, usually help children to feel more at ease and less threatened. When the primary aim is communication it is important to understand that, when such communication begins, it is a process rather than an event. When approached with sensitivity and care it can represent the first part of a therapeutic process which begins with an opening out and sharing – a willingness on the part of the child to contact distressing and confusing experiences within themselves and share them with the listener. This process, encompassing the sharing of painful material, is often a necessary first step towards subsequent protection of the child. It can represent a first stage too, towards helping the child to enter into a therapeutic relationship with the listener, where that is appropriate, or with some other person who can go on to help the child make sense of these experiences. The primary aim of therapy may be described as one where: 'The emphasis is thus on enabling the individual to move from a sense of being at the mercy of hidden feelings to gaining some mastery [*sic*] over them' (Wilson et al., 1992, p. 2).

Although the promise of therapeutic help for such children may not fall within the scope of the adult listener – who may, for example, have a limited investigative role – it is nevertheless vital to acknowledge that such processes may already have begun. It is therefore crucial to ensure that roles are clear and that further opportunities are afforded for the child to continue the process within safe boundaries.

Our capacity to hear what children are saying, especially for inexperienced workers, can be limited by our sense of revulsion and distaste at the things we encounter when children reveal their abuse to us. The ubiquity of abuse as well as its nature are shocking to all of us who were fortunate to have had safe childhoods. Such events may fundamentally challenge our perceptions of society and parenting, particularly when we realize that the abusers rarely conform to the stereotype of the stranger with monstrous appetites, but are the apparently ordinary mothers and fathers who might pass by unnoticed and unremarked in any street or supermarket. Furthermore, we need to recognize that, while many children who have been involved in exploitative sexual experiences are aware of some sexual taboos and consequently may be unhappy about what has happened to them, they are often confused about sexual behaviour and the context in which it has occurred.

So, while the horrors of their abuse remain overarching and oppressive in the experiences of some children, for others it is confused by the fact that it may have taken place within a relationship which also contained some emotional comfort and warmth. The experience of abuse, for this latter group, confined as they are by their own limited experience of the world, may be that it is relatively 'normal'. After all, their parents/carers are the only ones most of them have ever had, and whatever else happens, they represent 'normality' and home. Consequently, abused children may develop confused and ambivalent feelings about their own sexuality and its implications for other people. In some instances, adult carers may find that gentle boundary-setting linked to sex education is the most effective response, whereas, in others, where children perceive themselves and their bodies as dirty or worthless, there may be a more fundamental task of re-establishing some basis for the child to begin to value him- or herself. Whatever the most appropriate response, in all cases the crucial first step is to seek to establish communication with the child on his or her terms, not ours. If not, a child's perception that he or she is somehow responsible for what has happened, coupled with an awareness of social taboo, can – when combined with a more or less explicit injunction against disclosure from a powerful adult – create a powerful barrier to disclosure and is often a major hurdle to be overcome in therapy.

Perhaps the most pervasive barrier to communication arises from the different social realities which adults and children inhabit. The tendency to interpret the behaviour and language of other people solely in our own terms frequently obscures the meaning it has for them, or debases the messages they are conveying, as in the case of Zoe, aged 5, who spoke of her fears:

> Well, this is getting more seriouser everyday. More seriouser. You've got to help the little girl. She has the spider disease. And there are poisonous spiders in her tummy. And it's full of, full of, poisonous spiders and soon her tummy's going to burst open and the poisonous spiders will fly out everywhere and poison every human in the land. (Bray, 1991, p. 115)

It would be easy for an adult listener to ignore the child's reality or immediately attempt to construe it in adult terms – and thus shape the dialogue in these terms – by asking the child to explain what the 'spiders' were. However, by accepting the child's subjective perception of events and attempting to explore it, in this case by asking how the spiders get into the girl's tummy, the worker elicits the following response: 'They came in a hole in her mouth and in her tummy and the naughty man put them in there with the white stuff.' It later became apparent that Zoe had been sexually abused by her father, and her ideas about what had happened to her were further confused by her lack of knowledge about human reproduction. This does not mean that, in coming to our considered view of what such narratives represent, we uncritically accept them, nor should we simply assume that such stories are necessarily metaphors for sexual abuse, but simply that, when children say things like 'a worm came into my bedroom last night', or speak of 'poisonous spiders', we should not automatically deny or attempt to 'correct' their accounts. Instead we should listen carefully to what they have to say and attempt to construe what meaning it might have for them.

Sexuality and listening to the narrative

It is well recognized that attitudes to sexuality are often conflicting, sometimes ambiguous and frequently uncertain. It is unsurprising, therefore, that in our dealings with children we communicate such varied and sometimes confusing messages. There are two central issues in respect of practice with abused children. The first is to acknowledge that we need to be aware of our own personal feelings and ideas about sexuality and thus do not allow these to obstruct our work with children. Being prepared therefore involves the development of an open and pragmatic acknowledgement of sexual language, taboo and behaviour. Workers should be prepared to use whatever language children feel happiest with and should learn to recognize how difficult it may be for children to speak out about their experiences. One training exercise which one of the authors of this chapter has used is to ask workers, in pairs, to discuss a recent sexual experience. Few find it easy. How might children feel, therefore, when we ask them to recount their own experiences? How can we listen to an abused child's account, if our own discomfort and inhibitions obstruct our 'hearing'? The following extract shows just how shocking some children's experiences may be, even to experienced workers, but also demonstrates how important it is to listen openly without attempting to deny or suppress the narrative:

> 'It were them little ones that hurted, weren't it, Jess?' James ventured matter-of-factly. 'You know, the ones you cut your nails with, with the pointy ends, weren't it, Jess?' He pressed his older sister for confirmation. 'The other ones what you sew with, the big ones with the jaggy bits . . . you know . . . round the sides, well they never really cut as much, did they, Jess? Cos there was no points on the end probably,' he added wisely. Jessica sat, detached, twisting a blade of grass around her finger . . . The scene was the foster carer's garden. I was collecting information for a court report. James, aged six, was explaining . . . the relative merits of pinking shears over nail scissors as instruments of anal

penetration. It was becoming clear that the children's father had not limited himself to penile or digital penetration in his sexual assaults upon them . . . Such events, it seemed, had been a matter of routine in James' life. I struggled to regain composure. In the meantime James' mind had moved on to another subject. 'Have you seen my hamster?' (Bray, 1991, p. xvii)

The second issue central to practice with abused children is to acknowledge that such children may themselves have sexual feelings. However, recognition of this possibility is potentially fraught with danger because it can be misused by abusers themselves. Consequently, we should not allow exploitative adults to expropriate this possibility and use it to legitimize their perception of children as sexual beings for their own purposes. Nevertheless, we need to acknowledge that not only has the behaviour of some children been sexualized by their abuse by adults or other children, but also that some victims of child abuse may have learned to take pleasure from sexual activity, and/or the intimacy which may have accompanied it.

This socially premature consciousness by some children of their own sexuality is not universal amongst abused children, nor, obviously, is the experience of abuse always pleasurable for them. In fact, the damaging and harmful consequences are usually all too clear. But we have to accept the reality that not only will some children repeat and rehearse the sexually inappropriate behaviour which they have learned, but also that some are potentially capable of taking pleasure from those activities. This realization is frequently a disturbing one for carers and workers to confront, for it erodes their idealistic notions of childhood innocence. After all, the most common construction of childhood is one which perceives children's bodies, minds and emotions as immature, and thus tends to preclude the possibility of sexuality, or, alternatively, views it as evidence of some deeper disturbance (de Mause, 1991).

While the difficult questions about whether we describe such sexualized behaviour as 'dysfunctional', 'precocious' or 'premature', and about how we should understand and theorize such behaviour, are beyond the scope of this chapter – especially since it requires some knowledge of what is perceived as 'normal' (Lindblad et al., 1995) – we cannot ignore its existence. A reluctance to recognize the fact that George, a 7-year-old, gets pleasure when he 'rubs his willy like Sam done' (Bray, 1991, p. 198) and is quite prepared to act sexually with other children, leaves us badly placed to discuss and respond to the problems this may cause – complaints from other parents, exclusion from school and rejection by ill-prepared, poorly informed and overwhelmed foster carers are unfortunately all too common in such cases. Apart from the obvious risk that such behaviour may pose to other children, it remains risky for the child who exhibits it, since its continuance unchecked and unaddressed almost invariably results in social condemnation and isolation.

Preparedness therefore requires that workers develop a professional persona which is authentic – in that it is genuinely based upon their own personality and character – but one that remains unshockable and allows them to hear the child's narrative with relative equanimity. There is, however, a danger that, in developing this aspect of professional persona, workers may become desensitized to the pain that children suffer. The implications for staff care are clear: it is vital that professionals are provided with opportunities for support and reflection upon the impact of their work upon their own lives. If children perceive that workers are shocked by or displaying revulsion at what they are hearing, or suspect that there is, however unwitting, any form of negative response, including insensitivity, then it is likely that their narrative will be inhibited (Glaser and Frosh, 1988).

Of course, there may be a clear need on the part of the worker to show the child that they disapprove of the actions of the abuser(s), but workers should be wary of unwittingly displaying judgemental attitudes and of rushing to offer judgement. This may be particularly dangerous in cases where a courtroom appearance may be in prospect, and where such responses may be open to scrutiny and challenge. It may have the effect of undermining the credibility of the worker's evidence because of the apparent prejudging of the issue. In this latter respect, as with all communication with children, one should attempt to move at their pace and take one's cues from them.

Based upon her own practice, Bray presents a model of disclosure which describes a typical process through which many children pass. This is by no means an inevitable sequence, nor even a necessary one, but it is common:

> At the beginning, blocking behaviour such as foot-tapping, hysterical giggling or averted eyes – the child would keep its dilemmas very close to its chest and would resist any adult attempts to make contact . . . Gradually, then we would move on until the child began to test the ground tentatively and trust began to develop, then would come the sharing part when we began to face the problem head on and share it, and I would learn for the first time precisely what it was and gain a measure of what the impact had been upon the child's life. Soon we would experience discharge when an outpouring would occur, often in the form of a torrent of words, anger and actions which led to confrontation . . . The end of the process saw a plateau, a calm resolution, a putting down of the baggage and moving on. Time and time again, we would move backwards and forwards across this continuum as the child's own inner healing strength offered its own answers and dilemma after dilemma sought resolution. (Bray, 1991, p. 46)

The crucial point is that, while workers may have sound ideas about the likely processes of disclosure and therapy, the cues for the content invariably come from the child themself. For example, one child, Tracey, who was being shown around a police station because she was worried about the consequences of revealing what had happened to her and – as became apparent later – wanted to know what would happen to her abuser, asked to be locked in a cell alone for a few moments. The adults present were understandably somewhat surprised by this request but acceded to it: 'After a little while she banged on the door. "Let me out now." We opened the door. She stood, a tiny form in the doorway. "He can't get out," she said triumphantly' (Bray, 1991, pp. 64–5). Thus, it is only from a close hearing and sensitive understanding of children's narratives that we can guess what their confusions and problems are. The worker, therefore, is not the possessor of the answers, but is a catalyst for change. As Bray later comments in regard to successful outcomes: 'The child did all the doing – I just made a place where it could happen, and let it be' (1991, p. 47). Given that the extended extract above describes a set of processes which children commonly undergo when a constantly listening adult affords them the opportunity to share in this way, it is perhaps salutary to note how difficult it can be for this to occur within existing 'unfriendly' adult-constructed frameworks of investigation and evidence-gathering.

The contradiction between professional procedures and the child's needs

The practice guidelines provided in the *Memorandum of Good Practice* (Department of Health and Home Office, 1992) ascribe a dual role to child protection agencies in respect of children at risk, one of 'protecting their interests and dealing effectively with those who would harm them'. However, there are two questionable assumptions which underpin the guidance protocol:

- Children like James and Jess will be able to talk about their abuse, accurately, at a time that is administratively convenient, and in a form that adults can use to protect the children's interests and deal effectively with those who cause them harm.
- This process of disclosure can be successfully achieved under artificial conditions, in front of a camera, in a short period of time, lasting little over an hour, since workers who wish to continue with disclosure will need to be in a position to justify further interviews from material obtained in the first session.

It is our contention that the protocols and the formal processes of gaining evidence ignore the reality of how children actually respond to formal intervention by child protection agencies. Put simply, such procedures ignore the reality of how children think, speak and act. Furthermore, the statutory emphasis – enshrined in the Children Act 1989 – upon participation and cooperation with parents, whose interests must be seen to be afforded demonstrable consideration and respect, introduces another complicating factor to this aspect of investigation in cases where it is the parent(s) who are under suspicion. James and Jess, for example, live their lives in a distorted world. Their abusive experiences may be so much a feature of their everyday normal life that it literally may become 'unremarkable' to them. Even when such children are aware of the distortions which beset them, they may develop coping strategies which deny or downplay the significance of what has happened, or is happening, to them. They may cope psychologically with the uncertainty, or the possibility, of overwhelming distress by, for example, distancing, denial or blocking: that is, by having it 'not happen to me'. Helping children such as this to express their pain, and thus providing us with the evidence and means to protect them, is often a lengthy and immensely delicate process.

The case of Michael, a small, undernourished 3-year-old boy whose eating patterns were unusual – sometimes biting but not swallowing food, and sometimes vomiting it up again and playing with his vomit as if he were trying to examine it – shows how ham-fisted existing procedural guidelines often are. Concern about Michael arose from circumstantial evidence that he would not let anyone take him to the toilet, nor take off his clothes to allow doctors to examine him, and appeared to be frightened and wary of men. Michael's mother, Annette, had reported that her partner, Stephen, was violent towards her and intimated that he also treated Michael harshly in comparison with his own children. There had also been earlier suspicion of possible sexual abuse of Michael's sister, Kerry Ann, but no conclusive evidence. Annette, though frightened of her partner, gave her consent for Michael to be interviewed without Stephen's knowledge. A specialist child abuse consultant was called in to conduct the interview with the aim of establishing whether there had been any abuse and, if so, to gain evidence which would justify statutory intervention. During the informal interview held at the day nursery Michael attended, he quickly became absorbed in playing with a number of different toys available in the consultant's specialist toy-box. Unprompted, Michael enacted a scene of considerable domestic violence. Amongst the ordinary toys were several anatomically complete dolls of which he was initially unaware, but which became the focus of his attention when he discovered them later in the session. Again unprompted, Michael began to play with the adult male doll:

Totally involved. He pulled the penis hard and twisted, jamming the now naked doll in between the radiator and the wall. He ran forward, picked up the yellow plastic sword and thrust it deep into the man's groin. He cut and twisted and pummelled at the genital area, twisting the penis round and round with furious grunting noises. The doll fell to the ground. I knelt down beside him. Silently he paused for breath, staring at the devastated spectacle on the floor. He looked at me. Glassily. Eyes empty. Mind elsewhere . . . For some time Michael considered my face. From the frenzied odyssey a victor was emerging . . . He stood across from me, still measuring my face. He reached out towards me and, still whispering (to himself), placed a small grubby finger on my lips . . . Michael had not yet spoken a word (to me). In his world, speech was superfluous. His language was the language of play. Michael was introducing me to his explosive and precarious world . . . He pulled my arm and, male doll in hand, beckoned towards the window . . . 'You open', he said . . . 'Michael, if we open the window I shall have to hold on to you. We're too high up and I can't let you fall.' He nodded . . . I opened the window and held on to him tightly, my hands around his tiny waist . . . he raised his arms. The cloth doll balanced momentarily above his head and then fell, hurled downwards towards the ground far below. 'Man dead', he said . . . 'Man dead. Naughty man dead', he repeated. 'Michael, has the naughty man got a name?' No reply . . . I tried again. 'Michael, can you tell me, where does this man live?' Michael shook his head. I could feel him withdrawing from me. Things were becoming unsafe. We both knew it. Now he would retreat to safety within himself, and close the door. Much against my better judgement, I persisted. 'Michael, does somebody hurt the little boy?' Panic flooded his face. He stood before me, eyes moving everywhere. His hands reached automatically to cover his penis. (Bray, 1991, pp. 82–3)

As feared, after the end of this session, which was suggestive of abuse but did not in itself provide unequivocal evidence of it, Annette appeared to respond to threats from Stephen and forbade any further contact with the worker. While 'common sense' might persuade us otherwise, we must not rule out the possibility that Michael was receiving adequate care and protection in his own family – no-one working in childcare can be unaware of the dangers of jumping to unpalatable conclusions, but the critical point is that further exploration of the possibility of Michael having suffered abuse was obstructed in this case, as the local authority's judgement was that an approach to the court was unlikely to be successful. Although Michael was a very young child, he was able to give us a glimpse of his fragmented world. Given further time, trust and confidence, he may have provided information about who did what to whom within this disrupted world he inhabited. With continued access to him, the provision of such information remained a possibility, but it could not, and would not, have happened in a single hour within a video suite.

Among the views expressed in the study of the implementation of the memorandum of good practice on video interviewing of child witnesses

(Department of Health, 1994, p. 16) one respondent stated that 'There is a lot of commitment, but also a lot of anxiety about the lack of results' and concluded that 'children don't tell stories the way the Memorandum suggests. They often tell some of it before and then repeat and expand on video. However, that is not technically how it is meant to happen.' Indeed, practitioners might wonder whether, in the current climate, exploratory play sessions should even take place at all. If Michael's case were being investigated today, he might well be considered too young to represent a view via an interview conducted in accordance with the memorandum guidelines, and the case might not proceed beyond this initial decision.

Conclusion

The Bridge Consultancy's report into Gloucestershire Social Services' handling of the children cared for by Frederick and Rosemary West (who were arrested on several charges of murder) once again emphatically reminds us of the crucial importance of listening to what children are saying. It concluded that this aspect of practice was: 'probably the single most important matter in this report' (1995, p. 20). The report stated that:

> The social work staff, lawyers and police who listened to the West children, evaluated their comments and acted, should be commended for their ability to respond objectively and for their willingness to risk their professional reputations on the basis of what they were being told. It would have been so easy to do nothing rather than take the risk because the comments of the children appeared bizarre. (1995, p. 19)

While the West case is admittedly extreme, even by the horrific standards of so much 'ordinary' child abuse, it is galling to realize that even the most recent review of the research into child abuse and protection (Department of Health, 1995), with one notable exception, makes little reference to the voices of children. This exception (p. 46) acknowledges children's disappointment at the lack of effective response in some cases. It notes their sense of powerlessness, and recognizes that they often blame themselves for what has happened to their families after social services and the police became involved. But in the practical exercises suggested at the end of this review, while there is one on communicating with parents and carers, there is no mention of actually communicating with the children themselves.

Current practice, both at the personal level of practitioner preparedness and in terms of the procedural guidelines for establishing and gathering sustainable evidence, may be incompatible with the practical reality of how children actually communicate difficult information. Unless we recognize and address this disparity by better preparing novice practitioners for their work, by lobbying for more child-friendly statutes, and by developing reality-based procedures which allow the child's voice to be heard properly, we should face the uncomfortable reality and acknowledge that current practice continues to leave some children in dangerous situations without adequate protection.

We acknowledge that 'the interplay between fulfilling the requirements of a legal or a therapeutic system presents a constant dilemma for those involved in sexual abuse assessment work' (Keary and Fitzpatrick, 1994, p. 547). However, we are firmly of the view that the current guidelines are unrealistic when working with young children because, in the most fundamental manner, they fail to observe one of the most basic tenets of sound practice – which is to start from an appreciation of where the client is, that is, the client's own psychological and emotional position in relation to the experiences they have undergone. Nevertheless, our view derives more from direct case experience, and we recognize that it is not unequivocally supported by research (although there are a number of studies which point up the importance of interviewing styles: Dent and Stephenson, 1989; Jones and McQuiston, 1988; Keary and Fitzpatrick, 1994; Quinn et al., 1989). In our view, the question of the 'balance of rights' in terms of what constitutes acceptable grounds for statutory intervention remains central. Contemporary practice does not best serve children's interests since the main arena for deciding such matters – the court system in England and Wales – is premised upon an adversarial contest instead of an inquisitorial search for 'truth'. This system is often destructive of children's testimony, because it sets out, not with the primary aim of establishing the veracity of such testimony through inquiry, but with the presupposition that this can only be tested by a process of challenge.

Finally, while professional practice in cases of child abuse is most obviously conceptualized in terms of adult notions of protection, safety, respite and prevention, we should also consider the child's position and perception of events. In many interventions their position of powerlessness is continually confirmed by the processes which swamp them – their voices remain unheard. We know that some children are wary of disclosing what has happened to them for fear of the consequences for, and from, their families, and that others having disclosed abuse are sometimes unhappy about the ways in which allegations are investigated. For example, a small study of older children who had reported abuse while they were in public care, which uniquely asked them to talk about what they thought of the investigation, revealed that the children felt considerable dissatisfaction with what happened to them (NSPCC, 1996).

It is our contention that listening to children and appreciating what they are saying is not simply a matter of getting better evidence, but is a small step towards empowering relatively powerless people. Since most abuse, whether of children or adults, is readily understood in terms of the abuse of power, we should always consider this dimension in our work with children. Simply listening carefully demonstrates our appreciation of their position. Hearing their narrative in the way in which they wish to tell it signals respect. This alone can begin to help some children regain a sense of personal worth because, apart from the cathartic effects of ventilation and disclosure, they have some element of control in their interactions with us. Let us not forget that it is we adults who, by dint of our age and understanding, mandate politicians and public servants to establish the statutes, structures and processes which purport to respond effectively to the pain of some of our most vulnerable children.

Footnote

While reference to anatomically complete dolls is made in the description of the case of Michael, we acknowledge that, since that time, there have been considerable misgivings and a vigorous debate about whether, or when, such dolls should be used. Nevertheless, it is our view that they remain a valuable aid to communication in some circumstances, but that workers should not use them as if they were a diagnostic test of abuse, especially because of the dangers of adult imposition of meaning which might be mistaken and unjustified. For a fuller account of the issues we recommend Everson and Boat (1994). None the less, it is worth noting what a curious and fascinating phenomenon it is, that 'ordinary' dolls routinely do not represent the reality of the human body. This 'bowdlerization' of the human form for the most part passes unremarked. What does the desexualization of the doll signify – an adult perception of idealized childhood, or a manifestation of adult fears and sexual taboo?

References

Boyle, S. (1991) 'Introduction' to Bray (1991).

Bray, M. (1991) *Poppies on the Rubbish Heap: Sexual Abuse – The Child's Voice*, Edinburgh: Canongate Press.

The Bridge Consultancy (1995) *Part 8 Case Review – Overview Report in Respect of Charmaine and Heather West*, Gloucester: Gloucestershire Social Services Department.

Dent, H. R. and Stephenson, G. M. (1989) 'An Experimental Study of the Effectiveness of Differing Techniques of Questioning Child Witnesses', *British Journal of Social and Clinical Psychology*, 18, pp. 41–51.

Department of Health and Home Office (1992) *Memorandum of Good Practice on Video*

Recorded Interviews with Child Witnesses for Criminal Proceedings, London: HMSO.

Department of Health (1994) *The Child, the Court and the Video: A Study of the Implementation of the Memorandum of Good Practice on Video Interviewing of Child Witnesses*, London: HMSO.

Department of Health (1995) *Child Protection: Messages from Research*, London: HMSO.

Everson, M. D. and Boat, B. W. (1994) 'Putting the Anatomical Doll Controversy in Perspective: An Examination of the Major Uses and Criticisms of the Dolls in Child Sexual Abuse Evaluations', *Child Abuse and Neglect*, 18 (2), pp.113–29.

Glaser, D. and Frosh, S. (1988) *Child Sexual Abuse*, London: Macmillan.

Jones, D. and McQuiston, M. (1988) *Interviewing the Sexually Abused Child*, London: Gaskell Psychiatry Series.

Keary, K. and Fitzpatrick, C. (1994) 'Children's Disclosure of Sexual Abuse During Formal Investigation', *Child Abuse and Neglect*, 18 (7), pp. 543–8.

Lindblad, F., Gustaffson, P. A., Larsson, I. and Lundin, B. (1995) 'Preschoolers' Sexual Behaviour at Day-care Centers: An Epidemiological Study', *Child Abuse and Neglect*, 19 (5), pp. 569–77.

Mause, L. de (ed.) (1991) *The History of Childhood*, London: Bellew.

NSPCC (1996) *Safe and Sound*, London: National Society for the Prevention of Cruelty to Children.

Pugh, R. G. (1996) *Effective Language in Health and Social Work*, London: Chapman and Hall.

Quinn, K. M., White, S. and Santilli, G. (1989) 'Influences of an Interviewer's Behaviors in Child and Sexual Abuse Investigations', *Bulletin of the American Academy of Psychiatry and the Law*, 17, pp. 45–52.

Wilson, K., Kendrick, P. and Ryan, V. (1992) *Play Therapy: A Non-directive Approach for Children and Adolescents*, London: Bailliere Tindall.

12 Short-term focused groupwork for young male abusers

Alix Brown and Jackie Jennings

Introduction

Many intervention programmes with adolescent males who sexually abuse have been carried out in group format. Programmes used in the USA by Ross (1987), O'Brien (1992) and others have a large component of groupwork in their make-up. Many programmes in this country have used groupwork as well, sometimes for assessment as well as intervention.

The advantages of groupwork have often been listed. Ryan and Lane (1991) suggest that many of the common characteristics exhibited by young offenders are effectively addressed in a group. These include: denial and minimization, isolation, poor social skills, inaccurate sexual education, distorted beliefs and victim stance. Ryan and Lane feel that connecting with other group members and using confrontation and challenge, together with role play, support and education, can help deal with many of these issues. They are particularly keen on the 'combination of confrontation and support' as it 'originates in the peer group [as] adolescents are less resistant when challenged by their peers than in similar interactions with adults' (1991, p. 257). While groups are often used to work with adolescents who abuse, there is very little in the way of evaluative work to suggest how effective they are compared, for example, to individual interventions.

For the confrontational aspects of a group to be effective, they need to be genuinely created by the group members themselves and not simply put to the group by the facilitators. Groups of adult sexual offenders involved in long-term intervention – and probably under a legal mandate to attend – often can provide such challenges, especially when some members of the group have been involved in the intervention programme longer than others. Adult groups, such as those run in the past by the Gracewell Institute

157

on a residential basis, and by various probation services throughout the country, can provide not only such challenging but also a level of support (Beckett et al., 1994). One of the major concerns in looking at groupwork with adolescents was the possibility that such groups would be less likely to create appropriate challenges and could even become counterproductive.

There are a number of reasons for this. The first of these relates to the power imbalance in the adolescent group situation. Such a group is always facilitated by adults who have a level of power and control over the young people involved. However it is presented, the adults are in charge of the group. While this may be acceptable to adults who have been convicted of abuse, adolescents may be more likely to respond to their own peer group pressure and attempt to challenge the adult facilitators or take over control of the group. Given that adolescents do respond readily to such pressures, and given that many of them do not have the impulse control to avoid or recognize the negative nature of such a response, it is possible that working with a group of adolescents who had abused could become a very difficult and unhelpful experience.

The second difficulty, in our specific setting, arose because many of the adolescents were not, in fact, on criminal orders. Some were in care, but most were cautioned for their sexual abuse, and any intervention carried out was done solely on the sanction of the case conference and with the agreement of the young person and their carers. This means that there was little compulsion for them to attend the groups. While some workers who run groups may feel this to be a disincentive, it can be seen in a positive way: if the young people involved in groups have a personal commitment to attending, then the work they do is likely to be much more effective. However, this means a good deal of hard work in making the groups very positive without losing the challenging nature of the work and, certainly, without colluding in any way with the offending. It also suggests the need to keep the groups relatively short. An adolescent's attention span is limited in any case, and a long-term group would seem destined to fail unless there was a compulsion to attend. On the other hand, a long-term group whose members *were* compelled to attend would seem likely to be much less effective as the young people would either seek to take over the group and disrupt it (subtly or directly) or simply 'opt out' and take little part in, or pay little attention to, what was going on.

Previously, one of us had acted as a consultant for a longer-term group which had tried to cover issues relating to offending pattern, sexual education, relapse prevention and victim empathy work. In the dozen or so sessions, it was very clear that these issues could not be covered appropriately and that some of the young people simply 'opted out' and avoided certain areas altogether. Because the schedule was so full, many issues were not covered. In discussing the difficulties raised by this group, it was obvious that a longer period of time was needed to deal with each issue, but that this would then make the entire group unacceptably long in its duration.

The answer, then, appeared simple. Shorter groups, dealing with specific parts of the abusing behaviour, would enable us to provide a concentrated input, allowing group members opportunities for both challenge and support but avoiding any bid to disrupt the group due to the novelty or initial motivation wearing off. A shorter period would commit the young people to a definite number of sessions with a clear end in view and this, if presented in the right way, should enable workers to hold their interest right to the end.

It was also clear that there were some parts of the work which should not be undertaken in groups. Fantasy work is a good example – there were fears that young people would share fantasies or become aroused by each other's descriptions of the abuse. There seems to be little or no direct research evidence on this point, but it is easy to imagine adolescents trying to outdo each other in their descriptions of abusive fantasy just as they do in reality in boasting about their sexual exploits. It would be likely that there would be some offences – such as rape of a girl of nearly the same age as the offender – where such boasting (once the offence had been discovered) would enable the young person to minimize the abuse and place the blame on the victim. Although most sexual offending against children is secretive and not usually shared with peers, there is a significant risk that simply using groupwork to address such offending could 'normalize' it to an extent and, ultimately, be counterproductive. It is important that individual work gives a young person the chance to examine their own motives and recognize their own patterns without distractions from others.

Setting up the groups

In setting up the short-term groups we were clear that individual work with a young person should continue alongside any groupwork. We were also clear that, for each group, there would be specific requirements and that a young person would have to have achieved specific goals before attending a group.

We decided that there were four areas in which groupwork could enhance the individual work we were already undertaking with young people: Sex Education, Planning the Offences, Victim Empathy and Relapse Prevention. These four areas would provide four short-term, focused pieces of groupwork. Young people could progress through each group, if that was felt to be appropriate, but it seemed more important to be able to feed them into groups at a time that fitted with their own needs. While the group was operating, individual work would continue, and feedback to the individual worker would be given from the facilitators. We were able to set out quite clearly the requirements for, and the aims of, each group, and both local authorities involved put forward the names of young people to be considered for each group.

The requirements and aims were as follows:

Overall aims

1　To add a further dimension to individual work with young people who abuse by enabling:

   – support from peers and peer group challenge to take place, as appropriate;
   – young people to make quicker progress, thus supporting individual work with them;
   – intervention methods to be used which can enhance individual work with young people who abuse.

2　To assist in training workers by:

   – increasing skill and confidence in groupwork situations;
   – providing appropriate support and supervision for designated workers.

3　To provide a new and cost-effective resource for each participating area which it would be unlikely to provide on its own, in line with 'Working Together' and the provisions of the Children Act 1989 to cater for 'Children in Need'.

Objectives for groups

Objectives for each group focus on specific issues, but overall objectives include:

1　Assisting group members to change their behaviour in the context of taking responsibility for their actions.
2　Improving self-esteem and social skills for group members.
3　Enabling group members to challenge each other appropriately about their excuses and rationalizations for offending.
4　Enhancing and emphasizing the individual work being carried out by local authority workers.

Objectives for workers

1   To utilize the four suggested group modules in intervention with those young people who abuse who, it is felt, will benefit from groupwork.
2   To evaluate each module both through the self-report and questionnaire responses of the young person and through the worker's own evaluation.
3   To feed back information to individual workers to enhance and focus their interventions with young people.

Aims of groups

1   Sex Education group   At the conclusion of this group, a young person should be able to:

   – demonstrate that they understand the following terms: abuse, mutuality, cooperation, compliance, consent, relationship, rape, sexual assault;
   – distinguish between sexually appropriate and sexually inappropriate behaviour and explain the reasons;
   – demonstrate an understanding of the way attitudes towards men and women, boys and girls affect behaviour;
   – question some of their own attitudes about sex, sexuality and gender;
   – understand the legal situation with regard to sexual offences and abusive behaviours;
   – demonstrate an appropriate understanding of contraception and sexually transmitted diseases;
   – discuss, with tolerance and understanding, issues around developing sexuality and sexual orientation.

2   Planning the Offences group   At the conclusion of this group, a young person should be able to:

   – describe in full their offending pattern and the ways in which they were able to set up and carry out their offence(s);
   – describe and challenge their original excuses, rationalizations, justifications and minimizations;
   – identify other areas where they may be reluctant to take full responsibility for their actions and the consequence of these actions.

3   Victim Empathy group   At the end of this group, a young person should be able to:

   – demonstrate a real and genuine understanding of the thoughts and feelings of their victims(s);

- write an appropriate letter to their victim which does not use blame, excuses or justifications;
- demonstrate an understanding of the short- and long-term effects of sexual abuse for victims;
- identify the questions and concerns which victims will have about their abuser;
- incorporate an appropriate concern for past and potential victims into their strategies for avoiding reoffending.

4　Relapse Prevention group　At the end of this group, a young person should be able to:

- clearly state alternatives to offending;
- identify various practical ways out of their offending cycle;
- demonstrate the existence of external supports in preventing reoffending;
- have an appropriate and rational view of their potential for reoffending;
- state and understand the consequences of further offending for victims, family, self and society;
- have a positive view of themselves in a future without abusing.

Initial requirements for short-term focused groups

1　Initial requirements for Sex Education group:

- assessment has suggested that relationship and attitude education work is needed;
- young person has skills in reading/writing and understanding to cope with several written questionnaires;
- young person is willing to participate in a group;
- young person is able to make a brief statement to the group (can be worked out with individual worker) about their reason for being there.

2　Initial requirements for Planning the Offences group – the young person:

- has completed Sex Education group and achieved its aims *or* has achieved similar aims through individual work;
- is able to draw out their cycle of offending and to include some (i) grooming/targeting behaviours (ii) excuses and rationalizations;
- has acknowledged the importance of fantasy and masturbation in setting up their cycle.

3　Initial requirements for Victim Empathy group – the young person:

- has completed Planning the Offences group and achieved the aims of that group *or* has achieved the aims required of that group through individual work;

- is *not* a bullying or sadistic offender – workers need to be clear that the young person does *not* gain pleasure directly from hurting or overpowering others;
- is prepared to acknowledge responsibility for offending directly to the group.

4 Initial requirements for Relapse Prevention group – the young person:

- has completed Victim Empathy group and achieved its aims *or* has achieved the aims required of that group through individual work;
- has recognized and acknowledged to the group that there is a real chance they could reoffend;
- has at least started individual work on fantasy modification if appropriate.

From the management side, it was important to have an agreement that allowed this 'cross-boundary' model to succeed. Given the current financial position, the only type of agreement which was possible was a no-cost agreement. Each local authority agreed to release two workers to be involved with the groups. The time required included meetings to plan the groups, the group sessions themselves and additional time after each session for debriefing and final evaluation meetings. In addition, while one local authority provided the premises for the group (a room with video recording facilities and an observation room), the other undertook to transport its young people. This was always done separately from the workers – it is not feasible to run the group and debrief afterwards if young people have to be transported home as well. From both workers' and managers' viewpoints, the other benefit of this groupwork system was in training workers. We used four workers for each group. Workers with little experience or workers who had groupwork experience but had not worked with young people who abuse were able to become involved in observing, facilitating and planning alongside others who had had significant experience in both areas. This was a very real 'plus' for workers and for managers, who thereby created inexpensive training for their own workers.

In each session, therefore, we had two facilitators and two observers – the observers being, for the most part, in the observation room and not present in the group. However, because we alternated facilitators, all the young people knew all the workers, and we met together at the start, at the end and during the break in the middle of the session. From the feedback after each of the groups this approach was seen as positive by all the young people.

Gender balance of workers

After much discussion, we decided that the only group where it was important to have both a male and female co-facilitator was the Sex Education group. It seemed essential that this group, designed to examine attitudes to men and women, should provide an appropriate role model. In subsequent groups, this model was not pursued as we felt that there the gender balance was much less important and preferred to mix up the workers according to their own interests and skills.

Running the groups

One of the difficulties often faced by workers in creating groups is that there are not enough young people available at any given time to form a group. This means that young people can wait around for a group when all the evidence suggests that, to avoid build-up of denial, avoidance, minimization and justifications, work needs to be started quickly, and the impetus of the initial assessment should not be lost. By combining two local authority areas, this becomes much less of a problem. We felt that a group should be composed of between three and eight young people – certainly no larger.

The basic session plan for the groups was devised to allow for the short-term concentration of the young people and to make each session as interesting as possible. We therefore included a number of different activities. The group started by talking briefly about the positive or negative experiences they had had during the week. This was followed by a group game, not necessarily a serious one, and then the first part of the working session. A short break – for drinks and crisps, at which all observers and facilitators were present – was followed by the second working part of the session. A final game, either to calm the group or to get them moving about, followed by feedback from the observers and (usually) five minutes' relaxation, brought the group to a close. The techniques used in the working sessions included discussion, video, drawing and drama.

The Sex Education group

The main aim of the Sex Education group was to begin to challenge attitudes to males and females, but it was also designed to provide updated sexual knowledge. We evaluated this group by means of a simple questionnaire about sexual knowledge – in fact, most of the group had the basic knowledge before the group began and there were no major improvements on what were reasonable scores initially. We used video clips, discussion and games to disseminate information and worked in a 'soundbite' way which seemed to hold the attention of the young people involved. Two of the group were dyslexic, so we built into our group model ways of working which did not pick out or disadvantage those two young people. This involved, for instance, always reading out any written information and sometimes utilizing all four workers to ensure that everyone understood their tasks.

The Planning the Offences group

This was probably the most demanding group – the 'cycle' group. In it, we aimed to work through a typical offender's cycle, with each young person identifying the parts which related to their own offending pattern. This involved some careful work around the 'fantasy' part of the cycle to ensure that young people did not share their own fantasies, and it also involved some specific role-play work around parts of their offending. This was very draining, both for the young people and for the workers, but it enabled some young people to add a good deal to the cycle that they had already recognized in their individual sessions.

The challenging that we got was not extensive but the group did seem fairly supportive of each other (although not collusive). We created an 'excuses board' which the group challenged during the last session, but direct challenge during the group itself was rare. It was our conclusion that many of the young people involved in this sort of group would not directly have the courage to challenge their peers.

The Victim Empathy group

This group relied almost entirely on role-play work and, as such, appeared very successful. Some of the comments from the young people afterwards were: 'You get to see what it's like from the other person's point of view'; 'It makes you feel better in the group – working it out'; 'The hardest part was at the start . . . introducing yourself and all that'; 'The worst bit was being the abuser in the role play.'

We asked them what they thought they would remember in ten years' time: 'Role plays'; 'About victims'; 'The other group members'; 'The way you've been working with other people.'

We had decided that it would not be appropriate for the young people to role-play their own offences. Partly this was to avoid re-creating fantasy and memories of the experience, and because we felt that it could put too much pressure on each young person. In any case, with five young people in the group we would not have time in six sessions to role-play each individual offence effectively. We therefore created two composite offences, incorporating elements of each person's offending, and spent parts of two sessions on each 'offence', casting, discussing, playing and videoing each one. We were careful in the selection of roles and ensured that each young person had an experience of playing a victim. When a young person played an abuser, we ensured that they were not playing a role which was similar to their own abusing behaviour. This group was set up with the same basic session plan as the other groups.

One of us had also worked extensively with groups for young women who were victims of abuse. She was interested in the comparisons between the two types of groups, not having worked before with a group of young abusers. In the use of role play, for instance, it was clear that the young abusers' group took readily to the idea and were keen to participate. Using the 'freeze frame' technique to elicit thoughts and feelings at different points enabled the young people to go beyond the here and now in their thinking and to consider gender, societal and cognitive influences on victim responses to abuse. All of the young people felt that it was uncomfortable playing the victim but they also said that they very much disliked playing the abuser. In retrospect, this is exactly the result we would have wished to achieve.

Our facilitator who had worked with the young women's groups observed that, in such groups, while role play was a very useful tool to develop freedom of expression and disclosure of 'real' feelings, the participants were generally difficult to engage in this activity. It appears that victims have difficulty in taking on a 'tough' role and do not easily adjust to assertive, dominant character parts. However, the women's groups did use peer support to challenge oppression and gained strength from helping each other.

Relaxation and games were used by both groups, with the young male abusers engaging readily in both activities with little apparent embarrassment. The young women, on the other hand, appeared to feel much less safe and found it hard to relax and let go. Avoidance tactics were applied to this part of the schedule, and the group as a whole viewed this as an unhelpful activity.

Attendance at the abusers' group was 100 per cent, without any mandate. This was surprising because it indicated a real level of commitment to the group which might not have been expected. There was real sadness when the group ended. For the young women, it seems that many of them attended because of pressure from their non-abusing parent or from their social worker. Very few believed that attendance was for the benefit of themselves or that it would be helpful. Numbers fell within the first month and 30 per cent, on average, of the membership were lost.

A concern that is often expressed about working with young abusers in groups is that they could create a 'hierarchy of offending'. In the case of this specific group, there was some discussion of each person's offences but there never appeared to be a problem in relation to a hierarchy or a comparison of offending behaviour. We felt that this would only become a possibility if the group had gone on for much longer and that using a six-week group session was one way of avoiding difficulties in this area. The group for victims of abuse was, of course, longer and, in the early stages, it seemed that a 'tariff' of experience evolved, leading to one or two members questioning their group membership. This led to two possible responses by the young women: putting extra effort into group members felt to be more 'hurt' than themselves, or minimizing and dismissing their own need for help and support. The young women needed reminding that the degree of abuse was not the issue and that their feelings were the common denominators, whatever the individual experience.

The Relapse Prevention group

As far as the local authority programme was concerned, this was to be the fourth group but, at the time of writing, it had not been operated. Several workers moved on and the impetus was lost. Relapse prevention runs through all the intervention programmes in any case, but this group was designed to reinforce the positive, offence-free lifestyle and to enable young people to role-play difficult situations and avoidance techniques. Plans for the group were made and included a number of visual ways of looking at how to avoid reoffending. A 'relapse prevention' game was created, and it is envisaged that such a group would include role-play work to reinforce coping strategies devised and developed by the young people and their individual workers.

Conclusion

The three groups seemed to run successfully. With one exception (due to circumstances not within our control as the young man was from a third local authority) we had 100 per cent attendance. Only one young person was under any compulsion to attend. He was on a deferred sentence for the Planning the Offences group, but he also attended the Victim Empathy group after he had been conditionally discharged. One young man attended all three groups, another two attended two, but the others came in for groups as indicated by their progress on their individual programmes.

We did feel at times that the groups were not long enough, even though they dealt with one specific aspect of the abusing. On reflection, however, these short-term groups seem to hold the attention of the young people, quite effectively enabling them to concentrate on a particular issue. In addition, the programme provided positive and invaluable 'hands-on' training experiences for workers. The young people's feedback indicated a level of enjoyment which seems more likely to ensure that they relate to and remember the issues discussed. The young people also indicated that the most difficult part of the programme was having to talk about their abusing behaviour by being open and accepting responsibility for their actions.

From our own point of view, the experience of planning and running such groups has been very challenging, but the cooperation and links with other workers who are doing the same has been very positive indeed. The element of training during the time the groups were operating was also important and enjoyable.

From our observations of abuser and victim groups we would suggest that adolescents who abuse are as much in need of a safe, supportive environment as are victims of abuse. Their cognitions, attitudes, values and fantasies need challenging and checking out, but there remain the issues of isolation, rejection, disgust, self-devaluation, guilt, blame and family breakdown which are also experienced by the victims of abuse. This observation does not minimize their behaviour but reinforces the idea that, in order to avoid their reoffending, a whole series of other issues need to be tackled along with the confrontation and change of the behaviour itself. In the victim empathy work, in particular, it was clear that the group helped the young people to rethink their perspective and to create some empathy and understanding, and that this was by far the best way to enable them to make long-term, positive behaviour change.

Immediate feedback on the groups suggested that the young men involved felt that the experience of attending had been an important one for them. Measuring long-term behaviour change is clearly difficult and, in any case, the groups were always intended to run alongside a full programme of individual intervention. None the less, the short-term groups focused the young people on specific issues and enabled them to examine their cognitions and feelings along with others who had also abused, but without the dangers of creating an 'abuse subculture'. Such groups enhance the individual work but are not a substitute for it. Group participants need to be selected carefully and, just as with individual work, workers need to remain fully in control of the content and direction of the sessions. With these provisos, however, short-term focused groupwork with young sexual abusers appears to avoid the pitfalls of other types of intervention programmes involving adolescent groups, and provides a positive experience which can only aid young people in making confident choices not to abuse in future.

References

Beckett, R., Beech, A., Fisher, D. and Fordham, A. S. (1994) *Community-Based Treatment For Sex Offenders: An Evaluation Of Seven Treatment Programmes*, London: Home Office.

O'Brien, M. (1992) 'Cognitive Behavioural Techniques in the Treatment of Adolescent Sex Offenders', paper presented at the NOTA Conference, Dundee, 30 September to 2 October.

Ross, J. (1987) 'Treating the Adolescent Perpetrator', paper presented at the 16th National Symposium on Child Abuse and Neglect, Colorado.

Ryan, G. and Lane, S. (1991) *Juvenile Sexual Offending: Causes, Consequences and Correction*, Lexington, MA: Lexington Books.

With acknowledgements to Chris Wake, Nigel Wake and Mark Stokes from Shropshire Social Services and John Lees and Ann Wheeldon from Dudley Social Services, all of whom were involved in planning and running the groups.

13 The groupwork support of sexually abused boys
Andrew Durham

Introduction

This chapter discusses issues relating to a groupwork project which was set up to support a group of boys who were victims of organized sexual abuse. The boys had to wait for almost two years following their disclosure before giving their evidence in court.

The first part of the chapter relates to factors around male child sexual abuse and initially considers problems relating to its under-reporting. Subsequently the problem of *some* male victims of sexual abuse sexually victimizing other children is explored. It is strongly emphasized that there is a substantial majority of sexually abused male children who *do not* sexually abuse others, and that this issue requires sensitive consideration when working with sexually abused male children. Finally, the influence of structural pressures and societal definitions of masculinity in exacerbating the problems experienced by sexually abused boys is debated.

The second part of the chapter considers the incompatibility between the evidence demands of the legal process and the therapeutic needs of sexually abused children. The *Memorandum of Good Practice* (Department of Health, 1992) has tried to address this issue with the introduction of guidelines for the production of video-taped evidence. However, because this is based only on partial implementation of the Pigot Committee's proposals, children are still required to attend court for cross-examination.

Finally, I offer an example from practice which tries to show that, in spite of problems in the judicial system which can hinder supportive, child-centred practice, it is possible to identify and execute certain areas of positive intervention before a trial, without interfering with the reliability of evidence.

Factors relating to the sexual abuse of boys

From the review of research by Watkins and Bentovim (1992) and others, it would appear that there is a considerable under-reporting of the incidence of sexual abuse of boys (Peake, 1990; Mendel, 1995). The reasons identified include: the victims' fears of homosexuality; a response to the stress caused by abuse through externalized behaviour; the culture of masculine self-reliance, and ideas about youthful male sexuality. There are also arguments that there may be an inadequate response to allegations because of a tendency to blame the boy or even because of a denial of abuse by professionals. In addition, the influence and possible power of the paedophile lobby has to be acknowledged. Other factors which may be involved include loyalty to the offender and pleasure in aspects of the abuse.

The fact that, within a homophobic society, homosexuality engenders widespread fears, confusion and taboos about sexual identity may also discourage openness about the subject. It is important that these and other possible factors in under-reporting should be considered when designing programmes of intervention.

Watkins and Bentovim (1992), in their review of research relating to the sexual abuse of male children and adolescents, quote research (Rogers and Terry, 1984) which describes three behavioural responses which were seen as more or less unique to male victims:

1   Confusion or anxiety relating to sexual identity.
2   Inappropriate attempts to reassert masculinity (compensatory aggression).
3   Recapitulation of the victimizing experience.

Confusion or anxiety relating to sexual identity is described as involving homophobic concerns. Attention is drawn to the importance of distinguishing between fear of homosexuality and the development of homosexual preference. The former is a contributory factor to non-disclosure, possibly enhanced by societal factors and compounded by confusion relating to arousal during abuse. In many cases, sexual abuse is experienced prior to a full understanding or development of sexual identity, which may create the myth that the experience dictates the identity.

Compensatory aggression is described as the most common behavioural reaction. Such behaviours would include fighting, destructiveness, disobedience and hostility. Alongside the research by Rogers and Terry (1984), additional research by Summit (1983) supports this finding. The majority of the research evidence discussed by Watkins and Bentovim (1992) supports the view that sexually victimized males are more likely to show externalized responses than females.

Recapitulating the victimizing experience is described as identifying with the aggressor in preference to adopting a victim identity. That most perpetrators are male enables boys to become more likely to develop such identities.

Watkins and Bentovim (1992) quote conflicting research on the extent to which victims go on to sexually victimize others. One study by Conte and Schuerman (1988) quotes a rate of 2 per cent, although the study is not gender-specific. Other studies, relating to boys alone, ranged from a rate of victimization of others of 13 per cent (Friederich et al., 1988) to a rate of 50 per cent (Sansonnett-Hayden et al., 1987). The pooled prevalence of these studies was 22 per cent.

Statistics quoted in the media and in other arenas sometimes relate to the proportion of adult sex offenders who were themselves victims of abuse. Often these statistics are quite high and can instil considerable anxiety into the male child victim, who may not have sufficient understanding of statistics to realize that the particular example quoted does not accurately relate to the proportion of victimized boys who go on to abuse.

Furniss (1990) refers to sexually victimized males having fears of themselves becoming abusers. The path of victim to victimizer is described as a circular and self-reinforcing process in which fears relating to the abuse prevent the development of normal adolescent relationships. Ryan (1989) refers to victims of sexual abuse experiencing many dysfunctional outcomes: emotional; developmental; behavioural; an inability to communicate; feelings of helplessness; depression, and somatic complaints. She refers to learned behaviour where victims re-create their own experience of abuse. Such 'traumatic sexualization' is referred to as developmentally inappropriate sexual behaviour (Finkelhor and Brown, 1986). Long-term victims of sexual abuse may have been exposed to the distorted rationale of the perpetrator. This can lead to ritualistic patterns of sexual behaviour that become more rigid and more secretive over time, nurtured by an emotional climate of fear and anxiety. The child's anxiety and confusion lead to an incorporation of the offender's rationalizations and distortions:

> 'The conflicting physical and emotional sensations, psychological confusion, and feelings of intrusion may create a sense of powerlessness and lack of control that reinforce the helplessness inherent in any exploitative experience' (Hiroto 1974). The lack of control may lead to control-seeking behaviours (e.g. eating disorders, self-destruction, or exploitation of others). (Ryan, 1989, p. 327)

Secrecy and isolation prohibit the child from validating feelings or correcting distorted assumptions (Finkelhor et al., 1986). This is supported by Furniss' (1991) reference to entrance and exit rituals which deny the reality of the abuse taking place in terms of being validated by events outside the abuse itself. This may lead a child into irrational thinking, a declining self-esteem, guilt, confusion, powerlessness and anger. Ryan (1989) refers to such developing fantasies as retaliation in order to regain control. This, in turn, leads to planning negative behaviour such as offending. The identity of an aggressor becomes more comfortable than the pain and anxiety of a victim. Aggression becomes the means of dominating helplessness.

For such a child, the triggers for negative behaviour or sexual offending may be those situations where the child feels out of control or experiences situations which resonate with the abuse. The cycle towards a sexual assault may take the form of a pattern of negative feelings and cognitive distortions coupled with a need to take control. These children may often feel persecuted not only by their own experience of victimization but by other factors such as social isolation, poor peer group relationships or family disruption. According to Furniss (1991), the physiological reward of sexual offending constitutes its addictiveness. The pairing of sexuality with fear, anxiety, helplessness and aggression may lead to future experiences of those feelings becoming the trigger for a cycle that leads to sexual arousal. This reinforces the pairing and can lead to the sexualization of non-sexual problems. For some children, remembering experiences of abuse may entail high levels of arousal. Over a period of time, sexually aggressive fantasies followed by sexually aggressive behaviours become the means to regain control, albeit temporarily, until the initial feelings which triggered the cycle recur and move the child towards repeated sexual offending. For the victim, this loss of control and subsequent emotional turmoil is the *outcome* of being abused. For the offender it becomes the *trigger* for future offending.

Minimizing one's own abuse, denying the abuse, retracting disclosures, accepting the pleasure of the abuse without question, and repressing any subsequent trauma arising from the abuse all serve to create the deception that sexual abuse is not harmful and can be enjoyed by its victims. They are dysfunctional, irrational defences and serve to move a victim along the path to victimization.

Therapeutic intervention must work towards accountability for both the victim and the offender. Any intervention with victims of sexual abuse must focus on placing blame with the offender and must emphasize empathy with the victim. The victim is helpless and needs to be helped to regain control. Ryan (1989) argues strongly that victim empowerment must be based on cognition rather than on feelings. The victimization of another can create a feeling of power but it is difficult for such an act to create an open, rational cognition of power. Ryan is cautious about some of the traditional therapeutic methods of helping a victim. Encouraging a child physically to act out anger may reinforce aggression and support retaliatory behaviours.

Victims need to be helped to rethink situations in order to cause a reduction in negative feelings, as scenarios of anger and retaliation can become role plays for future aggression and victimization. Ryan uses the term 'legitimate privacy' to replace the dangerous secrecy of the facts of a child's abuse. It is emphasized that the victim must be helped to identify his own pain and that victim empathy is a key element in therapy: 'The child's power is in self-discovery, strength discovery, and the ability to identify and rely on supportive, protective adults' (Ryan, 1989, p. 333).

When dealing with child sexual abuse, children and adults may be presenting themselves in states of trauma and distress which require an immediate response in terms of individual support. However, it is important in terms of being able to apply the most appropriate and effective intervention to keep structural factors in mind. For example, feminist perspectives see child sexual abuse in the light of power and gender – an unequal distribution between men and women in a patriarchal society. Child sexual abuse, then, is seen as an abuse of male power and trust. This perspective relates male sexuality to power, control and dominance. Scraton (1990) refers to Connell's concept of 'subordinated masculinity' by citing examples of younger men subordinated to their seniors and the subordination of homosexuality to explicitly heterosexual, hegemonic masculinity. Hegemonic masculinity is central to cultural beliefs and orientates policy and formal politics:

> Further, they become the basic currency of entry into the world of work, leisure and social commentary, deeply ingrained in the initiation of induction procedures of political and economic institutions, social clubs and gatherings, and forming the basis of laws, conventions and practices. (Scraton, 1990, p. 16)

Helping an abused boy contextualize abuse may prevent him from developing some of the compensatory aggressive behaviours mentioned above. The secrecy and shame of sexual abuse may serve to 'subordinate' a survivor's masculinity to the 'hegemonic masculinity' of wider Western culture. Treatment should consider forms of 'alternative masculinity' which help young people become aware of these cultural forces and develop a sense of choice which does not by necessity conform or subordinate itself to enforced stereotypes. Gender, of course, is only one aspect of discrimination which forms the context for abuse. Other aspects of structural disadvantage should also be borne in mind, such as age, race, class and disability.

Sexual abuse is a multifactorial problem implying multifactorial solutions which take account of the interaction of individuals within a cultural framework. It is also necessary to be aware of matters which relate specifically to the male experience of sexual abuse. As with all situations of intervention relating to sexual abuse, it is important to take account of the gender of workers and of the need to avoid creating therapeutic scenarios which resonate the experience of abuse.

For children and young people who have sexually abused other children, their offending behaviour needs to be addressed as a primary focus. When helping boys address their own experience of being sexually victimized, the therapeutic task is to identify and name the experience of sexual abuse as a harmful and painful one whose recipient requires support, understanding and healing. The victim becomes not a victimizer but a survivor. Dangerous secrecy becomes legitimate privacy through a process in which the individual regains rational control.

Children, evidence and therapeutic intervention

The incompatibility between the evidence demands of the legal system and the needs of children in child abuse cases has been well documented in the literature (Spencer and Flin, 1990; Davies, 1992; Aldridge and Freshwater, 1993). It is generally agreed that children's attendance at such trials is at least stressful, if not traumatic. In cases of sexual abuse, where a child may be in need of therapy, the experience may be particularly traumatic. In such cases, any pre-trial discussion of matters relating directly to the evidence of the alleged abuse is likely to prove difficult if the reliability and spontaneity of the evidence is to be preserved. The child is required not to discuss the evidence but to keep it freshly in mind for repetition at the trial and wait until after the trial before being able to talk through the abuse and receive help.

This problem has not been resolved by the introduction of the *Memorandum of Good Practice* (Department of Health, 1992) following the Pigot Committee, as it is still necessary for a child to appear live in court for cross-examination after admitting evidence in the form of a video-recording. This has been only a partial implementation of Pigot's proposal. He had suggested a second video-recording of the child's cross-examination in chambers soon after the first video interview. This would have solved the problem of therapeutic work being delayed by slow-moving legal processes.

The current system has the therapeutic needs of abused children and the evidence requirements for a successful prosecution locked in opposition to each other. The task is to maintain a balance throughout a very difficult waiting period. If the decision has been made for a child to go to court, then the balance is already moving towards evidence. The task then becomes a damage-limitation exercise as, inevitably, the child will suffer stress as a result of such a decision.

A practice example

The boys served by this project had attended computer clubs set up locally by a man named Harry, who was a computer studies lecturer, and another man named Gordon, who was a legal clerk. These men were known to each other. Harry's club was for boys aged under 11 whilst Gordon's was for 11 and over. Some of the boys had attended both clubs, as moving from one club to the next was an established process. The club evenings involved computer activities, games and trips out. Occasionally there were residential trips during school holidays and at weekends.

After concerns had been raised relating to the continued presence of boys at Gordon's house and the behaviour of one of the boys, a joint social services and police investigation was set up – over thirty boys were interviewed. There were clear statements from 11 of the boys relating to acts of sexual abuse which had been committed against them by either Harry, Gordon or both over a period ranging from two months to, in some cases, four years. Most of the boys were loyal to Harry and Gordon, some out of fear, particularly in relation to Harry, while some of the loyalty was a genuine friendship, particularly in relation to the boys who attended Gordon's club. This made the investigation both confusing and difficult.

Because of the legal system, the complexities of the case and possibly the professional status, knowledge and skill of the offenders, the process of prosecution lasted for almost two years. During this period there were several 'warnings' for court appearances, some of which involved the boys attending court sessions which resulted in adjournments. These repeated delays caused the boys a great deal of anxiety and stress. Both men were eventually convicted on a number of counts of sexual abuse and given short prison sentences.

When the Crown Prosecution Service (CPS) had decided to proceed with a trial, a multi-agency meeting was set up. At this meeting the setting up of a support group was proposed by myself and social services colleagues. Following this, it was necessary to negotiate with the CPS about how it would be possible to run a support group without influencing or causing problems with evidence. It was also necessary to advise them that this practice would be in accordance with the child welfare recommendations of *Working Together* (Department of Health, 1991). A close liaison with the CPS was established and maintained throughout the pre-trial phase. The defence lawyers were made aware of the group and were given a basic outline of the programme. There were no specific challenges about the support groups in court, although the accusation of collaboration was an aspect of the defence case.

It was recognized that there needed to be a speedy acknowledgement of the difficulties the boys had experienced so far, and their need for a support system for the future which would reduce their anxieties and break down any isolation. There was also an emphasis on giving the boys a choice about appearing in court.

I was introduced to each family by a member of the initial investigation team. After I had given each boy an initial support interview which gave him and his parents an opportunity to raise questions, further interviews were arranged, at their request, in groups of two or three. This was necessary in order to break down further any fears and anxieties the boys and their parents might have before entering into a full group. The boys chose particular friends from the proposed group with whom they felt they would like to discuss the idea of a support group. This suited the pace of events, as the social services department were still in the process of identifying co-workers for the groups. Two support groups were set up – one for six boys aged 14 and the second for five boys aged 10 to 13. The members of Group One were an established peer group, all members living on the same estate. Group Two members were only acquainted through occasional computer club sessions and some residential trips. I led the group with two female co-workers, one for each group, in order to provide a mixed gender leadership.

The boys welcomed the prospect of attending a support group, especially in view of their not attending any group activity since the closure of the computer clubs. The boys also welcomed the proposal that attendance at a support group was a decision independent of attending court, and that the decision on attending court could be made during the life of the group. This was particularly important for some of the boys who were struggling with their loyalty to Gordon. In some cases, this situation was causing family conflict. Most of the families expressed concern about the boys. Some boys were suffering from disturbed sleeping patterns, were often moody and appeared unsettled. As soon as the boys began to feel that they were being involved in a process of exercising choices and were not being seen simply as court witnesses, their commitment to the process developed and their anxieties began to reduce.

The pre-court stage of the groupwork programme was as follows:

1   *Identifying support and building self-esteem*

This involved the presentation of the group programme with discussion around issues to do with choice. Activity-based sessions were designed to enhance self-esteem and to develop a group identity. These sessions generally alternated with the work-based sessions to offer support through a difficult and distressing programme.

2 Going to court

Sessions included the giving out of basic information about the court and the nature of the adversarial process. Also included were visits to local courts, role plays, identifying personal strengths and discussions emphasizing the importance of telling the truth. Also included were stress-reducing techniques.

3 Sexuality and sex education

We embarked on a basic sex education programme using the 'Man's World' board game to facilitate discussions about sexuality, sexual orientation, gender roles, sexism and so on. In addition, these sessions attempted to identify the pre- and post-court areas to be worked on, including the difficulty of not discussing the abuse before the trial. The boys were asked to approach me in the event of any distress which they felt could not be addressed within the group sessions.

4 Protection issues

This part of the process focused on discussions about knowledge of good touching and bad touching and the importance of being able to say 'No' to inappropriate contact. In addition, activities were used to help the boys learn to identify safe adults to tell. This whole area attempted to ensure a continuation of understanding and support from families.

This pre-court phase of the programme was characterized by the need to balance evidence requirements and welfare/protection issues. The boys were asked not to discuss aspects of the abuse with each other. The pre-court phase addressed issues relating to the context in which the abuse had occurred. Most notably, issues were discussed relating to developing masculinity in a society which emphasizes dominance and self-reliance as expressions of masculinity, and which generally supports the expression of homophobia. Such issues have the potential to exacerbate and deepen the anxiety of an abused male. We took pains to talk about such issues supportively but without any direct reference to sexual abuse, with the knowledge that it was likely to be the case that privately held anxieties were being addressed. When, during the post-court phase, these issues were fully addressed in the context of the actual sexual abuse, it was clear from some of the comments and reactions of the boys that they had listened carefully to, and benefited from, the earlier discussions. They demonstrated understanding and made reference to the earlier sessions, and were able to enter into the discussions with some degree of ease.

A group leader attended each trial and supported the boys throughout. Prior negotiations had already been made with the court for the provision of suitable waiting facilities.

The post-court programme was as follows:

1   Discussing the court experience

This session involved discussing and explaining the outcome of the trial and acknowledging everybody's contribution as well as sharing feelings.

2   Secrecy

Here we looked at the role of secrecy in sexual abuse as a means of maintaining silence, and explored together the advantages of breaking down such secrecy. Again, feelings, anxieties and events were shared.

3   Abusers

The characteristics of abusers and their behaviour were explored by the group, focusing on how an abuser can present different faces to different people. Discussions centred on abusive processes, targeting, grooming, and the maintaining of silence. The session also talked about how the abusers set up sexually-oriented games and asked about the boys' feelings towards the abusers now. The session ended with a discussion of how one might identify abusers in the future.

4   The abuse

There was an open discussion by each young person of the abuse they suffered. This allowed group members to compare and corroborate their experiences as well as challenge denial within the group. There followed a discussion of feelings about the abuse and a sharing of difficulties as a result of the abuse. We also highlighted the importance of the safety of the group and the advantage of talking.

5   Further issues of sexuality and sex education

This part of the programme looked at the nature of sexual assaults on children and compared them to the group members' own experiences. To help in ensuring protection in the future, we identified and addressed sexualized behaviour and sexual messages. Discussions covered a variety of issues, including masturbation, sexual fantasies and memories of the abuse, along with problems of tension-relief and the possible sexualization of non-sexual problems. The session concluded with talks about relationship attitudes, sexism, gender roles and stereotypes.

6 Fears arising from the abuse

We explored at some length the fears around enjoying some aspects of the abuse, and concerns around homosexuality. Issues around loyalty to the abuser and the mixed feelings that were aroused were addressed, as was the fear of becoming an abuser. We emphasized issues of choice and sexuality as a developmental process and the need not to become fixed by one's experiences. The group talked about the importance of talking through difficulties and solving problems, as opposed to hiding them and building up fears. The session also emphasized the harm of sexual abuse and the need for help and guidance in recovery.

7 Sources of future help

This session acknowledged the importance of family, friends (each other) and the availability of local resources. Members were encouraged to contact group leaders in the future, if necessary, or any other member of the social services department.

8 Evaluation

The whole experience was evaluated by the use of questionnaires, discussion and the comparison of earlier group material with more recently completed work. The discussions centred on feelings and the extent of recovery, and the ultimate ability of group members to be able to protect themselves and be protected in the future.

Throughout the unexpectedly long lives of both groups, the group leaders observed increased levels of confidence and self-esteem. This was borne out by comments from the young people to the effect that they felt better and had valued being a member. Topics which had been the subject of personal fears and secret anxieties were finally discussed openly and to the full. Some boys showed a greater level of initiative and independence, becoming more able to take part in discussions and make decisions about group events and topics. There were comments on the evaluation forms about the value of being listened to and having the opportunity to take time to discuss feelings and have questions answered. The attendance rate for both groups was close to one hundred per cent. The artwork towards the end of the group was much more relaxed, relating to hobbies and interests, and no longer showed any sexual comments or sexually explicit drawings of the abuse. Most of the tensions and conflicts between group members had also subsided.

That the boys had to wait for almost two years before giving their evidence meant their having to hold on to deeper anxieties of the abusive experiences for an intolerably long time. This was a clear example of the incompatibility between the demands of the legal system and the therapeutic needs of victims of sexual abuse. Several of the boys openly stated that they felt that their enjoyment of the support groups had to some extent compensated for this. At times, however, their actual experiences and responses spoke against this. Furthermore, these comments were made after the court process had concluded and were a sharp contrast to the anxieties expressed in response to news of further adjournments. The boys had to cope with the knowledge that a stressful event was still to occur at some undefined point in the future, and that this was preventing a full therapeutic discussion of personal experiences and feelings relating to the abuse.

If it had been known at the outset that the delay would be two years, then the process may have been considered to be contrary to the welfare of the boys, and it is likely that the topics of the post-court programme would have been dealt with much sooner. Such a decision, however, would have damaged the prospect of a successful court outcome to the extent that the case may have been dropped. Many sexual abuse investigations fail to reach the court system for reasons relating to the weakness or lack of evidence. This case could have been one such example.

Inevitably, a programme of this length and nature will have an impact on its leaders. This impact will possibly differ between genders. A male worker has to face comparisons with the abuser and needs to identify boundaries and highlight the absence of any personal complicity in sexual abuse. A female worker has to face possible stereotyping and sexist attitudes and can feel isolated in an all-male group. These factors dictate the need for close communication between workers and a well-worked-out and agreed consistent response to situations which may arise. All the workers discussed ways of demonstrating non-oppressive, respectful relationships in their behaviour with each other and with the boys. These factors also highlight the need for the leaders to provide mutual support and to receive joint and individual supervision on a regular basis. Unfortunately, the supervision occurred more on an individual basis than on a joint basis. The mutual support and cooperation between the group workers, to some extent, compensated and replaced this. In view of the unexpected length of the groups, each group worker required and benefited from the sustained support of colleagues from their respective teams.

Conclusion

The incompatibility between the therapeutic needs of sexually abused children and the demands of the legal system was vividly demonstrated by the experience of the boys in the groups. Throughout the process there were clear expressions of anxiety from all of the boys in relation to the delays in the court process. This highlights the need for social workers involved in this area of work strongly and consistently to advocate and negotiate for priority to be given to the needs of children who are caught up in this manner.

The experience of the boys in this project supports the view expressed in the literature that groupwork is an appropriate and desirable response to male sexual abuse, particularly in relation to organized abuse involving several children. The proposals for such work are likely to require strong negotiation for acceptance by members of the legal system. Detailed plans justifying how the work will give priority to the children without jeopardizing the reliability of evidence are needed.

The project has shown that it is possible to carry out therapeutic work before a court trial, without interfering with evidence – most notably, areas of work which address issues relating to the context of abuse which have the potential to exacerbate and deepen the child's level of anxiety. The split of a therapeutic programme into pre-court and post-court phases was helpful to all parties but particularly to the boys, who were able to see that difficult areas of work were on the agenda for discussion at a later stage. Such a split is, of course, a compromise and not a solution. The solution requires an adjustment of the legal system to enable a child's role at court to be concluded at a very early stage, to free the child to receive a full therapeutic programme.

The project has demonstrated that many of the problems identified in the literature in relation to male sexual abuse were experienced by the boys in the groups – most notably, the anxieties relating to the legal processes as well, of course, as the personal emotional distress and turmoil already highlighted.

The extension of the group process as a result of the delays had a compensatory spin-off in therapeutic terms, although direct therapeutic work relating to the abuse itself did not take place until after the court appearance. Both groups continued until the full therapeutic programme had been implemented. The workers and boys believed that a degree of therapeutic healing took place through the positive group experiences, in the form of increased self-esteem and, ultimately, empowerment through knowledge and confidence-building. There was visible relief after a positive court outcome when responsibility was finally placed where it belonged.

It is hoped that the boys involved with the project will continue to recover and readjust to a life without court cases, secrets and fears, and will continue to develop along the path of transition from victim to survivor.

References

Aldridge, J. and Freshwater, K. (1993) 'The Preparation of Child Witnesses', *Journal of Child Law*, 5 (1).

Bolton, F., Morris, L. and MacEachron, A. (1989) *Males at Risk: The Other Side of Child Sexual Abuse*, Newbury Park, CA: Sage.

Connell, R. W. (1987) *Gender and Power: Society, the Person and Sexual Politics*, Oxford: Polity Press.

Conte, J. R. and Schuerman, J. R. (1988) 'The Effects of Sexual Abuse on Children', in Wyatt and Powell (1988).

Davies, G. (1992) 'Protecting the Child Witness in the Court Room', *Child Abuse Review*, 1, pp. 33–41.

Department of Health (1991) *Working Together Under the Children Act 1989: A Guide to Arrangements for Inter-Agency Cooperation for the Protection of Children from Abuse*, London: HMSO.

Department of Health (1992) *Memorandum of Good Practice on Video Recorded Interviews with Child Witnesses for Criminal Proceedings*, London: HMSO.

Finkelhor, D. and Browne, A. (1986) 'Initial and Long-term Effects: A Conceptual Framework', in Finkelhor et al. (1986).

Finkelhor D., Araji, S., Baron, L., Brown, A., Doyle-Peters, S. and Wyatt, G. E. (1986) *A Sourcebook on Child Sexual Abuse*, London: Sage.

Friederich, W. N., Beilke, R. L. and Urquija, A. J. (1988) 'Behaviour Problems in Young Sexually Abused Boys', *Journal of Interpersonal Violence*, 3, pp. 21–8.

Furniss, T. (1990) 'Groupwork Therapy for Boys', in Hollows and Armstrong (1990).

Furniss, T. (1991) *The Multi-Professional Handbook of Child Sexual Abuse: Integrated Management, Therapy and Legal Intervention*, London: Routledge.

Gelsthorpe, L. and Morris, A. (eds) (1990) *Feminist Perspectives in Criminology*, Buckingham: Open University Press.

Hollows, A. and Armstrong, H. (eds) (1990) *Working with Sexually Abused Boys*, London: TAGOSAC.

Mendel, M. P. (1995) *The Male Survivor: The Impact Of Sexual Abuse*, London: Sage.

Peake, A. (1990) 'Under-Reporting the Sexual Abuse of Boys', in Hollows and Armstrong (1990).

Porter, E. (1986) *Treating the Young Male Victim of Sexual Assault: Issues and Intervention Strategies*, Orwell, VI: Safer Society Press.

Rogers, C. N. and Terry, T. (1984) 'Clinical Intervention with Boy Victims of Sexual Abuse', in Stuart and Greer (1984).

Ryan, G. (1989) 'Victim to Victimiser: Rethinking Victim Treatment', *Journal of Interpersonal Violence*, 4 (3), pp. 325–41.

Sansonnett-Hayden, H., Hayley, G., Marriage, C. and Fine, S. (1987) 'Sexual Abuse and Psychopathology in Hospitalised Adolescents', *Journal of the American Academy of Child and Adolescent Psychiatry*, 26, pp. 262–7.

Scraton, P. (1990) 'Scientific Knowledge or Masculine Discourses? Challenging Patriarchy in Criminology', in Gelsthorpe and Morris (1990).

Spencer, J. R. and Flin, R. (1990) *The Evidence of Children, The Law and the Psychology*, London: Blackstone Press.

Stuart, I. R. and Greer, J. G. (eds) (1984) *Victims of Sexual Aggression: Treatment of Children, Women and Men*, New York: Van Nostrand Reinhold.

Summit, R. (1983) 'The Child Sexual Abuse Accommodation Syndrome', *Child Abuse and Neglect*, 7.

Watkins, B. and Bentovim, A. (1992) 'The Sexual Abuse of Male Children and Adolescents: A Review of Current Research', *Journal of Child Psychology and Psychiatry*, 33 (1), pp. 197–248.

Wyatt, G. E. and Powell, E. J. (eds) (1988) *Lasting Effects of Sexual Abuse*, London: Sage.

Part III

The staff dimension

Introduction

Child protection can be seen to be a labour-intensive form of work in terms of both the number of people involved across the multidisciplinary spectrum and the intensity of demands upon those who are engaged in this challenging aspect of childcare practice. Consequently, there would seem to be little difficulty in making the case for paying attention to the staff dimension of such work – the issues that arise in relation to the demands upon workers, the needs of staff and the problems that arise when such questions are ignored or dismissed.

It has long been recognized that organizations rely very heavily on the quality of their workforce to achieve their corporate aims. As it is often expressed in the context of human resource management, an organization's most important asset is its staff. An organization that fails to pay serious attention to staffing or 'human resource' issues is one that seriously risks a breakdown in its ability to achieve its ends. Where this applies to a child protection system, there is a very real danger that children will be unnecessarily harmed as a result of important staff-related issues not being addressed.

It is relatively easy in the human services to attach considerable importance to the needs and concerns of service users and yet to devote little or no time, thought or energy to the needs and concerns of the staff who are charged with the demanding duties of professional practice. For child protection in particular, this is especially the case, with the emotional demands of the work often being neglected (Morrison, 1994). It is therefore necessary to challenge organizational cultures that neglect the staff dimension and allow discontent and other problems to fester (Thompson et al., 1996).

Part III of this book therefore examines five aspects of the staff dimension, each with important issues that merit much closer attention than has hitherto been the case. In Chapter 14, Tony Morrison explores the question of 'emotionally competent organizations' and asks whether they are fallacy, fiction or necessity. His analysis raises a number of important issues about the harm that can be caused by employing organizations that are unaware of, and insensitive to, the complex emotional dynamics that characterize child protection interventions. He succeeds in challenging a number of common assumptions that can be seen to underpin organizational practices and stresses the need for child protection interventions to be understood in the context of organizational dynamics.

John Bates examines a number of points arising from the debate about men's role in childcare practice in Chapter 15. He cautions against the tendency to look for simple solutions to complex problems. Recognizing the need for men to play a part in developing anti-sexist childcare practice, he considers some of the steps that staff need to take to bring this about. In so doing, he highlights some of the complexities of this important aspect of practice. He argues that both men and women have a part to play in developing forms of childcare practice that do not rely on discriminatory stereotypes or oppressive actions and attitudes.

In Chapter 16, Malcolm Jordan draws on his experience as a panel member on numerous inquiries in residential childcare settings. He addresses the important question of risk assessment and the issues surrounding the measures relating to the appointment and support of staff that are designed to play a part in protecting children from institutional forms of abuse. In doing so, he brings into clear focus many of the significant challenges facing residential childcare staff and managers, and provides helpful insights into how these can be effectively managed.

In Chapter 17, Val Capewell makes a contribution that considers the need to recognize foster carers as colleagues with needs and rights, rather than simply a particular form of social service department client. She focuses on the particularly difficult issues that can arise when foster carers are accused of being the perpetrators of abuse. Her insightful analysis poses a number of questions that concerned employers will need to address if they are to avoid some of the very harmful mistakes of the past. She acknowledges that the private nature of fostering offers potential abusers unrivalled opportunities to exploit children in their care, but points out that for most foster carers their position is one of isolation and vulnerability, a position which becomes all too obvious when they are made the subject of allegations of abuse. Capewell offers practical advice gleaned from research by the National Foster Care Association about contracts, training and support, and exhorts workers to recognize and redress the imbalance of power between foster carers and social work agencies by treating them as colleagues not clients.

In the final chapter, Michael Murphy, an experienced child protection trainer and coordinator of staff care services, provides an important discussion of what goes to make up a 'package' of necessary measures in order to ensure at least a basic level of staff care. If the pressures inherent in child protection work are not acknowledged and addressed positively and constructively within a framework of staff care, the costs for all concerned can be very high indeed.

References

Morrison, T. (1994) 'The Emotional Effects of Child Protection Work on the Worker', *Practice*, 4 (4).

Thompson, N., Stradling, S., Murphy, M. and O'Neill, P. (1996) 'Stress and Organizational Culture', *British Journal of Social Work*, 26 (5).

14 Emotionally competent child protection organizations: Fallacy, fiction or necessity?

Tony Morrison

Introduction

A couple of years ago a middle manager summed up the culture of her social work organization in terms that have resonated with every audience that I have subsequently shared it with. She described herself as paid for 'doing' – outputs, tasks and so on; as far as 'thinking' was concerned she should do that at home or at the weekend, but as for 'feeling' she should not bother to do that at all. In other words her organization, typical of many social care organizations in the early 1990s, was one in which two-thirds of the domains of human experience – that is, thinking and feeling – were off organizational limits. The consequences for any social care institution are deeply damaging in terms of critical reasoning, planning, working relationships, reflective analysis, staff stress and motivation. The consequences within a risk management environment, such as child protection, are more worrying still: blunted emotional responsiveness, reduced sensitivity, inadequate reflection, and dangerous decision-making.

Emotional competence is therefore not simply a challenge for individual managers or practitioners, it is also a corporate issue for organizations. Indeed, one might ask whether individuals at any level in the organization can remain emotionally responsive and literate in an agency environment that is emotionally illiterate, blunted, or sometimes more deeply disturbed.

The purpose of this chapter is to explore a number of related themes: the philosophical and emotional context in which child protection organizations are currently operating; the impact of anxiety on agencies, practice and practitioners; and the interplay between client-generated stress, practitioner stresses, and agency culture. It concludes with a number of ideas for promoting healthier organizational conditions. It is hoped, therefore, that the material will be of relevance not only to practitioners, but also to those managing these difficult processes, who are only too aware of the increased toll that child protection work is exacting on the workforce.

The current context of child protection work

It would be hard to overestimate the extent to which the context in which child protection work is operating has changed in the space of only a few years – and certainly since the Cleveland crisis in 1987, and the publication of the subsequent inquiry. There have been fundamental changes both in the philosophy of child welfare and in protection work, as well as in the organizations and structures through which such work is carried out.

As far as child protection is concerned, and sexual abuse more particularly, whilst in the early 1980s the accusation was that intervention was 'too little, too late', post-Cleveland this has given way to a deeper public disquiet that intervention is 'too much, too soon'. Olafson et al. have described such societal responses to sexual abuse in terms of cycles of discovery and suppression in which:

> We behave somewhat like those victims who protect themselves by splitting off and sealing over the memory of their childhood traumas ... despite substantial contemporaneous research on child sexual abuse. (1993, p. 8)

In other words, there is no consensus from society as to how sexual abuse should be managed.

Events in Cleveland became in turn one of the most potent catalysts to the Children Act 1989, which was designed to redress the balance of power in favour of the preservation and support of the family, and away from paternalistic state intervention. 'Partnership' philosophy was thus seen as the solution to the deficits of the child protection process.

However, the Act also retained much of the previous framework for investigating suspected abuse and intervening to protect children, albeit with more robust safeguards to limit what decisions social services can take without the court's sanction. Fox Harding (1991), in her analysis of the Children Act 1989, describes two contrasting tensions within the Act: first, increases in the state's right to intervene in family life are juxtaposed with the 'no order' principle of judicial non-intervention. Secondly, the Act's strong emphasis on working with parents, and defence of the natural family, is counterbalanced by the strengthening of children's rights. Thus, three years after the Act's implementation, whilst figures showed a dramatic reduction in the numbers of *emergency* applications for the removal of children from home, the percentage of children on child protection registers who were looked after by social services had dropped by only 3 per cent, from 23 per cent in 1989 before the Act, to 20 per cent in 1993 two years after the new legislation (Department of Health, 1994). Similarly, figures for numbers on child protection registers reveal that despite a substantial 30 per cent decrease between 1991 and 1993 – mainly due to the removal of one general criterion, 'grave concern' – during the same period there had been an underlying increase of 23 per cent in registrations for the other more specific criteria such as physical and sexual abuse and neglect (Department of Health, 1994). In other words, while gatekeeping has generally improved, there remains a fairly consistent cohort of abused children in need of statutory protection, and an increase in some areas of reporting.

Given the philosophical tensions within the Act, and the trends described above, it is perhaps not surprising that it has proved so difficult to find a consistent definition of 'partnership'. In fact, neither the statute nor official guidance defines the term. So why is this apparently 'user-friendly' and straightforward term so problematic to define and express in practice? The lay person's definition would equate the term with 'joint business' (*Concise Oxford Dictionary*, 1976), sharing, and equality.

However, it is very clear, both in the statute and in the accompanying guidance, that partnership in this context does not mean equality. The state has not abdicated its right to intervene in family life when a child is deemed to be seriously at risk of harm, particularly in cases of sexual abuse, which are seen in the first instance as criminal acts. The UK has not, for example, adopted the principle of family group conferences as in New Zealand, whose legislation is based on a more radical belief in a non-adversarial response to family difficulties.

Further analysis of the concept of partnership by Howe explores distinctions between notions of participation and empowerment:

> To what extent should helpfulness, empowerment and participation be mentioned in the same breath? Is to speak of one to speak of the others? Although they develop similar characteristics, they ought not to be confused as members of the same species. Their evolutions are quite separate but occupying similar ideological niches they have assumed similar shape and form. Practice is likely to become muddled if workers are attracted merely by a concept's looks rather than its intellectual origins. So for example it might be that clients experience participation as fair rather than helpful or that empowerment is a weaselword in child protection if good practice is to be characterised by honest dealings. (1992, p. 39)

He also contrasts a *therapeutic* definition of partnership based on a psychological contract between the parties for change, and a *social justice* contract based on respect, sharing, openness, clarity of roles, responsibilities, accountabilities and involvement in decision-making. So, whilst there has undoubtedly been a sea change in our approach to child protection, with the shift to a partnership ethos, many unresolved questions remain as to precisely what this means in contested situations.

Organizational change

Alongside these philosophical shifts there has been a parallel upheaval in the structures and relationships between all the main child protection agencies. Reforming legislation in health, education and social services against a backcloth of harsh fiscal cutbacks has resulted in extensive decentralization, and the creation of internal markets and competition which have fundamentally altered the relationships between those who purchase services and those delivering them. There has been a shift to competitive market solutions based on the primary values of efficiency, effectiveness and value for money, an erosion of state welfare, and a reappraisal of the very nature of professionalism (Yelloly and Henkel, 1995). These forces have in turn placed an almost intolerable strain on interagency work and the ethos of collaboration which has been at the heart of modern child protection work. Given that, even under reasonable conditions, multi-agency work is not easy, current conditions mean that it is facing its sternest test since its importance was first recognized in the early 1970s.

Hallett and Birchall summarize the situation when they describe the:

> atmosphere of chronic overstrain, unrealistic expectations of staff, desperately inadequate resources to cope with rapidly increased reportage of cases and a limited fund of skills and knowledge confronting rising expectations that abuse should always be successfully managed. (1992, p. 303)

Child protection work is thus being undertaken in an organizational environment which, for many staff, is characterized by rapid and continuous change, occupational insecurity and a preoccupation with survival at both institutional and personal levels. It is the particular impact on practitioners and practice, and the dynamics of managing child protection in an anxious environment, to which we now turn.

The anxious organization

Anxiety runs like a vein throughout the child protection process. It is present in the anxious or unrewarding attachment that forms the family context in which abuse may occur. It is present in the highly charged atmosphere of the parents' first encounter with professionals concerned about their child. It is present too within the professional system, as child abuse represents a crisis not only for the family, but also for the professional network. But anxiety exists not just at the level of the individual but also, as Menzies (1970) has pointed out, as an *organizational* phenomenon, in the organization's struggle for its own survival.

Menzies' research on 'Social Defence Systems' provides a compelling description of the organizational and human effects of managing in such an environment. She states:

The success and viability of a social institution are intimately connected with the techniques it uses to contain anxiety. The needs of the members of the organisation to use it in their struggle against anxiety leads to the development of socially structured defence mechanisms, which appear as elements in the structure, culture and mode of functioning of the organisation. A social defence system develops over time as a result of collusive interaction and agreement between members of the organisation in order to avoid the experience of anxiety, guilt, doubt and uncertainty which are felt to be too deep and dangerous for confrontation. (1970)

Failures at an organizational level to contain anxiety appropriately can permeate all aspects of the agency's work as well as affecting its relations with the outside world and other agencies. This is demonstrated in the Dysfunctional Learning Cycle described by Vince and Martin (1993).

In this environment, anxiety is seen as unprofessional, a sign of weakness or not coping. As a result, uncertainty is suppressed through fight and flight mechanisms. The absence of forums where feelings and doubts can be safely expressed leads to defensiveness, and a resistance to share and reflect on practice. It also undermines confidence to experiment with new forms of practice. (This may go some way to explain why it has proved so difficult to enable staff to relinquish paternalistic practices in favour of more innovatory and participatory approaches.) Emotional defensiveness then deepens into cognitive distortion whereby the painful reality is warded off via denial of dissonant information and attitudes, offering a temporary but false sense of security. If this process worsens with more wilful and sustained ignorance, it may lead eventually to total disengagement. Such systems have the appearance of being psychologically impregnable. The consequences of prolonged engagement in such a dysfunctional coping cycle are deeply damaging for all involved: families, staff, agencies and, most of all, abused children.

These consequences include:

1 *Depersonalisation* as clients cease to be individuals and become statistics;

2   *Detachment and denial* of feelings as the language of intervention becomes bureaucratised into packages and throughput;
3   *Ritual task performance* concerned only with procedural compliance;
4   *Constant counter-checking* in which cases never get beyond assessment;
5   *Redistributing responsibility* through projection and blaming of individuals or other agencies;
6   *Reframing and minimising* the true nature of concern;
7   *Clinging to the familiar* even when it has ceased to be functional (Menzies, 1970).

As Menzies comments, in an observation that rings very true of the child protection system:

> The difficulty has tended to be handled by increased prescription and rigidity. The greater the anxiety, the greater the need for reassurance in rather compulsive repetition. It is unfortunately true of such defence systems that they prevent true insight into the nature of problems and their real seriousness. Thus too often no action can be taken until a crisis is very near or has actually occurred. (1970)

There is of course a powerful link between organizational and personal anxiety, as external insecurities impact on the internal worlds of individuals, and resonate with their own historical and childhood experiences, fears and fantasies. To quote Menzies again: 'The organisational worlds we inhabit reflect the psychic world, the internal society of images and fantasies, conscious and unconscious' (1989, cited in Yelloly and Henkel, 1995, p. 9).

For those working directly with abused children and their families, all the above simply compounds an already highly complex and emotionally demanding process. Indeed, it is the contention of this chapter that the processes of transference and counter-transference which occur for practitioners in direct work with abused children are acutely exacerbated by the parallel processes and dynamics which occur in the organizations in which such work is undertaken. As we look now at some of the processes arising from direct work with abused children, we can begin to draw parallels with similar organizational dynamics.

Gil and Cavanagh-Johnson (1993) identify a number of core transference and counter-transference themes in work with abused children. Transference is the process whereby the client transfers or projects feelings, perceptions or behaviours arising from a previous relationship, onto the worker. Parental relationships are a prime source of transference, especially in the client's current relationships with quasi-parental figures such as social workers or other professionals. Counter-transference can be described as the feelings, perceptions or behaviours generated in the worker either in response to the client's transference or the worker's own unresolved issues.

Transference issues in working with abused children: Worker seen by child as:

1 *Parent/caretaker*: child tests out, or attempts to provoke abusive responses from, the worker.
2 *Sexual object*: child uses sexual behaviour as strategy with the worker to manipulate meeting of child's needs.
3 *Persecutor*: worker seen or perceived as controlling the child.
4 *Judge*: worker seen or experienced as having range of other powers over child, thus making it harder for the child to invest trust in the worker.
5 *Rescuer*: worker seen as all-powerful, and able to prevent any harm.
6 *Colluder in denial*: especially by abusing children or adolescents.
7 *Focal point for all needs*: thus the child needs to behave compliantly or look after worker to ensure she/he is not rejected or abandoned.

These dynamics, with perhaps the exception of being seen as a sexual object, mirror many of the conscious and unconscious expectations that practitioners may have in relation to their own agency. Few new entrants to social work or healthcare are adequately prepared for the realities of organizational life, and often come with idealized hopes of what working for a 'caring' profession will mean. Sadly, this mismatch between expectation and experience is a major cause of stress at a crucial point in their career, and intensifies the nature of the worker's counter-transference responses to children such as described below.

Counter-transference responses by the worker:

1 *Overidentification*: the worker needs to absorb the child's pain, resulting in an absence of psychological boundaries. The child's and the worker's pain are inseparable.
2 *Rescuing*: the worker believes they alone can 'save' child.
3 *Helplessness*: the worker resonates with, and joins, the child's sense of futility and loss of hope.
4 *Anger*: the worker's anger on behalf of the child or him- or herself is, however, suppressed because of lack of permission to express this, and guilt about feeling it in the first place.
5 *Over-controlling behaviour*: This is designed to ward off the worker's anxiety and reflecting of the child's own attempts to control their world.
6 *Victim behaviour*: This is especially likely if the worker has suffered similar traumas to the child, leading to the worker seeing their own abuser in the child, or feeling actually abused by the child. This may result in feelings of isolation, and fears such as 'Sex offenders are everywhere', 'Something is wrong with my child', or 'Something is wrong with me.'

A poignant example of helplessness was provided in a workshop when participants were asked to draw a road map of their own life history, indicating experiences or themes which may have motivated them to enter social work. One woman, a very experienced childcare worker, soon became distressed, as she realised for the first time why her interaction with children whom she had to take into care was so emotionally cold. She had spent extended periods in hospital as a child and recalled the painful memories of her parents leaving when the visiting period was up. When years later she was required, for the first time, to remove a child from home, she could not stop crying. The transference from the child in terms of abandonment, rejection and loss had provoked an overwhelming counter-transference in terms of helplessness in this worker. The worker resolved never to cry again, as a result of which she had learned to switch off emotionally whenever she was involved in similar tasks, a process which she had long felt guilty about. If a tutor, supervisor or trainer had thought to ask her to reflect on what personal issues childcare work was likely to generate for her, this scenario might well never have occurred.

Many of these dynamics are further mediated by factors of gender, race, disability or sexuality, through which personal and agency responses are differentiated and made more problematic. Thus female staff may well identify strongly with the child's experience of men as violators, whilst male staff may struggle with issues of generalized guilt and shame resulting from the same issue. For both, the experience is one that attacks their sense of confidence, self-trust and safety in doing the work, as well as their ability to work with others.

It is also not hard to see the potential impact on the management of risk. Unattended to, such processes can all too easily result in: distorted perceptions and bias; acting out of unexpressed feelings; impaired communication; blurring of facts, feelings and opinions; ignoring information; inadequate analysis; untested assumptions; action based on personal agendas, and polarization of professional networks. It is a prime source of dangerous practice.

Professional dangerousness

Reder et al.'s (1993) analysis of child death inquiries has considerably enriched our understanding of the ways in which the dynamics of abusing families interact with professional systems to increase the dangerousness of such situations, resulting in the mismanagement of high-risk families. Two specific characteristics of abusing families, unresolved care and control problems, are discussed. Many parents of seriously abused children have themselves been subject to emotionally depriving care and/or physically abusive punishment, which are subsequently manifested in their own adult and own parenting relationships in the form of unresolved dependency needs, and major conflicts about control. However, Reder et al. suggest that these care/control problems are further played out through the interactions between such families and the child protection network. Four specific processes in family–professional relationships are identified – dependency; closure; flight, and disguised compliance:

1   *Dependency*: Professionals are drawn into meeting more and more demands from parents, thereby obscuring the child's needs and issues of risk. When, for resource or other reasons, such intensive support is withdrawn, this triggers in the parents early feelings of abandonment, anger and withdrawal.
2   *Closure*: Parents who have a precarious feeling of control over their own lives, when forced to engage in mostly involuntary relationships with the child protection system, may respond by distancing, and closing in on themselves, either temporarily or completely, in an attempt to regain control of the outside world by keeping it out.
3   *Flight*: Parents move home, in some cases travelling to another part of the country, in an effort to maintain control over their relationship with child protection agencies by running away from, and thus fragmenting, the professional network.
4   *Disguised compliance*: Parents neutralize professionals' demands by offering an overt verbal compliance whilst maintaining a covert agenda of delinquent and rebellious behaviour towards the child protection agencies. (Reder et al., 1993)

Thus professionals' well-intentioned attempts to provide care and nurturance for deprived parents, and/or to set boundaries to protect children, may, unintentionally, trigger more dangerous responses from the parents as they struggle with the crisis that threatens to overwhelm their fragile defence systems.

There is, however, a parallel narrative to Reder et al.'s story of the way in which professionals can be drawn into dysfunctional family processes. This parallel narrative has its starting point not in the family, but in the dysfunctional organizational processes, described earlier (see Figure 14.1). For, in agencies where anxiety is not attended to, where feeling and thinking are off-limits, and where management processes may be experienced as non-contingent, neglectful or punitive, care and control conflicts can be an endemic feature of agency life. Thus, when such agencies encounter child abuse, their staff's own organizational and personal care and control conflicts may unwittingly be triggered by the very same dynamics in the families whose children they seek to safeguard (Figure 14.2).

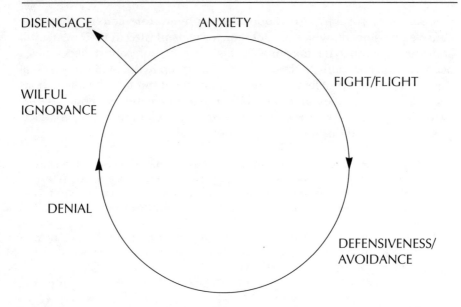

Figure 14.1   Dysfunctional Learning Cycle (Vince and Martin, 1993; reproduced with permission of *Management Education and Development*)

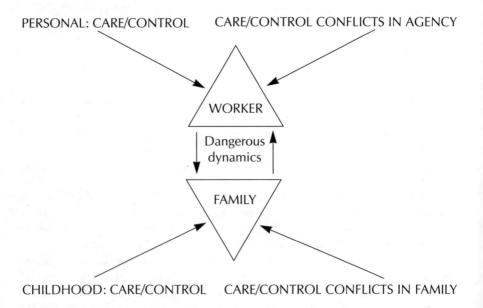

Figure 14.2   Family–agency care/control conflict model

In summary, the front line of today's child protection work is potentially a partnership between two parties, families and professionals, neither of whom feels understood, valued, respected, prepared or supported. This has potentially highly damaging consequences not only for practice, as we have seen, but also for the well-being of staff. To explore this I will to refer to, and elaborate on, an earlier model, the Professional Accommodation Syndrome (Morrison, 1990), to promote an understanding of the interaction between the primary stress of working with abused children, and the secondary stress stemming from the agency's response to these primary stresses.

Professional Accommodation Syndrome

In 1983 Roland Summit published a seminal paper, 'The Child Sexual Abuse Accommodation Syndrome', which offered a model to explain both why children took so long to disclose sexual abuse, and the reasons for some children subsequently retracting their statement (see Figure 14.3).

Briefly stated, Summit showed how the sexually abused child, living in a family system regulated by the perpetrator's dominance and by secrecy, feeling helpless and entrapped by the abuse, sought to resolve this psychological crisis by shifting responsibility for the abuse from the adult(s) to the child. The function of this accommodation is that by choosing to take responsibility for their own abuse the child can attempt to regain some control over the situation – for example: 'It's too awful to contemplate that my father is abusing me, and that my mother knows about it (even if this is not true), as I am powerless to act. If I assume instead that it is my fault (which is what my father has been saying to me) then, if I am good, and do what my father says – that is, keep the secret – then maybe it will stop.'

The effect of accommodating in this way is, unfortunately, further entrapment in the abusive relationship and ensuing delays in disclosure. Because of this, and the conditions under which a disclosure may emerge (family crisis, running away, psychosomatic complaints), the eventual disclosure may be seen by professionals as unconvincing and thus be disbelieved. Faced with doubting professionals and the mounting family crisis surrounding the disclosure, for which the child is now also made responsible, the solution is for the child to retract. The perpetrator's denial and the rule of secrecy are thus sustained, both of which serve to deepen the child's future vulnerability to abuse. The inadequate response of the professional system acts as a secondary form of victimization, and worsens the damage done by the original primary source of victimization.

However, Summit's powerful model can be adapted to enable us to understand more general processes of victimization and staff stress, and it is

---

(5) RETRACTION

(4) DELAYED OR
UNCONVINCING
DISCLOSURE

(3) ENTRAPMENT AND
ACCOMMODATION

(2) HELPLESSNESS

(1) SECRECY

Figure 14.3   Sexual Abuse Accommodation Syndrome (Summit, 1983)

particularly useful for child protection staff because it draws on the dynamics of abuse. It can be applied to managers, teams and organizations, not just in social work agencies but in virtually any care setting. Thus, in its reworked version, the Professional Accommodation Model works as follows, based on the same five stages:

1   *Secrecy*: Many staff hesitate to speak about the impact of the work on them because they feel or know that the agency or colleagues covertly or overtly deny them permission to do so.
2   *Helplessness*: Staff who feel helpless in relation to their work, or in the face of stress arising from it, feel a sense of shame. They experience the agency's rejection and dislike of their helplessness, and receive the message that those in the helping professions are paid to be copers. The agency's belief system is that uncomplaining workers are OK. Myths exist that trained staff should act logically, rationally and objectively. Gender stereotyping in agencies sees women who express stress as 'hysterical' or 'victims', and men as 'wimps' or 'little boys'. Features of race, disability or sexuality create yet other pejorative stereotypes.
3   *Entrapment and accommodation*: Staff are trapped in a dilemma in which telling the truth about their stress is seen as 'unprofessional', whilst denying that they feel stress is seen as coping and professional. In the face of this, staff are forced to accommodate by then deciding that the fault lies not with the agency's insensitivity, or with the nature of their work, but with themselves for feeling as they do, failing to cope, and generally not being sufficiently robust. The answer appears then to lie in suppressing their feelings, invalidating their experiences, and working harder.

4 *Delayed or unconvincing disclosure*: Disclosure of the distress may eventually be triggered by conflict, training, illness or talking with colleagues. Where conflict is the trigger, this may be in the form of unpredictable behaviour such as atypical aggression, lateness, sickness or sudden resignation. If this behaviour is only understood at a superficial level, and not as a signal of a more prolonged underlying distress, it may result in actual or perceived responses such as 'She should never have been a social worker/teacher/nurse anyway' or 'If you can't stand the heat get out of the kitchen.' The difficulty for managers and the agency is that, as Figure 14.4 shows, it is not until this point that any obvious signs of problems appear, and the fact that the presenting behaviour may well be a problem in its own right. The surface behaviour, however, is like the tip of the iceberg, below which there may lie a history of distress which has progressed through secrecy, helplessness and accommodation, and whose diagnostic signs have been both subtle and ambiguous. If the worker does leave the agency, he or she may well take to their new job these unresolved experiences, which will, unbeknown to their new employer, render the worker additionally vulnerable to stress. Some career patterns seem to be driven by a series of ever more rapid cycles of delayed disclosure-flight.

5 *Retraction*: The delayed or confusing nature of the disclosure, if followed by insensitive, ignoring or disbelieving responses in the agency, leaves the worker psychologically and professionally abandoned, fearing that he or she will now be written off as incompetent. In the face of this threat

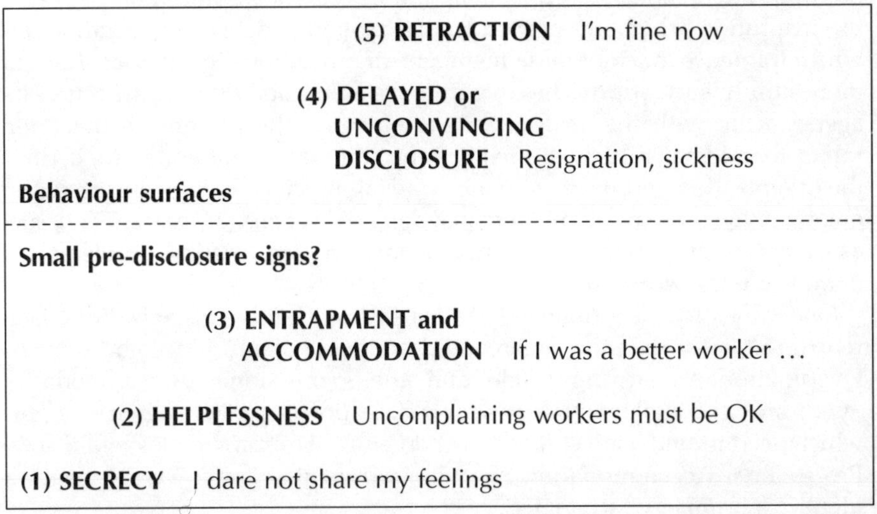

---

(5) RETRACTION   I'm fine now

**(4) DELAYED or
UNCONVINCING
DISCLOSURE**   Resignation, sickness

Behaviour surfaces

- -

Small pre-disclosure signs?

**(3) ENTRAPMENT and
ACCOMMODATION**   If I was a better worker ...

(2) HELPLESSNESS   Uncomplaining workers must be OK

(1) SECRECY   I dare not share my feelings

Figure 14.4   Professional Accommodation Model (Morrison, 1990, adapted)

to their whole career the only solution appears to be retraction: 'I'm fine now, it was just the time of the month' or 'I'm fine now, it was nothing to do with work.' Secrecy resumes and the entrapment deepens as a result of the experience of being punished for disclosing, which, of course, confirms the original belief system about the agency.

This model suggests that, with the exception of traumatic forms of primary stress, for example assault by a client, the critical dimensions of stress in child protection work do not arise primarily from work with clients, but in the agency's responses to the strong but normative feelings and fears which such work engenders. Normative anxieties become pathologized in such agency cultures, and solutions, if restricted to the provision of counselling, serve to reinforce the same message – that only 'inadequate' workers complain.

Towards emotionally competent organizations

Although approaches to organizational theory have tended to stress directional and structural aspects as being crucial to organizational well-being, other literature (Menzies, 1970; Vince and Martin, 1993) has emphasized the emotional and cognitive life of the organization operating at both conscious and unconscious levels. These approaches, drawing from group analytic and open systems theories, explore the impact on the agency of group interactions, and the acting out of the images and fantasies about the institution which are carried by the members of the organization and which influence much of these members' organizational behaviour. To put it more simply, such approaches integrate the *feeling* and *thinking* aspects of the agency's life with the *doing/task* focus. Indeed, the premise is that more rather than less is achieved if feeling and thinking are attended to, because the organization and its staff are not wasting precious energy and resources on organizational, social and personal defence systems (Menzies, 1970), such as denial or projection, which in fact only worsen existing problems and demotivate the workforce.

One way of conceptualizing the nature of healthy organizations is to return to two of the models already described, namely Vince and Martin's Dysfunctional Learning Cycle and the Professional Accommodation Syndrome, and explore strategies for the creation of positive agency cultures which need to underpin child protection work. Thus, if we look again at the Professional Accommodation Syndrome, from this angle we can begin to identify a number of strategies:

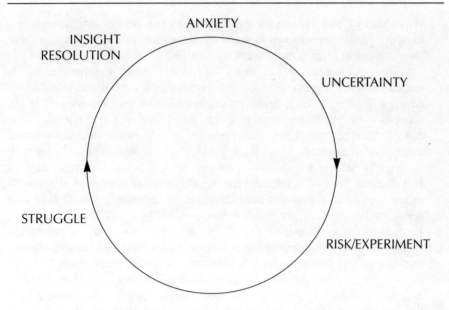

Figure 14.5 Functional Learning Cycle (Vince and Martin, 1993; reproduced with permission of *Management Education and Development*)

1 *From secrecy to openness*: If secrecy is where problems start, then the promotion of openness, by a variety of means, is the first objective in a healthy organization. This can be linked to Vince and Martin's Functional Learning Cycle (Figure 14. 5).

In this culture, anxiety and stress are openly acknowledged and seen as normative, allowing for the expression of healthy uncertainty, and difference, where problems and 'mistakes' are opportunities for learning, not punishment. Risks are taken and innovations are attempted. The unresolvable nature of many issues is openly acknowledged and struggled with, from which unexpected or creative resolution may come. In consequence of this, staff are empowered to tackle further demands.

In other words, the organization is managed in ways that acknowledge anxiety as an institutional, and not just an individual, phenomenon. This approach is therefore not primarily about the provision of staff counselling services, although this has a place, but is much more about the quality of management, so that the organization knows what its job is, knows where it is going, and equips its staff to get there. This happens through the provision of an effective infrastructure for practice: goals; values; leadership; structures; policies; resources, and effective human resource management. Time does not permit a discussion of these elements but, clearly, agency culture and structures are interdependent. Healthy processes will not happen in agencies that do not know where they are going or how they want to get there.

However, one specific element that does require mentioning is the critical role of supervision in the creation of a positive climate for practice. It is essential to reaffirm, as a profession, that supervision is the worker's most important helping relationship, and is, for the organization, the most important process by which thinking, feeling and doing are integrated. At an individual level, supervision is the vehicle through which anxiety is contained and held. It is also, far more so than training, the primary means for the development of competence and self-efficacy in staff. Openness cannot thrive in the absence of skilled and sensitive supervisory processes (Morrison, 1993).

2 *From helplessness to empowerment*: Helplessness needs to be combated through a range of empowerment strategies, central to which must be the notion that a primary buffer to stress and burn-out is self-efficacy. It is of little value to allow staff to ventilate feelings if they are not enabled to acquire sufficient knowledge and skills to do the job. They will remain helpless in the face of their incompetence. However, empowerment is also about acknowledging, valuing and utilizing difference within the workforce, and therefore it is concerned with making explicit issues of inequality and power. Working together means contact between differing emotional realities, different systems of meaning and different types of bias. Consequently, women and men, black and white, disabled and able-bodied, gay and straight have to address differential experiences of power and powerlessness as aspects of the organizational practice and learning (Vince and Martin, 1993).

3 *From accommodation to clarity*: Entrapment and accommodation is essentially a process of cognitive distortion whereby responsibilities and distinctions between 'me' and 'not me' become blurred and confused. The result is individuals taking too much responsibility for processes that are not within their control: 'If I had visited that child, she wouldn't have been abused.' However, because these are cognitive processes they may be well hidden, revealing only the most subtle of clues. The underlying strategy here must be about making the worker's thinking, beliefs, assumptions, fantasies or fears explicit so that they can be tested against external realities, facts, values, limitations, policies and expectations. Only by doing so can clarity and an appropriate sense of role and responsibility be regained. At an organizational level, continuing attention to role clarity is essential, given that role ambiguity and confusion are highly correlated with stress and burn-out.

4 *From delayed disclosure to restoration*: At this point there is a dual need. First, the presenting behaviour needs to be understood, as a potential

sign of distress, and as a consequence of the worker going through the previous stages. However, it is also possible that the worker's problems in fact do not originate within the workplace, but elsewhere such as at home. It is very important, then, that a sensitive and intelligent analysis is sought as to the reasons for the behaviour, in order that the worker feels that any cry for help is heard, and to identify any organizational/supervisory deficits or problems that have contributed to the behaviour. Secondly, it is vital to restore the worker to positive functioning as quickly as possible, even if this includes making clear the need to change the behaviour, alongside the provision of support, training, co-work or possibly counselling where appropriate. The overriding aim is to prevent a move to retraction.

5 *From retraction to prevention*: Once retraction has occurred, the aim is primarily preventative, to open up communication and make opportunities for openness and sharing of feelings more accessible in the future, accepting the worker's current statement that everything is now OK. Particular attention should be paid to the quality and safety of the supervisory relationship, and any specific support needs required by the worker. For example, black workers should be entitled and assisted in establishing support groups. It may be useful to examine with the worker whether they have had similar experiences in other settings which have not been resolved. However, as with the previous stage, every effort needs to be made to enable the worker to regain their confidence and sense of self-efficacy in the workplace as soon as possible. This may mean a sensitive review of the size and appropriateness of their workload.

Many of these strategies need to be implemented at a corporate level, for Pearlin and Schooler (1978, p. 18) state: 'Work problems are intertwined with the social structure and organisation of the workplace, and thus require collective, rather than individual solutions.' These must start at the organizational level, and clearly senior managers have a major responsibility, but the strategies must also work their way down to smaller work units. At a strategic level, there are four priorities as far as combating stress is concerned:

1 Raising awareness.
2 Developing interpersonal management skills.
3 Redesigning unhelpful structures.
4 Training. (HEA, 1988)

At a team level, one simple suggestion is for each local work unit/team to use the Professional Accommodation Model to analyse unhelpful processes, and then to generate a Team Health Plan based around the five stages described above: openness, empowerment, clarity, restoration and prevention.

Conclusion

Plainly there are no quick fixes or standardized remedies for the complex emotional turbulence of child protection work. What is clear, however, is that such processes are best understood as a triangular interaction involving agency, clients and workers. As such, the question is not whether organizations should be concerned for their emotional health but how to grow healthy organizational environments. This chapter has sought to provide models that may catalyse discussion, energy and action towards a vision of emotionally competent organizations. But, through it all, we should keep Tonnesman's words in mind:

> The human encounter in the helping professions is inherently stressful. The stress aroused can be accommodated and used for the good of our clients. But our emotional responsiveness will wither if the human encounter cannot be contained within the institutions within which we work. Defensive manoeuvres will then become operative and these will prevent healing. By contrast if we can maintain contact with the emotional reality of our clients and ourselves, then the human encounter can facilitate not only a healing experience, but also an enriching experience for them and us. (1979, cited in Morrison, 1993, p. 117)

References

Department of Health (1994) *Children and Young People on Child Protection Registers, Year Ending 31 March 1993*, London: Government Statistical Service.

Fox Harding, L., (1991) 'Underlying Themes and Contradictions in the Children Act 1989', *Justice of the Peace*, 15 September.

Gil, E. and Cavanagh-Johnson, T. (1993) *Sexualized Children: Assessment and Treatment*, Rockville, MD: Launch Press.

Hallett, C. and Birchall, E. (1992) *Coordination and Child Protection: A Review of the Literature*, London: HMSO.

HEA (1988) *Stress in the Public Sector*, London: Health Education Authority.

Howe, D. (1992) 'Theories of Helping, Empowerment and Participation', in Thoburn (1992).

Menzies, I. (1970) *The Functioning of Groups as a Defence against Anxiety*, London: Tavistock.

Morrison, T. (1990) 'The Emotional Effects of Child Protection on the Worker', *Practice*, 4 (4).

Morrison, T. (1993) *Supervision in Social Care*, London: Longman.

Olafson, E., Corwin, D. and Summit, R. (1993) 'Modern History of Child Sexual Abuse', *Child Abuse and Neglect*, 17 (1), pp. 7–24.

Pearlin, L. and Schooler, C. (1978) 'The Structure of Coping', *Journal of Health and Social Behaviour*, 19 March, pp. 1–23.

Reder, P., Duncan, S. and Gray, S. (1993) *Beyond Blame*, London: Routledge.

Summit, R. (1983) 'The Child Sexual Abuse Accommodation Syndrome', *Child Abuse and Neglect*, 7 (2), pp. 177–93.

Thoburn, J. (ed.) (1992) *Participation in Practice: Involving Families in Child Protection*, Norwich: University of East Anglia.

Vince, R. and Martin, L. (1993) 'Inside Action Learning', *Management Education and Development*, 24 (3) pp. 205–15

Yelloly, M. and Henkel, M. (1995) *Learning and Teaching in Social Work: Towards Reflective Practice*, London: Jessica Kingsley.

15 Men, masculinity and childcare

John Bates

Introduction

This chapter discusses the nature of masculinity, particularly in relation to men and their relationship with women and children, and in their roles as workers in the personal social services. In terms of safety and the risks involved, the issue of the appropriateness of men working with children is not a new one, as Pringle has noted:

> a recognition of the role of gender in the occurrence of sexual abuse calls into question the safety of children in any welfare setting where males are present as carers and/or therapists, not merely the residential sector. The implications for such an analysis in terms of policy and practice may be dramatic as regards the future role of men in welfare systems. (1992, p. 4)

Nevertheless, this chapter begins with the premise that tighter guidelines for men working with abused and 'damaged' children may only be one part of a more complex issue. This complexity arises from a recognition that many aspects of the social and psychological construction of masculinity are highly problematic in the ways in which they are manifested within the personal social services. The chapter explores some implications of this recognition and concludes with a selection of strategies for working which attempt to begin the process of revising and realigning the nature of men's work with men, women and children.

The development of awareness

During a recent workshop on anti-discriminatory practice a male residential childcare worker related an interesting story. He was an experienced worker in a senior position who was wrestling with the complex issues around practising in an anti-discriminatory way. He was attempting to challenge traditional stereotypes and introduce practices into his unit that were less oppressive to both the young women residents and his women colleagues. On duty one day, he was asked to intervene after several of the other staff had failed to calm a disturbed young man who had become abusive and violent, and who had begun to mutilate himself. Although the worker was a gentle man and physically small, the young man's behaviour became so risky that it became necessary to resort to physical restraint. After some time, when the young man had calmed down and been reassured, the incident appeared to be over. However, later on, three colleagues (two women and one man) came to him and complimented him on his actions in restraining this difficult resident. Superficially this might seem unremarkable but for the fact that their praise was not for his social work skills but for his physical prowess, and by implication his masculinity. Over the next few days, this scenario was repeated as several other of the young male residents also appeared to reassess their perceptions of him in a similar fashion.

This worker's experience was confirmed by other social workers in the discussion group, who also anecdotally confirmed the predominance of the perception that residential childcare was primarily a masculine activity, with women workers often being regarded as being too weak and fragile for the rigours of the job. This chauvinistic perception has been noted by other writers. Ruxton, for example, reports one male worker as stating: 'they didn't want me because they wanted a caring man, they wanted me primarily as a strong disciplinarian father figure . . . wait 'till your dad gets home – that's what it felt like' (1992, p. 27). Similarly, Bowl observed that: 'residential social work can be an aggressively male ritual, revolving round strong masculine father figures' (1985, p. 6).

Within the workshop, the discussion moved to the alarming number of scandals over recent years, mostly involving men abusing children in their care. All of the participants had at least one recollection of abuse being committed by welfare professionals on children they had worked with. Their concerns about men as abusers are confirmed by studies both in Britain and the United States (NSPCC, 1992; Nunno and Rindfleisch, 1991; Rosenthal et al., 1991). For example, Finkelhor (1990) estimated that 98 per cent of abuse on female children and 83 per cent of abuse on male children was carried out by males, and McFadden and Ryan noted that one of the few factors to show a reliable relationship with the incidence of sexual abuse is the gender of the head of the household. They stated that 'there was a very low incidence of sexual abuse in families headed by a single woman' (1991, p. 221). Rosenthal et al. (1991), in their study of abuse in residential homes, found that the perpetrators were predominantly men. Of course, some women do abuse, and this is an aspect which needs more attention, but, as a proportion set against male abuse, it remains a very small part of the picture.

The male participants in the workshop expressed their deep unease at the apparently unending series of scandals which had been revealed during the 1980s and 1990s. Events in Clwyd and Leicestershire children's homes and other incidents in schools, church organizations, residential units for people with learning difficulties and youth clubs had created a sense of despair and despondency amongst many of the workers. They felt that much of what was good about their services and their jobs was being devalued by this procession of malpractice and abuse. However, their unease had deeper roots. In part, it stemmed from a growing awareness that perhaps these events were not simply the actions of a few bad apples, but derived from more complex roots. They were beginning to realize that neither the problems nor the 'solutions' lay solely with other people, that they themselves might be implicated in the need for change. This, as Pugh has noted, is a characteristic feature of anti-discriminatory perspectives on practice – that is, the realization by social workers that 'their work is not automatically beneficial in its consequences: that they might be part of the problem, not the solution' (1996, p. 108). The influence of feminist theory is clear: the decentring of the worker dramatically switches the focus from workers 'as the agents of change', to their becoming 'the subjects for change!' (Pugh, 1996, p. 91).

This glimmering of consciousness in the male participants in the workshop heralded the realization that perhaps they were embarking upon an uncomfortable exploration of the patriarchal values and sexist ideologies embedded in their own personal, social and cultural patterns of identity and existence. As Mason and Mason have noted:

> While men who work in the 'helping' profession are not stereotypical macho heroes and may appear to be more sensitive than many men, we have not escaped this socialisation . . . men in the helping profession are probably just more subtle about sexism. (1990, p. 212)

Cause and culpability?

Clearly, the group were beginning to realize that these problems of abuse involved much broader issues of causality and, ultimately perhaps, a reframing of the very nature of masculinity. As the facilitator, my role was to build positively upon this insight and keep the group from getting stuck in an overly simplistic position of blaming. While blaming may seem like an attractive proposition, especially to those who have suffered the depredations inflicted by men, it is ultimately futile. Instead of stimulating positive change, it encourages either defensiveness or hopelessness. Nevertheless, as these men were beginning to realize, sexism is not a phenomenon constructed solely by 'monsters'. They, like all men, had a responsibility to examine their own actions as well as those of other men.

Many men still prefer to consider male abusers as aberrant 'perverts', beyond the boundaries of normal experience, and that stricter professional criteria, better training, clearer rules on appropriate touching and more rigorous police checking should be sufficient to eliminate abuse. However, this can be seen to be a mistaken conceit, one which may be employed to avoid any self-critical examination of the nature of masculinity. For, as Cameron and Frazer suggest, there is a common thread uniting male abusers: 'a shared construction of masculine sexuality, or even more broadly, masculinity in general' (1990, p. 9). Teague (1993), in a study of convicted rapists, showed the 'normality' of most rapists' personalities. For the most part, they were not the 'beasts' portrayed in the media, but men alarmingly like the rest of the male population. Teague accepts the premise most notably stated by feminist writers like Brownmiller (1975) and Chesler (1990), that rape is not primarily about sexual satisfaction but is about power. It is about men demonstrating and inflicting their power on women. From this premise, it is possible to see how rapists, while committing apparently deviant and depraved behaviour, can be conceptualized as being merely at the furthest extreme of a continuum of attitudes which also encompasses 'normal' behaviour. Teague quotes Ussher (1991):

> [these men] . . . don't sprout horns. Rapists, sexual murderers and paedophiles do not look like monsters. They cannot be identified by . . . their marked difference from other men. (1993, p. 8)

This is supported by Wyre (1986) who, in his direct work with sexual offenders, has noted that many of them hold views about women which reflect the views of most men in society at large. Of course, there might be other common factors but, as Pringle (1992) found in his review of the research into perpetrators, there do not appear to be common predictors of future perpetrators. For example, he challenges the notion that a history of abuse in childhood is in itself a reliable predictor of future behaviour. It is probable, therefore, that it is the feminist and social constructionist views of masculinity which offer more convincing accounts of the reasons for male violence and abuse. In these accounts, contemporary representations of masculinity are seen as intrinsically supporting the subjugation of women through the objectification of sexuality and, ultimately, through violence or the threat of it. The following section begins to unpack some of the strands of representation which tell particular 'stories' about men and women in our society.

Unpacking the narratives

The roots of the dominant masculine culture can be found in what Smart and Smart refer to as the:

> prevailing material conditions, cultural values, customs and social practices, such as the differential socialisation of male and female children within the family, schooling, forms of speech and language, media propagated stereotypes and other numerous seemingly innocuous processes. (1976, p. 12)

Many social scientists who write about male violence on women and children often present a narrative that belies blame or fails to attribute responsibility. Lamb, in a review of journal articles on men who 'batter' women, suggests that many social scientists tend to use the 'ubiquitous passive voice . . . which presents acts without agents, harm without guilt' (1991, p. 192). Often the severe injuries inflicted upon women were referred to as being the result of 'domestic' or 'spousal' violence, as if there were joint responsibility for what has occurred, rather than a violent act inflicted by one person upon another. This type of masking of actions by the use of language is frequently used to obscure the exercise of power (Pugh, 1996). Similarly, Hooper (1987) shows how the language used about incest often portrays men as 'victims' of their families. She notes how women are variously described as 'setting up' the conditions for incest by 'keeping themselves tired', or going to work, or into hospital. Hooper describes how some perpetrators who had been cast into the role of primary carers by unemployment gave masked accounts of their behaviour, in which they suddenly found themselves touching their daughters' genitals. In this way they sought to avoid culpability. Alternatively, the facts of abuse may be hidden behind the language of disease, being seen as a 'symptom' of family dysfunction rather than holding men responsible for the choices they make about their own behaviour.

The significance of language in constructing particular narratives or accounts of events cannot be underestimated, for not only can it be used to mask events, it can also be employed in ways which, intentionally or otherwise, disempower women. French (1992) refers to research into women's refuges and points out that the implications of portraying women as 'victims' when seeking funding continues to present them as being weak and 'helpless'. One further consequence is that such narratives conveniently support the mushrooming of professionals who become experts on 'family violence'. French points out that the clear association between masculinity, violence and indecency is rarely commented upon. In much of the media coverage of the horrendous murders of women by Frederick West, there was relatively little discussion of West's misogynistic views, and little analysis of the culture which may have shaped him. While some commentators did wonder how this apparently ordinary man could be capable of such vile acts, West was largely presented as an aberration, as someone beyond the normal realm of society. In terms of the scale of his atrocities, he clearly was 'abnormal', but in terms of the nature of his actions and his own accounts of them, his comments revealed that he was much like other perpetrators. During the trial, for example, tape recordings of West revealed his belief that all women were just interested in sex and that his victims had forced themselves on him. Teague's (1993) work with rapists revealed that many of them made similar comments, variously stating that they believed that women 'need to be raped'; 'want to be raped'; 'it teaches them a lesson'; 'shows them who is boss', and that 'they provoke it anyway so they deserve to be raped'. Teague develops this point by stating that: 'If these are simply cognitive distortions then the whole of male culture would appear to be distorted', because these views seem to be widely held beyond the ranks of convicted rapists and murderers.

Analysis of the actions of the media indicates some fundamental ambiguities in the representations of sexuality and gender. These were exemplified during the harrowing court proceedings in the West case. On one day in court, a frightened young woman gave evidence that Fred West had tried to look up her skirt whilst she was cycling home from school, and the media duly reported this as evidence of his perversion. Yet, the very next day, several newspapers pruriently printed a photograph of Hillary Clinton sitting down in a manner which accidentally revealed her underwear (Campbell, 1995). How is it that editors who reported the terror and embarrassment of a young schoolgirl failed to make any connection between the indecencies of West and their own actions in printing the photograph?

This was not an isolated instance of public dissociation and ambiguity. There have been many cases of horrifying violence perpetrated by men on women and children in which an insensitive judiciary and media thoughtlessly continue to present derogatory views of women. Teague (1993) cites the grotesque comments of the judge who, when sentencing Nicholas Boyce to imprisonment for manslaughter after killing his wife, described him as a *'man of reasonable self control'* (emphasis added) who had been provoked into killing her. The full obscenity of this description can only be fully grasped with a knowledge of what was said of Boyce's actions – that: 'You cut her up with a saw and boiled her skin and bones. You bagged up the pieces and over the next two days disposed of the body.'!

There have been numerous other examples of victim-blaming, especially in the reporting of offences against women. In one notorious case, a man received a light sentence because of the 'contributory negligence' of the victim who was portrayed as being reckless, as she had worn a short skirt. While these examples are conspicuous, in the sense that they were noted and remarked upon publicly, much of what the judiciary does passes without comment. Teague speculates that the judiciary have a structural role in maintaining the gender-based uneven distribution of power, and that their actions often implicitly legitimate male violence towards women.

Constructing gender and constructing masculinity

The constructionist analysis of gender adopted in this chapter is one which rejects the notion that there is any biological or innate disposition to attitudes and behaviours. However, it does recognize that this social differentiation is constructed upon the base of the biological distinction of male and female secondary sexual characteristics. Masculinity is therefore intrinsically a social construction which stratifies gender-specific roles and expectations by defining what is 'normal' behaviour for both men and women (Thompson, 1993), and this social structuring essentially subjugates women. This subjugation or derogation of women occurs in many different ways, but primarily it operates, not from the initial distinction of sex – that is, of male and female – but from the gender distinction, of masculine and feminine, of men and women. As Miedzan indicates, there is a prevailing 'sociocultural assumption, often unconscious, that male behaviour is the norm and constitutes a paradigm for human behaviour, female behaviour being viewed as deviant or defective' (1992, p. 25). From the outset, femininity is often defined as the absence of masculinity. This form of gender apartheid does not lead to perceptions of women as separate but equal, but to a perception of them as separate and inferior. The problem, of course, is the apparent 'normalness' of masculinity. Like the wallpaper, it is no longer noticed, so why bother to examine something that seems so self-evident? The answer is: because it is highly probable that male socialization and masculine culture are contributing factors to abusive behaviour by men.

Masculinity is a complex cluster of expectations that lay out the ground rules of how men should behave (norms), and how they should think (attitudes). The following subsections examine three of the most powerful aspects of masculinity.

Emotional 'hardness'

The reluctance of men to explore their feelings and express their vulnerability is well documented. Hite's (1987) survey of 4,500 women in the USA found that 98 per cent felt the biggest problem in their current relationship was a lack of emotional closeness with their male partner. For many men, the idea of masculinity revolves around the perception of being 'in control' of themselves and of other people and things. Thus, the direct expression of 'tender' emotions exposes their potential vulnerability to being hurt by other people. The implications of this are obvious. Because men are unlikely to expose their feelings if they think these will be abused, they may not only find it difficult to express the full range of emotions, but they will only do so in particular circumstances, and then often only with great difficulty. Hence, relationships with women and other men, which are not primarily sexual ones, will frequently be obstructed by the lack of direct expression of those feelings which could enhance trust, and facilitate support. Instead, men cultivate the carapace of 'hardness'. The iconic behaviour conveyed by Clint Eastwood in most of his earlier films epitomizes this desired persona.

This 'hardness' can also restrict close associations with children and colleagues, especially when combined with men's fears about their own sexual identity. Thus, while there may be sound reasons for being wary of emotionally close relationships with children in childcare work for fear of wrongful allegations, some men nevertheless often approach their work in ways which preclude even the possibility of effective relationships. Thompson (1995) has noted how the fear of being labelled as homosexual if a close relationship develops with another man also operates to limit the possibilities.

The instability of male identity

It has been argued that male identity is inherently unstable, being built around elements of masculinity that are themselves oppressive (Jackson, 1982; Bowl, 1985; Thompson, 1995). The centrality of competitiveness, competence, aggression and objectification creates a masculinity characterized by anxiety and instability. Failure to impress, compete or acknowledge competence, particularly in areas of sexuality, may well lead to inadequacies and fears which, not surprisingly, can then be projected onto women and children.

Other writers, like French, suggest that this instability is due to the fact that men strive for the appearance of manhood which involves postures of dominance and oppression. She continues:

Such behaviour suggests men believe 'manhood' is not inherent in a man, but depends on both the opinion of other men and the existence of a subjugated person. Male identity is therefore extremely unstable, and this instability creates anxiety, often expressed as rage. (1992, p. 183)

Socialization, stereotyping and derogation of women

The role of stereotypes in maintaining oppression and disadvantage is well documented (Thompson, 1993), and similarly the transmission of these stereotypes through the media, education and childrearing is also well known (French, 1992; Burck and Speed, 1995). The net effect, as Schein has suggested, is that: 'Boys and men are taught to despise and control the values and behaviours that are not considered masculine. As feminine traits are clearly not included in this category, this hatred transforms male behaviours and attitudes into violence and misogyny (hatred of women)' (1977, p. 69). The stereotyping of men and women into commonly accepted gender roles is clear for all to see in social work agencies and in children's services particularly. Ruxton (1992) talks of men working in caring situations who are afraid of being labelled homosexual. The perception that they have in some way 'failed' to make it in a real man's job is a fear acknowledged by Savage, writing of the male nurse:

He is emasculated by taking on 'women's work' in which he is expected to demonstrate 'feminine qualities' such as caring and gentleness and, in which, at least to begin with, he will be subordinate to women. And if his masculinity is in question, so too is his sexuality. (1987, p. 76)

Résumé

Before considering how we might change our practice, it is worth recapitulating the main points covered in the first part of this chapter, namely that:

- the majority of abuse on women and children is inflicted by men;
- guidelines and codes of practice are probably ineffective in protecting children in schools and welfare agencies;
- the profiles of violent and abusing men are indistinguishable from men in general;
- all men have the potential to abuse and violate;
- gender is a social construction not a biological or 'natural' one; because of this it can be amended;
- male workers may have to engage in a critique of the very essence of

masculinity at a personal, cultural and structural level if they are to retain credibility as childcare workers.

Changing our practice

Thompson (1995) argues that childcare workers must acknowledge the central role that male power plays in relationships with colleagues, children and the agencies in which they work, if the status quo is not to be perpetuated and reinforced. The six strategies that follow are based on Thompson's (1995) paper:

Avoid exclusion

This applies not only to the language men use which reinforces male supremacy but also to the way men behave. Men cannot dominate women without maintaining a unity against them, so it is important that men begin to learn to avoid exclusive male rituals and sexist terminology like referring to women colleagues as 'girls'. When male staff respond to a situation that may require physical restraint, it is essential that this is not done in a way that celebrates macho supremacy, for 'many women struggle to establish their competence as workers, or are hindered in their efforts to maintain or develop alternative forms of positive control when men behave this way' (Pugh, 1988, p. 14).

For men involved in childcare, it also means rejecting practices that involve the macho (and sometimes violent) initiation of young men into manhood or the treating of them as subordinates. It is grown men alone who initiate young men into masculine adulthood and the worst behaviour is usually practised in the company of other men. Male workers need to involve boys and girls and women colleagues on equal terms by rejecting the notion that men can only find meaning in other men through such things as clubs, cults and games.

Women, of course, also have a responsibility. The job of redefining masculinity and creating a more gentle, equitable society must be a joint activity. The increased divorce rate has ensured that more children are being brought up by women on their own, and many children in the welfare system will be cared for by women. Women too must become actively involved in order to try to give boys, in particular, an opportunity to grow and develop in ways which will allow them to become the sort of men our daughters will want to know.

Debunk stereotypes

The perpetuation of stereotypes is pervasive. It is vital to examine and challenge stereotypical assumptions such as the traditional roles people play in childcare and the differing expectations we hold for boys and girls. Childcare practitioners should encourage young women to take control of *their* sexuality and not have it decided for them by men. This may mean the discouragement of allowing the display of sexist posters or calendars by young males in children's homes, youth groups and so on.

In addition, social work with children demands that all staff – men and women – have to find ways to support young males in dealing with the impossible contradictory demands of growing up in a sexist society. As Phillips argues:

> What do you say to a twelve year old boy who is afraid to go to school because some kids have threatened him? How do you encourage a boy to stand up for himself when the only available means of doing so is to hit back? How do you protect a boy who has refused to fight and, as a result, been beaten up? (1993, p. 19)

Involve men in families and family work and women in organizations

The separation and allocation of different roles for men and women are evident. It is important to challenge the divide by encouraging men to become more active in family activities and women to become more involved in organizations. Men should encourage and support women, for example, in promotional struggles and be especially assertive in examining working relationships, pay scales and issues of power and status within the workplace.

The intrinsic sexism in some approaches to counselling and therapeutic models needs to be acknowledged and avoided. As the work of Lamb (1991) cited earlier indicates, some therapists discuss male violence and abuse as if both perpetrator and victim were jointly and equally responsible for the actions of the man. Feminist writers have offered valuable insights in analysing and deconstructing the received truths about family social work, and their work can provide useful material for workshop and discussion groups (Burck and Speed, 1995; Jones, 1995). As Burck and Speed point out, despite efforts to integrate anti-discriminatory practice into practitioners' mind-sets, the acquisition of knowledge does not, by itself, guarantee action. Without a profound change in our orientation to practice, it is likely that the critical insights of feminism will remain:

a tokenist addendum . . . a superficial nod in the direction of 'gender roles', leaving untouched the difficult and risky territory of the social and political construction of gender, and the role played by therapists in the maintenance, adaptation or subversion of family systems which may operate to the advantage or disadvantage of some or all of its members. (1995, p. 11)

Avoid 'masculinism'

For men to develop and to rethink masculinity, a great deal of unlearning is required. Masculinity provides a sense of personal wholeness or, as Giddens (1993) describes it, 'ontological security'. This holistic sense of a personal integrity becomes challenged at times of stress or when being confronted. The option to retreat behind male defences seems attractive but has to be avoided. As I discussed earlier, a common aspect of male socialization is the need to prove oneself in male company by taking risks, or showing fearlessness. Men in childcare have a unique vantage point from which to begin the process of undoing such damaging behaviour and offering models of masculinity that reject such practices. By giving young males models of manhood that are essentially gentle, non-confrontational and non-violent, there is a hope that this collective courage can begin the process of offering a more acceptable face of masculinity. For example, male workers who do not respond to provocation with macho posturing can offer young men a model of behaviour that shows it is possible to deal with problems without recourse to aggression or violence. Of course, women colleagues also have a responsibility to stimulate the changing atmosphere by reinforcing healthier, less stressful models of masculinity that allow young men to express anxieties and apprehensions without fear of ridicule or humiliation.

Another feature of 'masculinism' is the reluctance of men to seek help. This is already well documented in relation to men seeking help for physical and mental health difficulties (Cunningham-Burley, 1986; Verbrugge, 1985). Men are also conspicuous by their absence when it comes to families receiving family support (Berg and Rosenblum, 1977). This particular study reported that about 30 per cent of families turned up for their first session without the father and that in general fathers were more resistant than mothers about coming back to the clinic. Harris and Sullivan (1988) suggest that social work has been collusive in supporting the traditional demarcation of roles within the family where the male role is seen as private and inviolable. Many writers have pointed out the costs of maintaining the masculine front and have emphasized the potentially damaging burden of being unable to express feelings, of living in a world of distorted relationships, emotional illiteracy and of communicating at arm's length (Thompson, 1995; Harris and Sullivan, 1988; Bowl, 1985). The result is often an inability to see when things are going wrong, exacerbated by the man's contract with the world of work and the illusory comfort of a trouble-free, compensatory home life. As Tolson argues:

> More often, deeply troubled masculine feelings are swept away by feminine tension management, and the cost of harmony in the home can be a masculine superficiality towards feelings in general, in relationships within the family, and in a man's relationship with himself. (1977, p. 70)

The reluctance of men to seek medical and social work help spills over into their reluctance to seek support when overcome with stress (Morrison, 1990). For example, child protection work is a stressful activity, yet the culture of masculinity inhibits men acknowledging the heavy price of such work on their emotional homeostasis (Thompson et al., 1994). In addition, childcare workers can encourage young men to break down their emotional barriers and allow them to reveal their vulnerability without fear of humiliation or punishment. In beginning the process of rejecting 'masculinism', men can help each other to 'dump baggage' and begin to communicate their needs to each other and explore parts of their lives that have been traditionally out of bounds.

Reject heterosexism

Heterosexism is the received image of masculinity promoted by patriarchal ideology. As heterosexism is based on a typified image of masculinity, it is important for men in childcare to reject any notion of indulging in anti-gay or anti-lesbian activities, language or behaviour. This is especially important when working with young boys who may have been abused (see Chapter 13 in this volume). The acquisition of manhood depends on other men, and so it is especially important that the messages going out to boys and young men is a liberated one and not one which will continue to damage growing boys by initiating them into the destructive world of traditional masculinity.

Challenge sexism in others

Sexism is not just a personal prejudice. It is embedded in the cultural and structural building blocks of our society, thus demanding that men challenge the common representations of gender which uphold and reinforce patriarchy. For men in childcare it may involve the routine challenging of sexist language and behaviour through to contesting practice assumptions about the nature of a child's abuse by, for example, challenging an assessment that avoids male culpability. Men and women workers need to recognize the often oppressive nature of many models of family therapy and counselling techniques. Working with families where abuse has taken place demands a gender-sensitive practice. Lerner argues for an approach that 'does not minimise or obscure the role of fathers, the complexity of interlocking relationships, and the impact of culture on women's subordinate status' (1988, p. 264).

Conclusion

If we are to be effective in tackling the issue of abuse, we have to acknowledge that it is not sufficient simply to draw up guidelines about safe practice with children. A more fundamental exploration into the culture of masculinity is necessary if men are to remain credible workers with children. We need to begin what Mezirow terms 'perspective transformation':

> the emancipatory process of becoming critically aware of how and why the structure of psycho-cultural assumptions has come to constrain the way we see ourselves and our relationships, reconstituting this structure to permit a more inclusive and discriminating integration of experience and acting upon those understandings. (1981, p. 6)

This involves challenging the dominant assumptions of our culture and background and rethinking 'taken-for-granted' beliefs about our behaviour and the behaviour of others. Men need to understand that patriarchy damages them also. It becomes an emotional constraint that can lead to men failing to take responsibility for the part they play in both their private and public lives in the continuation of oppression and all the horrors that go with it.

Both men and women practitioners need to acknowledge that sexism, and its consequences, is not maintained solely by men. Women too, as recent writers have noted (Phillips, 1993), as well as being victims, are also participants in the everyday activities which either challenge or reinforce and reiterate our stereotypical images and patterned responses. As Thompson states: 'like any social formation, sexism has to be maintained, reinforced and consolidated if it is to remain a living force and not pass into history' (1995, p. 5). Failure to understand that the reconstruction of male roles and behaviour within social work is part of a much bigger project – the reconstruction of gender – means that we must comprehend that this is a joint enterprise between men and women, its ramifications going far beyond the realms of our day-to-day practice.

References

Berg, B. and Rosenblum, N. (1977) 'Fathers in Family Therapy: A Survey of Family Therapists', *Journal of Marriage and Family Counselling*, 3, pp. 850–91.

Bowl, R. (1985) *Changing the Nature of Masculinity: A Task for Social Work?*, Norwich: University of East Anglia Social Work Monographs.

Brownmiller, S. (1975) *Against Our Will: Men, Women and Rape*, London: Secker & Warburg.

Burck, C. and Speed, B. (1995) *Gender, Power and Relationships*, London: Routledge.

Cameron, D. and Frazer, E. (1990) *The Lust To Kill*, Cambridge: Polity Press.

Campbell, D. (1995) 'Nightmare on Cromwell Street', *The Guardian*, 25 November, p. 25.

Chesler, P. (1990) *Sacred Bond*, London: Virago.

Cunningham-Burley, S. (1986) 'Marital Status and Health', paper presented to the First Congress of the European Society of Medical Sociology, Groningen.

Finklehor, D. (1990) 'Sexual Abuse in a National Survey of Adult Men and Women: Prevalence, Characteristics and Risk Factors', *Child Abuse and Neglect*, 14, pp. 19–28.

French, M. (1992) *The War Against Women*, Harmondsworth: Penguin.

Giddens, A. (1993) *New Rules of Sociological Method*, 2nd edn, Cambridge: Polity.

Harris, J. and Sullivan, J. (1988) 'Addressing Men's Roles', *Social Work Today*, 8 September.

Helm, M. and Pringle, K. (eds) (1992) *Surviving Sexual Abuse*, London: Barnardo's.

Hite, S. (1987) *Women and Love*, Harmondsworth: Penguin.

Hooper, C. A. (1987) 'Getting Him Off the Hook', *Trouble and Strife*, 12, Winter.

Jackson, S. (1982) *Childhood and Sexuality*, Oxford: Basil Blackwell.

Jones, E. (1995) 'The Construction of Gender in Family Therapy', in Burck and Speed (1995), pp. 7–23.

Lamb, S. (1991) 'Acts Without Agents: An Analysis of Linguistic Avoidance in Journal Articles on Men Who Batter Women', *American Journal of Orthopsychiatry*, 61 (2).

Lerner, H. (1988) *Women in Therapy*, London: Jason Aronson.

Mason, B. and Mason, E. (1990) 'Masculinity and Family Work', in Perelberg and Miller (1990).

McFadden, E. J. and Ryan, P. (1991) 'Maltreatment in Family Foster Homes: Dynamics and Dimensions', *Child and Youth Services*, 15 (2).

Mezirow, J. (1981) 'A Critical Theory of Adult Learning and Education', *Adult Education*, 32 (1).

Miedzan, M. (1992) *Boys Will Be Boys: Breaking the Link Between Masculinity and Violence*, London: Virago.

Morrison, T. (1990) 'The Emotional Effects of Child Protection Work on the Worker', *Practice*, 4 (4).

NSPCC (1992) *Experience of Child Abuse in Residential Care and Educational Placements*, London: NSPCC.

Nunno, M. and Rindfleisch, N. (1991) 'The Abuse of Children in Out of Home Care', *Children and Society*, 5 (4), pp. 295–305.

Perelberg, R. J. and Miller, A. C. (eds) (1990) *Gender and Power in Families*, London: Tavistock/Routledge.

Phillips, A. (1993) 'The Trouble With Boys', *Everywoman*, September.

Pringle, K. (1992) 'Danger! Men at (Social) Work', in Helm and Pringle (1992).

Pugh, R. G. (1988) 'How to Build a System for Managing Violence', *Community Care*, September.

Pugh, R. G. (1996) *Effective Language in Health and Social Work*, London: Chapman & Hall.

Rosenthal, J. A., Motz, J. K., Edmondson, D. A. and Groze, V. (1991) 'A Descriptive Study of Abuse and Neglect in Out-of-home Placement', *Child Abuse and Neglect*, 15, pp. 249–60.

Ruxton, S. (1992) *What's He Doing at The Family Centre?*, London: NCH Research Report.

Savage, J. (1987) *Nurses, Gender and Sexuality*, London: Heinemann.

Schein, L. (1977) 'All Men are Misogynists', in Snodgrass (1977).

Smart, C. and Smart, B. (1976) *Women, Crime and Criminology: A Feminist Critique*, London: Routledge.

Snodgrass, J. (ed.) (1977) *A Book of Readings for Men Against Sexism*, CA: Albion.

Teague, M. (1993) *Rapists Talking About Rape*, Norwich: University of East Anglia Social Work Monographs.

Thompson, N. (1993) *Anti-Discriminatory Practice*, London: Macmillan.

Thompson, N. (1995) 'Men and Anti-Sexism', *British Journal of Social Work*, 25 (4).

Thompson, N., Murphy, M. and Stradling, S. (1994) *Dealing with Stress*, London: Macmillan.

Tolson, A. (1977) *The Limits of Masculinity*, London: Tavistock.

Ussher, J. M. (1991) *Women's Madness: Misogyny or Mental Illness?*, London: Harvester Wheatsheaf.

Verbrugge, L. (1985) 'Gender and Health: An Update on Hypothesis and Evidence', *Journal of Health and Behaviour*, 26 September.

Wyre, R. (1986) *Women, Men and Rape*, Sevenoaks: Perry.

16 Risk assessment in residential childcare

Malcolm Jordan

The considerable cost of the numerous formal inquiries into child abuse in residential establishments can only be ultimately justified in terms of their prevention of further instances of this kind of abuse. Institutional abuse has been long established, and any historical review of the literature will show that these cruelties have been more eagerly described than those contained in the more pervasive sphere of abuse within families. The enclosed scenario that residential abuse represents would seem to add dramatic value! More recently, interest has focused on abuse within the community. Very slowly the civil rights of children have been strengthened.

The Children Act 1989 has been seen by many as marking a peak in legislative provision designed to protect children and young people and enhance their civil rights. In general, those professionally concerned with the complex task of childcare have welcomed the provisions of the Act and the consequent empowerment of children. They have striven – through training, the adoption of clear policies and procedures, and changes in direct practice – to implement both the spirit and detail of an Act which itself reflects the ideology of a past and future political view rather than anything that held sway in the 1980s. Not surprisingly, the promulgation of policies which give prime consideration to the child have not been universally welcomed.

Consequently, implementation has not been entirely smooth, without challenge or fault. It would, however, be difficult to dispute the proposition that the Act, together with its subsequent guidelines and developments, has significantly enhanced the rights of many vulnerable young people.

In the public mind the main focus has continued to be on abuse within the family and in the community. Social work managers, however, have rightly and immediately given additional attention to children within institutions, whether these be on a day or residential basis. The power relationships here are so heavily weighted against the client, and the difficulties facing any

229

aggrieved child so great, that considerable attention has been given to strengthening the voice of the child – and awareness of their inherent civil rights – through the development of easily accessible complaints procedures, and so on.

These policies have not been welcomed by all other professions, particularly educationalists, or by some practitioners who understandably feel themselves the more powerless as their charges become more powerful. The situation was succinctly expressed by a care worker who, in addressing the issue of abuse within a residential school, explained that 'the 1989 Children Act gave children rights, but this deprived us of our threats'. Staff have been placed in extremely ambiguous and painful positions, usually during the unsocial hours when the policy-makers and procedural pundits are soundly asleep. Headteachers find the requirements of the Act difficult to reconcile with the need to retain control over large groups of lively adolescents, a regime traditionally reliant upon a fragile hierarchy of assumed authority.

What can we learn from those situations in which things have gone badly wrong? We should be able to answer this question by highlighting the issues that emerge from recently completed and published official inquiries into abuse within establishments whose prime purpose was the care and the emotional, social and intellectual development of children (Levy and Kahan, 1991; Independent Review for Sheffield Child Protection Committee, 1992; Smith, 1992; Hereford and Worcester County Council, 1993; Kirkwood, 1993). Other unpublished material identifies the same issues. In many respects, these issues are neither remarkable nor surprising, although they strike at the heart of residential care in the last decade of the 20th century.

None of the institutions that were the subject of abuse inquiries had been successful in incorporating the philosophy underlying the Children Act, and none had, for various reasons, put new ideas into practice. Each of the institutions was controlled by an individual whose management was based on the exercise of personal power and the imposition of unquestioning obedience from staff. A natural consequence of this, and sometimes exacerbated by location, was the fact that these institutions were isolated and had developed a powerful internal culture. Staff, often care staff and women, saw themselves as powerless.

Central to these events was the personality and performance of the head of the establishment. Their powerful position had been achieved, in some instances, through the development of a range of special knowledge and skills built up over many years. Their reputation therefore enabled them to command unquestioning respect from staff and gave them a unique position within the establishment, agency and community. The delegations of power essential to the running of any normal establishment was not tolerated in such individualistic regimes. The extent to which such expertise had developed from many years of experience reflects the difficulty that these establishments had in embracing new ideas and current practices. Such heads were heavily identified with their establishments. They remained rooted in the past.

Training and development are not welcome in such homes. Staff are recruited, often in an arbitrary manner, because their personality 'fits' with the head's ideas, and any contamination with new ideas would threaten the whole internal belief system. Internal management requires dependency on the one and only available model as advanced by the leader. Alternative approaches have to be rejected and their legitimacy denied. The internal culture is strengthened by the perception of all such outside influences as threatening. Visitors are given only limited access, imposed policies and procedures are ignored or complied with in a token and meaningless way, and the role of the visiting 'expert' is derided. Not surprisingly the stress levels and consequent sickness rates among staff are high, although not attributable to the residents! This is particularly so for the heads of establishments and, over a period of time, as the pressures grow and the natural effects of ageing occur, they are variously described as 'paranoid', jaded, highly anxious and with acute feelings of persecution. This is often increased by long-standing threats of the closure of the establishment, and the destruction of a long-cherished and very personal enterprise.

What were the responsible authorities doing all this time? It would be trite to say that they were busy being reorganized, restructured and denied resources. None the less, this has been a significant factor in their failure to notice what was going on. These processes rob organizations of clear and consistent leadership. In all cases where abuse has taken place, there has been a failure to communicate across functional and departmental boundaries. In each case key people have been acutely aware that 'things are not right' in such and such a place, but there has been a failure to communicate clearly these concerns and to convince colleagues. Often, of course, each key person only stays in their post for a brief period before moving on or being moved. Reorganizations are extremely costly, particularly for vulnerable children and staff.

The role of the first line manager is vitally important and fraught with difficulty. It is not unusual for this person to have an administrative or management background rather than a professional one. Even if professionally qualified, they will be paid far less than the head of an establishment. For these reasons alone it is unrealistic for the unfortunate person in this post effectively to challenge the all-powerful role and personality of such heads. To some extent, their own judgement must be informed by advice received from professional experts, advisers, inspectors and so on, and proper action can only be achieved by effectively marshalling these forces. Unfortunately, this is a difficult operation, particularly as there is not always a unanimity of opinion about how an establishment is being run. Some advisers may support the ideology of the establishment, while others may avoid the place, having been damaged by past confrontations. They can always justifiably claim excessive demands for their attendance elsewhere.

The particular paradox of residential care, its value, its endearing nature and the challenge it presents to management theory and practice is that many of the characteristics outlined above are indicators of both the very successful and the very sick regimes. Indeed, in many ways the establishments identified in these inquiries were the victims of their own apparent success. A place where there is clarity of purpose, together with clear and committed leadership, is usually one which can deal with very challenging young people. As the anti-institutional dogma has swept through the land, there have been fewer and fewer residential places, and less choice for a hard-pressed social worker faced with a very hot potato, late on a Friday afternoon. Threatened by closure it is not surprising that the head accepts more challenging and more disturbed young people, although their needs can no longer be met from the resources available within the establishment. Often this results in an increase in inappropriate control systems, justified by a need to keep numbers up and thus stave off the ultimate threat of closure. The internal culture changes, to the great disadvantage of the more vulnerable residents, who are the eventual victims of layer upon layer of abuse. In this scenario it is hardly surprising that their complaints are not heard through the clash of ideologies, personalities and systems.

We know only too well the sad outcomes as documented by too many official inquiries: too few resources; too much ideology; too much power vested in one person; too little challenge by managers; and excessive incompetence within agencies, leading to repeated failures to grasp nettles.

It would not be wise to conclude this brief summary without mention of the role of the 'lay' person increasingly relied upon by government to exercise control, as governors or boards, as parents or inspectors. Clearly they have great potential value but, in these specialized areas of work, the learning curve is inevitably a long-drawn-out one, and they are largely reliant upon the advice of the head and other advisers who are the very source of the malaise with which they are being asked to deal. Inquiries have repeatedly called for lay persons to have access to independent advice to assist them in their task.

What lessons should be drawn from this heavy investment in repeatedly closing the stable door? What indicators can be developed to identify abusive regimes and thus help prevent repeated patterns of abuse? The personal cost of these abuses, whether they be to children – who have a right to expect good parenting – or to staff – who should expect good and safe management – is unimaginable. The degree of pain that lies behind all these situations is frightening.

There is currently a considerable debate about the value of some preventive strategies in child abuse work in general. There is a concern to define what is meant by abuse and to decide on the proper level and timing of possible interventions. Within institutions the issues are simpler and sharper. However abuse is defined, prevention can only involve the internal life of the institution and its management context. One problem is that many young people now coming into residential care present far more challenges to staff than was previously the case. Their experience along the route to the ultimate solution of placing them in such care often makes it much more difficult to work with them. Charismatic and committed individuals are therefore needed more than ever before to work with such clients. Residential establishments that are isolated, domineering and resistant to change are not required. Special places need very special management.

There is much to be gained from modern management techniques. We should at least have learned that imaginative professional practice is enhanced by simple structures that define the purpose of each unit and its function within the whole range of provision, and the importance of quality procedures that keep practice on the right path, or at least alert management to the fact that things are going wrong. If these simple requirements are put beside the issues outlined above, four key indicators are readily identified:

1 *Objectives*: Are the actual philosophies of care and the declared objectives of the establishment congruent and consistent with legislative requirements? Are actual admissions congruent with these objectives, and is the establishment appropriate for the challenges presented by the actual residents? Consideration of these issues should allow for and encourage the highly personalized and effective regimes that lie at the heart of good residential care. There are no excuses for the imposition of standardized and fashionable dogmas.

2 *Internal management*: What is the internal management style? Is the head of the establishment overidentified, is democracy or autocracy in vogue? How fragile does it feel? What are the communication patterns, do any upward messages ever get through to the top? What actually happens to complaints, how easy is it to complain? Are staff valued, are they offered training both in-house and externally?

3 *Boundary control*: How permeable are the boundaries of this place? Are they closed-off, resulting in an isolated community out of touch with the wider society? How many visitors – and of what type – actually penetrate the life of the establishment, and do they get messages out?

4 *Agency management*: How competent is the agency which carries ultimate responsibility for what happens here? Who is the 'key manager', what

are their qualifications, status and experience? What is the relationship between this person and the head? What is the quality of advice and support available to the head, and is it used? How effective are the communication patterns within the agency? Do they easily allow for a corporate approach which brings together knowledgeable professionals, inspectors and administrators? How have past issues been addressed? Have nettles been grasped?

These four critical indicators should provide a comprehensive view of the degree of risk for residents and staff within the establishment. Consideration under these headings can be written in non-technical language which is relevant to the past experiences of lay managers such as governors. It is a sad reflection upon the situations where abuse has taken place that conflicting or plainly wrong advice was given. Joint reports from a variety of professionals would help avoid these tragedies and afford lay board members some security during what is inevitably a long and steep learning curve.

How can such a programme be followed? The first two of these indicators – objectives and internal management – are currently well covered by good inspection teams using the legislation, regulations and guidelines of the Children Act 1989. Certainly residential care homes outside the public sector get full value from this approach and are required to follow every detail within a short timescale. It is not so clear whether the public sector is so firmly treated.

Problems arise with the last two indicators – boundary control and agency management. As currently set up, the inspection systems are not competent to examine these issues. It is a central argument of this chapter that they should be so competent. If this were the case, they would be much more effective in preventing abuse. In order to achieve this, there would have to be major changes in the existing system.

In the first place, inspections would have to be completely independent of any providing agency. They would have to be organized nationally and would be required to be multidisciplinary. They would have to include managers, residential experts, educationalists and well-established representatives of the professions relevant to the particular establishment (for example psychologists, therapists). Their brief would extend beyond the individual home to an examination of the agency and the main management systems outlined above.

These groups would have to have both the authority and the ability to penetrate deep inside the life of an establishment and the responsible agency. No doors should be closed; all information and documentation must be available on demand. This is a radical proposal but supports the view given by at least two heads caught up in abusive regimes. When the employers waved the final big stick of disciplinary action, the heads were aggrieved because they felt that those sitting in judgment were a main part of the problem, having denied the establishment proper resources, support and management over many years.

The inspectorial system would have to balance both the current detailed consideration of regulation and so on (the checklist), and a wider and free-flowing exercise of professional judgement. A witness recently likened one of these residential establishments to the court at the time of the Roman emperor Claudius. You knew whether it was a safe day by 'sniffing the air'. We need experts in sniffing out the truth of what goes on in each institution.

The reports presented on each establishment need to be clear, rather than long, and should use the indices developed here to indicate the degree of risk at each establishment, with particular emphasis on boundary characteristics and the managing agency. It will be argued that such a system is expensive and impractical. It will certainly be resisted by the main agencies, who will feel very threatened by an inspection of their role. Clearly, teams will have to draw on a wide range of expertise and be well trained. Such a fluid approach flies in the face of new methods advocated by existing inspectorates, where massive documentation leads to the checking-off of numerous boxes on printed forms in the search for some mystical and meaningless score.

The approach suggested here restores professional integrity and dialogue to its proper place, the restoration of professional wisdom rather than a concern with checking narrow competencies. In many ways it harks back to the original concept behind the Health Advisory Service established by Crossman in 1969: a strong multidisciplinary team giving an in-depth view and centred on the user. This service was itself established following a series of abuses within long-stay hospitals and proved a major catalyst of change and prevention for the following twenty years. In residential care it would represent a real effort to build a major bulwark against future abuse. It would show that these matters were taken seriously, and the cost of repeated inquiries would have borne some fruit.

References

Hereford and Worcester County Council (1993) 'Report of an Independent Tribunal into Rhydd Court School', Worcester: Hereford and Worcester County Council.

Independent Review for Sheffield Child Protection Committee (1992) 'A Review of Malcolm Thompson's Employment by Sheffield City Council: Report of an Independent Review for Sheffield Child Protection Committee', Sheffield: Sheffield Area Child Protection Committee.

Kirkwood, A. (1993) 'The Leicestershire Inquiry', Leicester: Leicester County Council.

Levy, A. and Kahan, B. (1991) 'The Pindown Experience and the Protection of Children', Stafford: Staffordshire County Council.

Smith, J. (1992) 'Report of the Scotforth House Inquiry', Lancaster: Lancashire County Council.

17 Foster carers: Clients or colleagues in child protection?

Val Capewell

Foster carers provide care for children in their own homes with little direct observation of their work. In addition to their direct childcare role, they are increasingly being asked to undertake extra tasks, such as arranging parental contact and providing information for court and children's hearings, case reviews and so on. To the birth parent, foster carers are often the public face of the agency, and may therefore be the target of their dissatisfaction and complaints. The relative isolation of foster carers, compared to residential workers, increases their vulnerability to complaints and allegations from both parents and children in their care. The corollary, of course, is that the comparatively private nature of the fostering situation does provide abusive foster carers with many opportunities to exploit their powerful position. In its most insidious form, this exploitation may commence with social workers at the recruitment, selection and assessment stages. It may then continue with the targeting and sometimes lengthy 'grooming' of the potential victim – where abusers develop an intensive relationship with a child, often over many months and years, eventually winning their trust and then abusing it.

When allegations of abuse are made against foster carers, during the subsequent child protection investigations their status changes from that of colleagues to clients. This change of status occurs following an allegation of physical or sexual abuse being made by a parent, or by a child who is either in their care or who is making an allegation retrospectively. Reliable figures on the number of complaints are limited and not up to date. However, a small study of carers in the Midlands found that 1 in 6 carers had had a complaint or allegation made against them at some point during their fostering career (Nixon et al., 1986). This chapter reflects the experience of the South Wales Advice and Mediation Service (SWAMS), part of the UK-wide charity the National Foster Care Association (NFCA), which has noted

237

a dramatic rise in both regional and national referral rates with regard to such allegations.

NFCA maintain that it is only a minority of foster carers who abuse children, although they recognize the selective nature of their contacts with foster carers, since not all carers who have been subjected to an allegation of abuse are referred to them. Their own survey of foster carers who had had such allegations made against them found that, of 519 questionnaires returned, 177 carers had experienced an allegation. Of these, 63 per cent of the allegations were 'not founded', 6 per cent were 'founded' and, in 8 per cent of cases, the agency involved had been unable to determine whether any abuse had taken place. In 10 per cent of cases the carers did not know the outcome, and a further 13 per cent of cases had other outcomes (NFCA, 1995). Most allegations were unsubstantiated, with insufficient evidence to prove or disprove them. The remainder were shown to be false accusations. The false and unsubstantiated allegations originated mainly from teenagers, and while they may be from boys as well as girls, the majority were made by girls against a male within the household, and concerned inappropriate touching, kissing and sexual innuendo, as well as sexual intercourse. Interestingly, foster carers who had been fostering for more than eight years were much more likely to be the subject of an allegation than less experienced carers. It is thought that this results from the greater complexity of the placements.

It is our experience at SWAMS that child protection workers when investigating allegations against foster carers follow them up more rigorously than with other members of the public. Relatively few social work departments have a clear policy and procedure for investigating allegations of abuse by foster carers. The NFCA questions the equity of this, since it appears to ignore Department of Health guidance on child protection and investigation which states that:

> It is important to understand that the Social Services Department's duty to investigate under Section 47, in line with established Area Child Protection Committee (ACPC) procedures, applies equally to children in foster care as it does to children living with their own families. (Department of Health and Welsh Office, 1991, Section 5.19.2)

Of course, one could argue that this clause was intended to ensure that social workers investigated allegations against foster carers as rigorously as they would with those concerning birth parents. Nevertheless, it is not unreasonable to suggest that social workers should apply the same standards of probity, proof and procedure equally in all cases.

Our experience is that the more stringent investigation of foster carers is more likely to be accompanied by the premature removal of the child, and the cessation of contact, despite the fact that many foster carers will have been significant figures in the child's life. In some cases, when children have made an allegation whilst out on a visit, they have not been returned and the foster carers have not received any satisfactory explanation at all. Unlike birth parents, foster carers who are the subject of allegations of abuse are often not allowed to attend the subsequent child protection case conference. The long-term effects on the carer's life can be enormous. They can find themselves suspended from employment, have their registration as foster carers terminated and their ability to work in any area of childcare impaired, even when there has been no finding of guilt. Furthermore, the position of foster carers is somewhat ambiguous since they rarely have access to the same complaints procedures as service users, nor are they always able to access the grievance procedures available to other workers.

NFCA has long maintained that there is a need for a thorough investigation into any allegation which follows a clearly defined policy and procedure, and in 1988 produced such specimen guidance for agencies. The guidance recommends that foster carers should be informed when an allegation has been made, should have the opportunity to answer any allegations, and that all investigations are formally concluded. Unfortunately in some cases, foster carers have been removed from the approved list without ever being made fully aware of the nature of the complaint, and without ever having had the opportunity to answer the allegations, although this right was enforced after a judicial review (*Regina* v. *Wandsworth*, 1988). This guidance was further refined in 1995 (NFCA, 1995). Prior to 1988, no agency had such a policy.

The following anonymized case illustrates the experience of foster carers. A couple had fostered two teenage girls; M had a severe learning disability and had been in their care for nine years. They had cared for the other girl, J, for eighteen months, having taken her as an emergency placement without any background knowledge of her highly sexualized behaviour. Prior to the sexual abuse allegation against the male carer, she had previously made an allegation of physical abuse against the female carer, which was proven to be unfounded. It transpired that, prior to this first allegation, J was unhappy with constraints that were put on her by her social worker, and she blamed the female carer who had had to implement these constraints. J was removed from the home, while M remained. J subsequently made allegations of sexual abuse against the male carer, which resulted in an unannounced evening visit to their home by the police and a social worker. M was removed that evening and placed in residential care. The male carer recorded his experience of this visit as follows:

> They had a duty social worker with them and she took M away from us. They
> proceeded to rip the house apart, searching all our clothing hanging in the

wardrobe, searching through drawers, suitcases, personal papers, etc. asking did we have any sex aids or pornography in the house. It was unbelievable, they stripped all the bedclothes off the beds and took them away for deoxyribonucleic acid (DNA) testing. They made a video film of every room in the house and then took me down to the police station locking me in a cell. I was asked if I had any objection to having samples taken of my body, which were duly obtained. It was all very degrading. I was then fingerprinted and had facial photographs taken, being returned to my cell prior to being interviewed. I explained about the problems we had had with J's sexual behaviour, how she had in the past made similar allegations against her father, her two elder brothers and two lodgers living in the house prior to being put into care. I was advised to engage a solicitor, which I had to pay for. No help was forthcoming from the Social Services.

After some three months, the male foster carer (as is common with most carers in this situation) received a bland message from the police stating that no charges were being made, due to insufficient evidence. He continues to profess his innocence, but is unable to prove it. Even if J retracts her allegations, he believes the cloud will still hang over him. He will, as do others in his position, 'take this with me to the grave'.

The emotions that this person and other carers express are similar to those of a sudden bereavement. NFCA workers find that carers ride an emotional see-saw during the allegations and investigations. Frequently, when allegations are made solely against the male partner, female carers are angry, and reject and seek to refute the charges. They will 'fight the world' to prove their partner's innocence. In contrast, the men are often in the depths of despair – almost suicidal, their minds race ahead to the possibility of a conviction and how they would survive prison. When the fateful words 'insufficient evidence for a prosecution' are uttered, the see-saw alters and often the roles reverse, with women becoming depressed and men angry. Workers have become aware of a pattern of response which many carers pass through, with the whole process taking up to two years. The pattern of stages of response mirror those reported after bereavement and other forms of loss, namely shock, denial, disbelief, anger, growing bitterness, and then, eventually, a more philosophical acceptance. These stages are not passed through in a neat sequence: carers may oscillate between different stages.

For carers who have been subjected to an allegation, there is 'nobody for us'. In the majority of cases, social workers and link workers are unable to give the support they need. Social workers experience role confusion and a lack of clarity in the procedures. There is a role conflict for them – are they an investigator or supporter? Their own professional judgement is in question, particularly when they have had responsibility for the assessment of the foster carer's abilities, skills and subsequent approval as carers. They may find that they are swept along by events which render them professionally impotent and leave the carers isolated. For example, they may be required to conduct a risk assessment on a carer's own children.

To return to the carers, some of the reverberating emotions demonstrated by carers are that they are initially devastated, numbed, shocked beyond belief. They have lost their standing as respectable citizens, within both the agency and the community. They realize, probably for the first time, the possibility of their own family being broken up if their children are removed in addition to the foster children. The possibility of the alleged abuser being asked to leave the home to safeguard the children is also extremely disruptive of ordinary life. The marital relationship may be placed under tremendous stress – a lack of sexual desire is common, as are other psychosexual problems. Following an allegation of unproven sexual abuse a male carer writes:

> I couldn't keep the sexual side of our marriage alive, I just didn't want to know. It has had this sort of effect on me and I know this is very hard on my wife, who now needs my love more than ever. We still love each other very deeply but the sexual side of our life is almost dead – can anybody help?

This writer was referring to his inability to obtain and maintain an erection, and of difficulties of retarded ejaculation, which indicated a need for psychosexual counselling. A woman always has the constant fear 'Did he do it?', even if she thinks he did not. They often confide: 'I believe my husband, but what if . . . ?' An allegation may reawaken a female carer's own suppressed childhood sexual abuse, reawakening dormant feelings. Again, the implications for the sexual relationship and the marriage generally are tremendous, frequently necessitating counselling support.

Additionally, carers may suffer financially by losing the income from fostering if the children have been removed, as payment usually stops immediately; in a few cases, they may lose their jobs. Above all, they suffer a loss of self-esteem and integrity, and immediate control over their own lives. Their role changes from one of colleague to that of client.

The children

It is widely accepted that many of the children placed nowadays have more difficult and disturbed patterns of behaviour than was hitherto the case. Many children coming into care and being accommodated with foster carers will have experienced abuse in the past, possibly in their own families. Carers are often unaware of a child's situation, and lack information as to whether:

- there is a possibility that the child being placed has been abused;
- the abuse is likely to have been by someone the child knew and trusted, who was in a caretaking role;
- the abuse began at an early age;
- it continued for a long period of time;
- the child may have tried to get help but may not have been believed or heard.

This lack of information, coupled with the variable quality of training offered to new and experienced foster carers, contributes to a potentially dangerous situation. Even when these issues are raised in initial training, some prospective carers fail to understand or absorb the information when their concentration is focused on gaining agency approval. NFCA firmly believe that it is this situation that is dangerous, *not* the child.

Over the last few years, agencies involved in protecting children have learned to listen more carefully to the voice of children in public care, and to be wary of dismissing even apparently minor complaints. While there is no automatic assumption that all accusations are true, there is, none the less, a presumption that all complaints will be investigated and taken seriously (Department of Health and Welsh Office, 1989). However, there are a number of reasons why children in foster placements may make false allegations. They may be in a placement in which they are unhappy. They may feel that they are not being listened to by their social worker. For example, they may resent their request for a placement nearer their home not being 'heard'. Unhappiness about social work decisions, or about their situation more generally, may be displaced onto the foster carers. To some powerless children the power of accusation offers a unique opportunity to attempt to influence and control events for once. They may not realize the consequences for the carers, and indeed may not care, if by making an allegation they feel that for once they have control over their own lives.

Some abused children may be confused about what has happened to them, and may have difficulty in dealing with their new situation. For example, one young girl, after being placed with a family with teenage sons, told her social worker that she was unsure as to whether or not she was being abused and wondered if she was dreaming or fantasizing. Unfortunately, when she was placed no background information was given to the carers and, by giving her what they thought was a 'beautiful attic bedroom' on her own, away from their bedroom and those of their teenage sons, they had unwittingly replicated a similar scenario to that of her previous abuse.

In her various studies of both the placement of abused children in foster care, and of the abuse of them while actually in foster care, McFadden has identified five factors which are commonly found in situations where abuse is alleged (McFadden, 1987; McFadden and Ryan, 1987). These are: overloading by the agency; the characteristics of the child; lack of matching; lack of support, and lack of training for the foster carers. The NFCA's own studies (1994b, 1995) confirm McFadden's findings – that it is often the placing agency's practice which contributes to abuse within foster families.

1 *Overloading by the agency*

This occurs either when foster carers are not looking after the number or type of children for whom they have been approved – in terms of, for example, the age range, the sex or the degree of disturbance exhibited by the child – or when the length of placement differs from that for which they have been approved. Short-term placements may sometimes be stretched into long-term ones without a full review of the needs of the child. Due to a shortage of resources, foster carers may be pressurized to accept such unwanted situations out of compassion for the child. Sometimes, foster carers who have shown that they can cope with difficult behaviour are 'rewarded' by the agency with even more difficult and stressful situations to deal with. Under pressure, many foster carers may be reluctant to seek help for fear of being thought inadequate or incompetent. As a result, in their isolation, some of them have been totally overstretched and have harmed children they wanted to help and protect. For example, under severe stress they may react harshly to children's soiling or aggression, or may 'freeze them out' emotionally. These apparently 'out of character' actions are, in my experience, more likely to result in physical or emotional abuse and are, in part, a result of social work agencies exploiting their foster carers and failing to support them adequately.

2 *The characteristics of the child*

Agencies may fail to take account of the characteristics of the sexually abused child and the effect these may have on the foster family. Most foster children bring with them patterns of behaviour learned in their previous families and are therefore likely to repeat these in their new homes. For example, some abused children display sexualized behaviour which can be extremely disruptive to the lives of unprepared foster carers. Such behaviour may be overt, such as inappropriate touching and kissing, or may be covert as in situations where the foster child draws other children into inappropriate sexual behaviour. Such children are often aware of the power of sexuality and may sometimes deliberately use it. These children have a tremendous potential for re-victimization. For example, a child will often mirror the same values and behaviour towards a female carer as he or she did towards the distanced mother whom, they think failed to protect him or her from previous abuse. These children have no boundaries – they are unable to distinguish between positive and negative relationships. The patterns of communications, especially in relation to generational boundaries, becomes distorted, which can lead to a child becoming closer to the male carer or another male who offers comfort, thereby potentially replicating the abusive situation. In such enmeshed relationships between one foster carer and the child, the other foster carer is excluded and may experience feelings of resentment and anger towards the child which they find hard to admit or control. Such behaviour, damaging as it is to the foster child, can obviously be disruptive of unprepared foster families, but may be disastrous in foster families whose members have pre-existing insecurities, or are already experiencing other difficulties in their relationships.

3   Lack of matching

When selecting appropriate placements, social workers, perhaps because of the pressure of work and the shortage of placements, may fail to carefully match the carer(s) and the child together. The main factors to be considered in matching should obviously derive from the needs of the child. However, as the example earlier illustrated, it is not uncommon for workers to overlook significant features of an abused child's previous experience. Furthermore, there should be a careful assessment of the potential impact of the child's behaviour upon the proposed placement family or household and, while it is recognized that there are no perfect placements, any existing areas of difficulty should be considered in the light of the likely behaviour of the foster child. For children whose notions of what are considered the acceptable boundaries of behaviour are erratic or problematic, it is vital that they are placed within families where there is clarity about these matters, especially with regard to adult/child relationships.

4   Lack of support

It has often been noted that, for a variety of reasons, social workers' efforts are channelled more towards the immediate danger to and protection of children than towards the children's welfare once they have been 'rescued'. The NFCA often hears foster carers complain that social workers visit infrequently and often fail to respond to messages left for them. Consequently, when pressures build, the isolation compounds the problems experienced by foster carers who lack other sources of professional support. We should acknowledge that carers care for children in the privacy and isolation of their own homes, and that both carers and workers collude in this isolation, especially that of the male carer in his caring role. If the male carer is working, he may not attend meetings, training or support groups, and he then becomes unwittingly excluded from discussions and decision-making. Because of his isolation, he does not develop relationships with other male carers, nor does he benefit from their support or that of the workers. Carers are frequently left unsupported by agency staff. Consequently, many foster carers who find themselves accused of abuse express bitterness about their treatment by social work agencies. They feel that they have done their best in difficult circumstances only to be abandoned in their time of need by the workers.

5   *Lack of training for the foster carers*

Few foster carers are adequately prepared for the unexpected dynamics which disturbed children may bring into hitherto 'stable' families. The NFCA booklet *Safe Caring* (NFCA, 1994a) provides advice as to how families may adapt their lifestyle to prepare themselves, their families and the children they care for. Foster carers need to be trained to cope with the difficult aspects of children's behaviour, especially when this is linked with previous abuse. For example, the boundary-seeking behaviour of some children can create considerable frustration for carers. But, while aggressive behaviour is usually recognized as being potentially problematic, perhaps the most difficult behaviour is that which is sexually inappropriate or provocative. Male carers may experience sexual feelings which they do not understand or know how to deal with, and which they may be ashamed to admit. The absence or inadequacy of training, together with the relative isolation of many male carers, may contribute to a dangerous situation for both the child and the carers.

In addition to the preventative training, SWAMS believes that foster carers need to be prepared for the possibility that, at some point in their work, they may be accused of abuse. Therefore, their training should encompass departmental policy as well as an understanding of the actual procedures which will be used to investigate any allegations. Foster carers need to know where their support and supervision will come from, and need to know that the process will have an outcome which will be clearly communicated to all parties.

Conclusion

A vital safeguard for both carers and foster children is a placement agreement which must be clearly established at the outset. Such agreements should state the aims and objectives, the length of the placement, the therapeutic plan and the foster carers' role in this. They should contain specific commitments to both support and training, as well as a clear statement of the policy and procedure for dealing with allegations of abuse. The approach to allegations must also be open to the acknowledgement of the agency's possible failings in matters such as the appropriateness of the placement, training and support. When allegations are made, even when abuse is found to have occurred, the procedure needs to ensure that carers are at least given the same level of advice and guidance available to other agency staff.

The carers need to feel that they are part of a team and to know that their feelings and opinions are valued. NFCA findings indicate that all carers who have had an allegation made against them want it fully investigated. It is imperative that a system is found which ensures that the foster carer's voice is heard, and where they are treated by other professionals in a professional way. The relationship between carers and social service departments and the status of foster carers must be addressed as a matter of priority. We must extend the principles of partnership to those people who are providing the foster care service for local authorities.

Unfortunately many allegations are difficult to prove or disprove, and at the end of the process a decision still needs to be made on both the balance of probability and risk in a particular family. Foster carers who may feel that they have been found 'guilty' without adequate means of redress may feel that their only route is to sue the department for slander or defamation of character. This is not helpful to the foster care service as a whole, nor is it financially effective. There are considerable costs in pursuing investigations of abuse, and the NFCA estimates that it costs at least £10,000 to recruit and train foster carers. Dealing with avoidable allegations and complaints is a costly business if the carer ceases to foster following an unfounded allegation. It is vital that agencies work in partnership with carers, recognizing that it is a minority of carers who abuse children in their care; the majority do not. Therefore, it should be recognized that unfounded allegations of abuse are a 'hazard of the job' just as they are for residential workers, and foster carers should not be misused, nor left unsupported and undertrained to tackle these risks. They should be treated as colleagues not clients.

References

Department of Health and the Welsh Office (1989) *The Children Act*, London: HMSO.

Department of Health and the Welsh Office (1991) *Working Together Under the Children Act 1989: A Guide to Arrangements for Inter-Agency Cooperation for the Protection of Children from Abuse*, London: HMSO.

McFadden, E. J. (1987) 'The Sexually Abused Child in Specialised Foster Care', paper presented at the First North American Conference on Treatment Foster Care, Minneapolis, August.

McFadden, E. J. and Ryan, P. (1987) 'Abuse in Family Foster Homes: Characteristics of the Vulnerable Child', paper presented at the Fifth International Foster Care Organization Conference, Leeds, July.

NFCA (1994a) *Safe Caring*, London: National Foster Care Association.

NFCA (1994b) *Advising Carers – Helping Children*, London: National Foster Care Association.

NFCA (1995) 'Allegations Against Foster Families', *Foster Care*, 83, pp. 13–16.

Nixon, S., Hicks, C. and Ells, S. (1986) *What Cost Movement?*, Birmingham: Birmingham Social Services Department and the National Foster Care Association.

Queen's Bench Division, *Regina v. Wandsworth London Borough Council ex Parte P*, before Mr Justice Ewbank, 2 November 1988.

18 Delivering staff care in a multidisciplinary context

Michael Murphy

Introduction

This chapter is concerned with the difficult task of delivering a staff care service to child protection staff. It critically reviews the need for, and the provision of, staff care services within child protection systems. It suggests that it is time for such a provision to become an integral part of the child protection system, rather than an occasional reactive response when staff problems become impossible to ignore. It argues that all agencies which are part of the child protection system need access to the same such service. However, I would go on to suggest that the provision of the service in itself is not enough – crucially, it is in the blockages to the use of staff care, promoted by agency and society, wherein lies the biggest challenge to the development of an effective service. One such multidisciplinary staff care service is used as a case study in which the difficulties and structural blocks to staff care provision that the scheme exposes are reviewed, and practical ways of combating these problems suggested.

Staff care in a child protection context

Twenty years after the government circular LASSL (74) 13 (DHSS, 1974) first confirmed the need for coordinated multidisciplinary action on child abuse, those same child protection systems are still in receipt of a steady flow of helpful government advice and guidance: *Working Together* (Department of Health, 1991) and the *Memorandum of Good Practice* (Home Office/DoH, 1992) being notable examples. Most of this advice deals with the regulation and proceduralization of the child protection system. Some elements concern the proper care and treatment of the child under investigation whilst others (particularly following the Children Act 1989) deal with the concept of partnership, or the care of parents. None of this advice is concerned with the proper care or well-being of those staff members who undertake the child protection task. This lack of consideration of the needs of the deliverers of the service might be seen as a consequence of this same proceduralization or depersonalization of the system. Thus, under child protection procedures, it is presumed that service deliverers leave their individual selves at home and become truly self-less parts of the child protection machine. It is presumed that there is no need to care for staff who are engaged in child protection work, as that comforting process should take place solely in the private life of the individual concerned. There is a paradox here – the child protection system is built around belief in the benefit of public intervention into the private sphere of the family in order to prevent undue suffering. But a similar belief in the efficacy of public intervention into the private sphere of the practitioner, in terms of staff care, seems to be denied. There is a need to consider the professional and personal needs of all the practitioners and managers within the child protection system. These needs should be the concern of government, the ACPC and the agency, as well as the individual member of staff. This care should not just be provided from a sense of altruism or moral duty, but from the acknowledgement that such care would have a major positive impact on the delivery of the child protection service: 'Stress is an important and costly issue not just for staff within an organisation but also for the organisation itself in terms of how efficiently and effectively it operates'(Thompson et al., 1994, p. 16).

Stress and child protection work

The contention that child abuse work is stressful and has a profound impact on the staff who undertake the work is not new: 'Child protection can cut across our feelings and experience in some of the most personal parts of our lives, those experiences and feelings can have a powerful effect on our professional behaviour' (Murphy, 1995, pp. 163–4). As child abuse work encompasses some of the most painful, private parts of some people's lives, the work can evoke powerful responses in the practitioner's inner, private self. The pain and stress of the child or the family can be mirrored in the feelings of the practitioner. For example, a letter from a 14-year-old survivor was read out at a recent conference, stunning and distressing the adult practitioners present. In the child abuse inquiries that have shaped the UK child protection system, the issue of staff stress has frequently been mentioned: 'There was a common acknowledgement of the heavy emotional demands and profound impact this area of work has on professionals' (Butler-Sloss, 1988, p. 216). However, although inquiries have been eager to press for procedural changes within child protection systems themselves, they have been remarkably silent about specific proposals for improving (or beginning) a system of caring for staff. Harmful effects of child protection work are noted but nothing is actually done about it in terms of proposals for staff care. This lack of agency provision is not helpful to staff and reflects society's doubts about the need for, and the appropriateness of, a staff care service (Balloch et al., 1995).

The multidisciplinary context

The literature on stress and social work has been concerned with the pressure that child protection work brings to social work staff (Fineman, 1985; Thompson et al., 1994; Balloch et al., 1995). But child protection work is not only a field social work responsibility: 'The primary responsibility of the SSD in relation to child care and protection does not diminish the role of other agencies' (Department of Health, 1991, p. 9). What is certainly true is that the personal costs of child protection work, in terms of stress and emotional distress, are felt by all participating staff. Bradley and Sutherland (1995) have confirmed that stress is a critical issue for groups as diverse as field social workers and home helps. If this is the case, it is essential that the resources that are put into staff care are also shared between all participants in the child protection process. Because of the intrinsically stressful nature of child protection work, and the multidisciplinary nature of that work, there is a need for a flexible multidisciplinary staff care service to be included as an integral part of each child protection system.

The experience of one multidisciplinary scheme

In 1989 the Coltown staff care scheme was established, on behalf of the local ACPC, for all staff involved in the child protection service. The scheme is jointly financed by the social service department and health authority as part of a multidisciplinary resource project. The service is free and confidential, and attempts to be flexible enough to meet the individual needs of practitioners and managers in the system. Use of the scheme is not limited to those staff involved with a particularly difficult child abuse case but is open to any staff member who is undergoing considerable stress at work or at home. Most controversially of all (following much debate in the ACPC), a special part of the scheme was made available to those staff members who have been suspended following an allegation of professional abuse. Access is through an initial contact with the project coordinator or administrator. Following this, the participant is put in contact with one of seven external counsellors and a first interview arranged. Up to six sessions are initially available, with the possibility of extending that provision by a further six sessions.

Although the service is primarily used by individual members of staff (52 in 1994/5) the scheme has also offered help to whole groups of staff who have been undertaking particularly difficult pieces of work, or who have been the recipients of particularly difficult behaviour (six groups in 1994/5). The use of the service has been slowly increasing each year.

Feedback on the scheme is obtained through formal evaluation and informal feedback from practitioners and managers who have used the service. Practitioners from all agencies have indicated that they have benefited from the scheme. The only exception to this is the police, who have their own extensive counselling service in the area. The positive effects that have been noted include the reduction of sickness absence, the increased ability to deal with stressful situations, an improved professional confidence and a vast improvement in the sense of personal well-being for most users of the service.

However, developing a positive, accessible service as recommended in the recent NISW study (Balloch et al., 1995) is only the first step in delivering staff care. There are equally serious problems in ensuring that a scheme will be appropriately accessed and used. When users and potential users were asked about their participation in the Coltown scheme, several important factors or themes were discovered that inhibited the appropriate use of the service. It was discovered that some staff who needed the service were not accessing the scheme or were coming forward to use it at a very late stage. After asking consumers what these inhibitory factors were, the project then tried to reduce the power of those factors so that access and effectiveness could be improved. These factors or themes were the:

- personal/professional divide;
- lack of awareness of the scheme;
- uneven demand for the service;
- 'be tough'culture;
- 'others worse off than me'/'givers or receivers' theme;
- lack of early referral.

By examining these themes I hope to be able to draw some general conclusions about staff care and child protection work and make some specific suggestions as to how to increase the accessibility of staff care schemes.

The personal/professional divide

In most practitioner groups that aspire to professional status there is a powerful expectation that the personal and the professional will remain strictly separate. Thus, the staff member's personal stress is left behind in their private sphere and their work stress is picked up on their arrival at the workplace. This presumption assumes that no matter how bad the work or home pressures become, the staff member will continue to perform perfectly well in the other sphere. In the Coltown project this division between the personal and the professional has proved to be completely illusory. It has emerged that personal stressors would automatically be carried into the professional environment and vice versa. It was also hard to draw a clear distinction between stress caused by unusual events at work (for example involvement in investigating child sexual abuse); stress arising from the cumulative pressure of work, or the stress caused by personal life events. Because home and work life clearly impact upon each other, stress from both spheres is included in the eligibility criteria. The scheme encourages use by those staff who are experiencing stressful periods in their private lives, as well as those people who have been involved in something which is quite obviously work-related, such as being threatened or assaulted whilst doing child protection work. It was discovered that, when staff members were experiencing cumulative stress in both areas of their lives, they would feel particularly vulnerable. Not only were they operating under an increased burden of stress, but they were often cut off from their normal sources of support at home and at work. A typical example was of a residential worker who received a particularly difficult disclosure of child sexual abuse at the same time as undergoing a period of considerable pressure at home. At first, support was somewhat limited, but this improved as the worker contacted the staff care scheme. Counselling focused on both his personal and professional stressors. After six sessions he was coping much better with his work tasks and had made several positive changes in his personal life.

Not only do the professional and the personal impinge upon each other but child abuse work may actually create a bridge across the personal/professional divide.

The lack of awareness about the scheme

One of the strongest inhibitors to use of the staff care scheme has been the lack of knowledge about the existence, extent and the means of access to it. This proved to be a peculiarly persistent problem. It seems that awareness of staff care services is only to the fore at times of necessity. Unfortunately, severe stress often produces a state of being that seems to preclude those suffering the most from actually asking for help. This scenario of low demand has been previously described in other staff care services (Hemsley, 1986). Practical action has included extensive advertising in workplaces, simple and clear access procedures, targeting staff groups obviously under pressure and making special efforts to inform and persuade managers about the benefits of the scheme. It must also be acknowledged that it takes time to build up credibility and trust within a staff care scheme. Frequently, knowledge of, and trust in, the service grew from positive word-of-mouth reports from previous users.

The uneven demand for the service

Although the scheme was determinedly multidisciplinary in outlook and available to all child protection agencies, some unevenness has developed in its use. Thus, social services staff are overrepresented in the client sample, while users from other agencies, although present in substantial numbers, were not equally represented (33 social services staff and 19 other agency users in 1994/5). Managers and males, particularly at the beginning of the scheme, were also underrepresented in the sample (14 managers and 38 basic grade staff and 10 men and 42 women used the scheme in 1994/5). These figures seem particularly significant when the NISW study indicates that male practitioners and managers are particularly vulnerable to stress (Balloch et al., 1995).

Targeting those parts of the service underrepresented in the scheme has been the main tactic for altering the unevenness of demand. This targeting has been both by publicity and by direct contact with underrepresented groups. For example, one manager, when contacted by the facilitator, was surprised, pleased and even 'touched' by the offer of the service. In the evaluation that followed, what had pleased the manager most was that the scheme had recognized that 'even managers' had individual staff care needs of their own.

The 'be tough' culture

Murphy (1991) and Wiener (1989) have suggested that a 'be tough' agency culture can reduce a practitioner's ability to seek help and, by individualizing the problem, can lead to the rejection of that help. Closely allied to this 'be tough' culture is the fear that use of the service will bring stigma and negative consequences. This fear of being labelled less-than-strong is a theme for most practitioners in the child protection system but seems particularly exaggerated for male staff or for those working in teams with a particularly macho culture. Thus Leadbetter (1993) describes a residential service where even to report a violent incident (never mind obtain help with the aftermath) was unacceptable. This factor is perhaps the greatest obstacle to appropriate use of the scheme encountered so far. The two interventions that have gone some way to help overcome this obstacle have been (1) the adoption by the ACPC of a policy encouraging use of the scheme by promising no adverse consequences to the user and (2) the practice, adopted by some senior practitioners in the system, of being open and positive about their own use of the service. This has served to reduce some (male) managers' and practitioners' anxiety about seeming to be weak.

The 'others worse off than me'/ 'givers or receivers' theme

Inbuilt into the culture of many caring agencies is the strict demarcation between being the provider and being the recipient of the service. This is the understanding that you can be either 'sheep' or 'goat' but not both (Doyle, 1991). The notion, therefore, that the carer might need caring for may be a difficult one to accept.

Closely allied to this factor is the characteristic that before you can use a service you must both be deserving and be in a state of obvious high need. Because practitioners in the child protection system work with children and families in great need, they often define themselves as being relatively unworthy of help and not deserving of the service. For example, one experienced practitioner, having arranged to use the staff care service, was heard arguing with herself about whether she really deserved or needed the service: 'I've got a partner, a good job, lovely children – I shouldn't really need this service, should I?'

Even 'undeserving' practitioners without obvious major stressors in their lives can have need of a staff care service. As Arroba and James (1987) point out, it is the subjective negative response to the objective stressor that is often crucial in determining levels of stress.

The lack of early referral

One of the strongest factors which can block the individual's ability to access the staff care scheme is that stress itself can so demotivate the individual that they are unable to make the decision to refer themselves. In the case of severe stress or exhaustion, the 'suffering skin' (Thompson et al., 1994) that protects the individual from outside pressures also prevents them seeking support. With this group of staff, it is important that the service does not wait for the individual to come to it but that the service goes out to the individual. It is essential to reach out to people who are shocked, frightened or upset, making the staff care service easily accessible and practically helpful.

Discussion

What is the source of these inhibitory factors? Although all are seen and expressed at the level of the individual, this expression seems to be the result and the reflection of attitudes and values that originate in the wider society and which are fostered and expressed within the agency. Although individuals may overcome these factors successfully to use and open up a service, thereby reducing the stigma for others, the inhibitory factors remain.

So it seems that the provision of staff care to multidisciplinary child protection staff is enmeshed in a circle of restraint. Central government seem reluctant to recommend such provision, and agencies and ACPCs are unwilling to fund or organize appropriate schemes. Once provision is established, participation is blocked by individual practitioners mirroring the anti-care messages that are present in their agencies.

Pottage and Evans claim that the causes of stress are often located in the agency rather than the practitioner: 'A shift from the traditional view of stress as a personal problem, located in individuals, towards seeing it as an indicator of the ineffectiveness of work environments, systems and practices is necessary' (1992, pp. 12–13). It seems that the reasons individuals do not seek help with stress are also located in the agency itself.

But the fact remains that some staff do feel able to use staff care services appropriately, even at the risk of suffering negative consequences. It is essential that the elements of any staff care service challenge those values that inhibit its use and encourage those that see it as a positive part of the child protection service. These values should be promoted at ACPC, agency and team levels through practical policies, including:

1 The integration of the staff care dimension into child protection procedure and operations. This begins at government level and proceeds through ACPC, agency and team.
2 Staff care provision should be flexible and proactive as well as reactive, should include both individuals and groups and should begin as close as possible to the 'trigger' event.
3 The provision should not just be confined to social services staff but should extend to all the multidisciplinary staff group.
4 The service should be well publicized throughout the system, but specific targeting and publicity should be aimed at underrepresented groups.
5 The scheme should emphasize the duality and inseparability of professional and personal need.
6 The service should reframe itself not as a response to individual weakness but as a need to invest in staff.

If the establishment of such schemes seems unrealistic at a time of financial cutbacks it should be pointed out that, compared to the substantial cost of child protection work to ACPC agencies each year, staff care has a cost that is infinitesimally low. Any costs would be easily recouped by improvements in the health, well-being and effectiveness of the child protection staff, as well as achieving a substantial reduction in the costs of absenteeism and stress-related illness.

References

Arroba, T. and James, K. (1987) *Pressure at Work: A Survival Guide*, London: McGraw-Hill.

Balloch, S., Andrew, T., Ginn, J., McLean, J., Pahl, J. and Williams, J. (1995) *Working in the Social Services*, London: NISW.

Bradley, J. and Sutherland, V. (1995) 'Occupational Stress In Social Services: A Comparison Of Social Workers And Home Help Staff', *British Journal of Social Work*, 25 (3).

Butler-Sloss, E. (1988) *Report of the Inquiry into Child Abuse in Cleveland 1987*, CM412, London: HMSO.

Department of Health (1991) *Working Together Under the 1989 Children Act*, London: HMSO.

DHSS (1974) *Non-Accidental Injury to Children*, LASSL (74) 13, London: HMSO.

Doyle, C. (1991) 'Caring for Workers', paper presented at the BASPCAN conference, Leicester University, 16–19 September.

Fineman, S. (1985) *Social Work Stress and Intervention*, Aldershot: Gower.

Hemsley, J. (1986) 'Slow to Come Forward', *Community Care*, 5 June.

Home Office/DoH (1992) *The Memorandum of Good Practice*, London: HMSO.

Leadbetter, D. (1993) 'Trends In Assaults On Social Work Staff: The Experience Of One Scottish Department', *British Journal of Social Work*, 23 (6).

Murphy, M. (1991) 'Pressure Points', *Social Work Today*, 13 June.

Murphy, M. (1995) *Working Together in Child Protection: An Exploration of the Multidisciplinary Task and System*, Aldershot: Arena.

Pottage, D. and Evans, M. (1992) *Workbased Stress: Prescription is Not the Cure*, London: NISW.

Thompson, N., Murphy, M. and Stradling, S. (1994) *Dealing with Stress*, London: Macmillan.

Wiener, R. (1989) 'Stress Within the Team', *Social Work Today*, 11 May.

Index